CRITICAL ACCLAIM FOR MELTDOWN

Top 10 of 2006 MajorSpoilers.com "Absorbing", "masterful" & "stunning". **"4 out of 4 stars",**

"Pick of the Month". Comic Buyer's Guide **"Not since Kurt Busiek's 'Astro City' has a comic**

brought so much impact into the comic book world. The unyielding power of Meltdown leaves the reader thirst-

ing for more, a solid 6 star comic in a 5 star world, and an early Christmas present for comic fans worldwide." Newsarama.com

"I have to say this is **one of the best titles I have read in a long, long time.** As the year quickly comes to a close,

Meltdown is on my list for one of the top titles of the year. Meltdown receives a well deserved 5 out of 5 Stars." MajorSpoilers.com

"One hell of a good read... I opened the book and was instantly pulled into the hero's tragic tale." "5 out of 5 stars"

ComicCritique.com **"You ever read a comic book that was so good that you knew that it was the**

debut of some major talent? That's exactly how I felt as I read MELTDOWN ... the comics world is all the better for having

David B. Schwartz and Sean Wang in it. These guys are going to be major players in the comics world in the next several years and

you read it here first... I honestly don't know if I can remember when I've read an introductory issue that's been this good.

MELTDOWN is, as the kids say today, the bomb." **"[G]enius"** Ain't It Cool News

"[A] slick, involving, emotional tale...

MELTDOWN delivers the goods, creating a super-hero epic with true heart and passion... **Hopefully, people will take**

heed when I say that this is a must-buy once this series hits the comic stands." "5 out of 5 Bullets."

SilverBulletComicBooks.com "Schwartz's characters have genuine depth and motivation. Sean Wang's art is at once charming and

dynamic. **MELTDOWN is the first comic book I've enjoyed reading in many years."** Barry Hoggard, South

"This book hits you like a blast furnace, and it does it on every level." **"I truly can't recommend this book any higher,**

and won't be shocked if this book sells out, and is tops on everyone's list come December." "A-Plus" PaperbackReader.com

“Written with a darkly unique sense of humor, MELTDOWN hits the spot every time.”

“The most surprisingly wonderful book in years.”

“[T]his was really, really good...done with forethought and intelligence. The story had a certain bit of realism that just drew me in immediately.”

“Schwartz...uses the book to look at how people's childhood hopes and dreams are often squashed by adulthood and the economic truths of this world. And if the story alone weren’t good enough, **the art by Sean Wang is stunning.**” – SilverBulletComicBooks.com

“I had heard that MELTDOWN was a great new title, but I decided to test the hype. It turned out better than I could have asked for **- great characterization, wicked concept and solid art...** Schwartz and co. have outdone themselves with this mini-series.”

“These characters seem real, which is almost anything you could ask for in a superhero-based book...**a superb book.**” **“Rating: Must read.”**

“Both the writing and artwork achieve levels of storytelling that are inherently human and painfully honest.”

“Schwartz [is] always playing with his reader’s expectations. Wang...does nothing less than stun with his artwork.”

“I suggest this for any and all superhero fans. A very nice surprise.”

“[A] really well-told superhero story, with an interesting protagonist and some eye-catching art. **Go ahead and pick one up and try to resist.**” – JPKComics.com

“Schwartz has a great handle on his character, his motivations and frustrations, as well he impressively nails the themes that he wants to hit. The art by Sean Wang is aces. The top-notch coloring by GURU-eFX brings it all together... A definite surprise, and **a must-read for superhero fans who think they’ve seen it all.**”

“MELTDOWN succeeds on a number of levels...Artistically, the book looks fantastic...Together, art and story work tightly, **and MELTDOWN makes for an excellent read** because of it.”

“This isn’t a typical super-hero story. It’s a tragedy about a man who’s been denied his dreams, his desires and a dynamic destiny.”

“It’s a surprisingly introspective story... **a strong, emotional story** about a hero who gets pushed to his limits and beyond...[and] **a great read.**”

IMAGE COMICS PROUDLY PRESENTS

MELTDOWN

THE DEFINITIVE COLLECTION

Written by	Artwork and Lettering by	Colors by
DAVID B. SCHWARTZ	**SEAN WANG** (www.seanwang.com)	**GURU-eFX** (www.guru-efx.com)
Issue 1 Cover by	Issue 2 Cover by	Graphic Design by
CHRIS BACHALO	**GREG HORN**	**RORY MYERS** (www.rorymyers.com)

Use of multiple art styles suggested by BERNARD CHANG. Special thanks to: all of the fine folks at IMAGE COMICS for believing in the project and for all of their hard work in making it a reality; JASON RAYMAN (www.jrayman.com) for his spectacular PR work; both BERNARD CHANG and JOHN PAUL LEON for their parts in the project's initial gestation; HEROIC PUBLISHING (www.heroicpub.com); all the reviewers and websites who helped us get the word out; and, of course, all the stores and readers who actually purchased the book. We hope you enjoy reading it as much as we enjoyed working on it! Sean would also like to offer special thanks to MARGRETTE TWARDOWSKI for being so supportive. David would also like to offer thanks to SEAN for being such an incredible collaborator and his wife AMY for all of her love and support. He dedicates this book to his own little hero, LANA MEREDITH.

IMAGE COMICS, INC.

Erik Larsen - Publisher
Todd McFarlane - President
Marc Silvestri - CEO
Jim Valentino - Vice-President
Eric Stephenson - Executive Director
Joe Keatinge - PR & Marketing Coordinator
Thao Le - Accounts Manager
Rosemary Cao - Accounting Assistant
Traci Hui - Traffic Manager
Allen Hui - Production Manager
Jonathan Chan - Production Artist
Drew Gill - Production Artist

www.imagecomics.com

image®

CONTENTS

Foreword by ROBERT KIRKMAN   7

MELTDOWN: BOOK ONE   9

MELTDOWN: BOOK TWO   59

Behind the Scenes: THE ORIGINAL SERIES PITCH   109

Behind the Scenes: DESIGNING MELTDOWN   113

Behind the Scenes: CREATING A COVER   119

Behind the Scenes: CREATOR COMMENTARY
(including deleted scenes, alternate endings, and more)   125

PIN-UPS   145

Creator Bios   153

FOREWORD BY ROBERT KIRKMAN

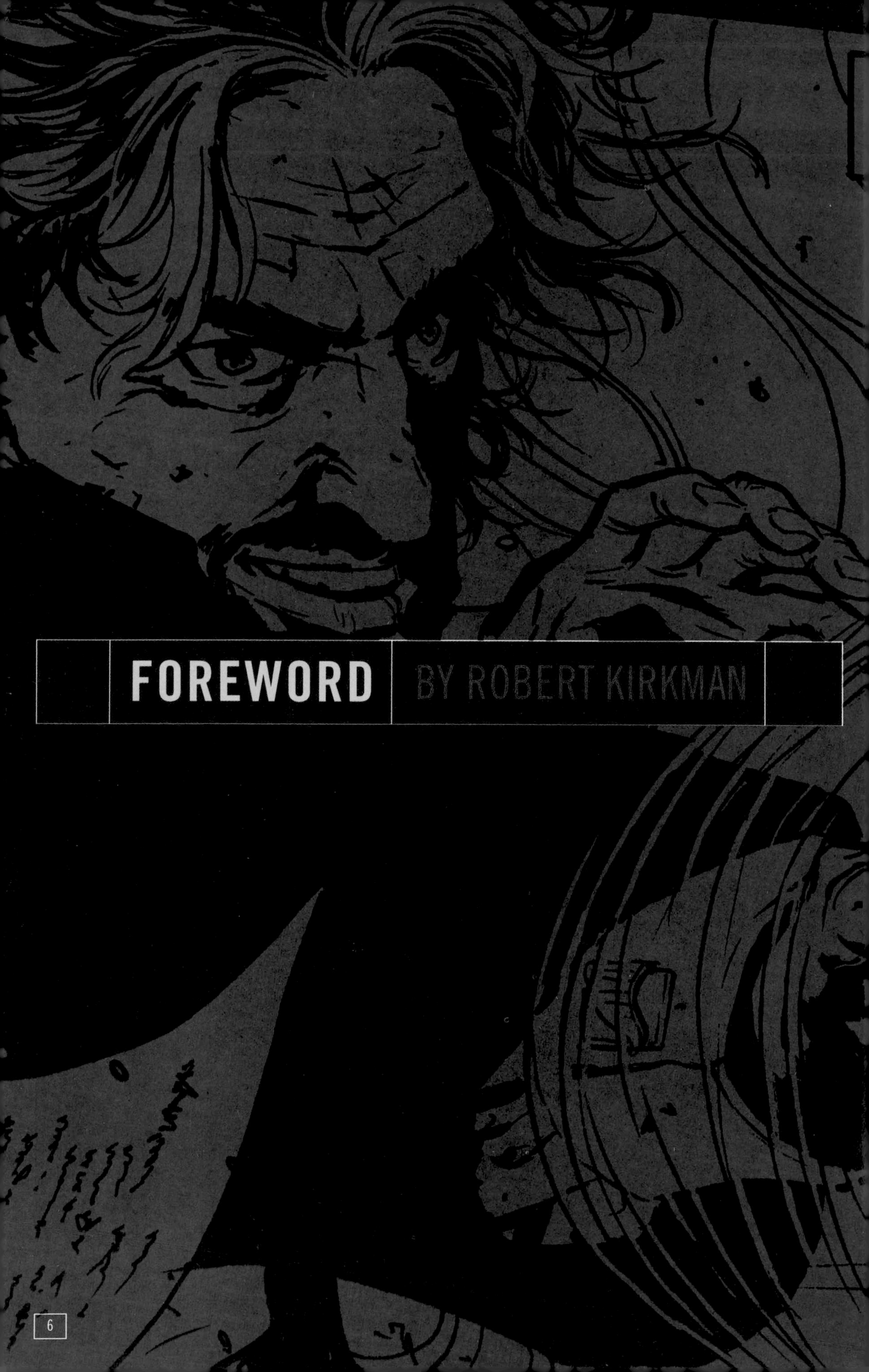

I don't presume to think that any of you reading this have any idea who I am. Some probably do. I'd certainly prefer if it were most if not all who knew, but let's face facts... I'm no Tom Cruise. So just to fill you cats in, I'm Robert Kirkman, and aside from writing some of your favorite mid to low-level Marvel books, I write comic books for Image Comics.

Image Comics is also the publisher of this fine book you hold in your hands, just in case you weren't paying attention. Image is a fabulous company, so great I'm actually compelled to say the word "fabulous." They have the ability to be all things to all people. There's no one in the world who wouldn't enjoy at least one Image book. They're just that diverse. They give young up-and-comers their start in comics (like Myself, or the writer of this very comic, young David Schwartz) and they allow seasoned pros who've been around a while a chance to shine (like the artist of this very comic Sean Wang). They're just an absolute joy to work with and I think they produce some of the finest comics on the market today.

There's just one little problem with Image. From time to time, not too often, Image will publish a crappy book. I dare you to find a publisher who hasn't, so I'm not attacking Image on this issue. It happens, I understand that. But every now and then Image will publish a book that makes you (or me) cringe. It's just a sloppy mess that isn't worthy of the paper it's printed on. It's just an embarrassing mark on the otherwise (in my opinion) fine tradition of a fabulous publisher.

When a book like this is released, I take it a little personally. Creating comics isn't an easy job to do. I work long and hard on my Image books making sure everything can be as close as possible to perfect. I slave over these things. I sweat the details and above all else, I CARE. I love all the comics I write, but at Image, I'm much more hands on, the final product is much more my product that the books at Marvel which pass through not less than two thousand hands (so that's one thousand people using both hands) before they reach yours.

So, I look at the rare bad books Image publishes and I think. "If MY book is an Image book... and this piece of trash is an Image book... how is anyone going to know the difference?" Granted, everyone has opinions and personal taste does factor into this a great deal... but to me every time Image publishes a sub par book (which I'll admit, these days are few and far between) I feel like it dings Image's reputation a little bit, and no matter how good I make my books... they'll still be hanging under that tarnished reputation.

What does happen at a more frequent pace is a book comes out from Image that is so unique and well conceived, designed and executed that I see it in Previews in the same section as my books and it makes me proud. Image sometimes does books that look so interesting and compelling that I just have to read them and I know others do too. Books like these bring the company up to a higher level and help tell the world just how special Image is. These books inspire me to work harder, to ensure that my books at least come close to living up to this level of quality.

MELTDOWN is one of these books. David Schwartz and Sean Wang were able to put together a solid, impressive package with MELTDOWN. The two issue series was a sight to behold – great covers, great interiors, high production values, compelling story, fantastic art and very professional lettering (which some creators these days overlook, but I think is a cornerstone of comic book production).

David's story is moving and dramatic. It's everything a superhero story should be. It's one of those stories that embraces superheroism in a shameless way and uses the genre to tell an in-depth character arc. I won't ruin anything for you here - but lets just say you're in for a treat.

Sean's art is both expressive & clean and gritty & detailed... whatever the scene called for. His use of varying art styles is seamless and meshes well with the story. Sean's work here has grown leaps and bounds since his time spent on "The Tick" and it was fantastic back then. The character designs are very cool and original and the entire book is just a joy to look at.

Together these two have produced a comic that stands shoulder to shoulder with the best of Image comics. I'm eagerly anticipating the release of this collected volume and I'll gladly display it on my bookshelf. Looks like you, dear reader, will get to as well. Enjoy!

-Robert Kirkman │ Backwoods, KY │ 2007 │

Robert Kirkman has been writing and producing creator-owned comics since 2000. He's the writer of The Walking Dead, Invincible and The Astounding Wolf-Man for Image Comics and his Marvel work, past and present, includes, Ultimate X-Men, The Irredeemable Ant-Man, Marvel Zombies, Marvel Team-Up and Captain America. He's been known to bench-press a Buick, but the feat has yet to be photographed and it is suspected that the "Buick" he mentioned isn't a car but is in fact something of little weight and bench-pressing it is not impressive at all.

MELTDOWN

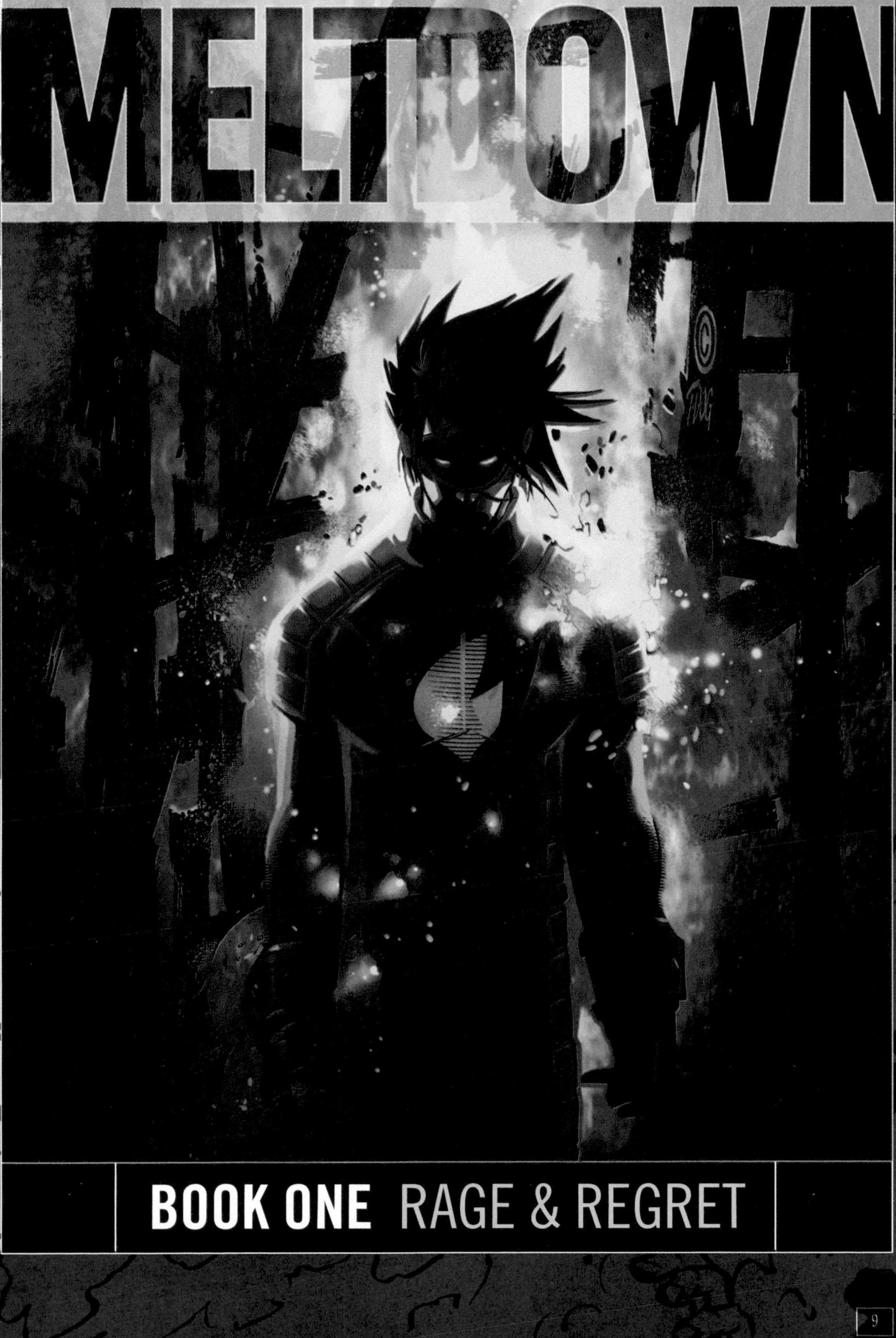

BOOK ONE RAGE & REGRET

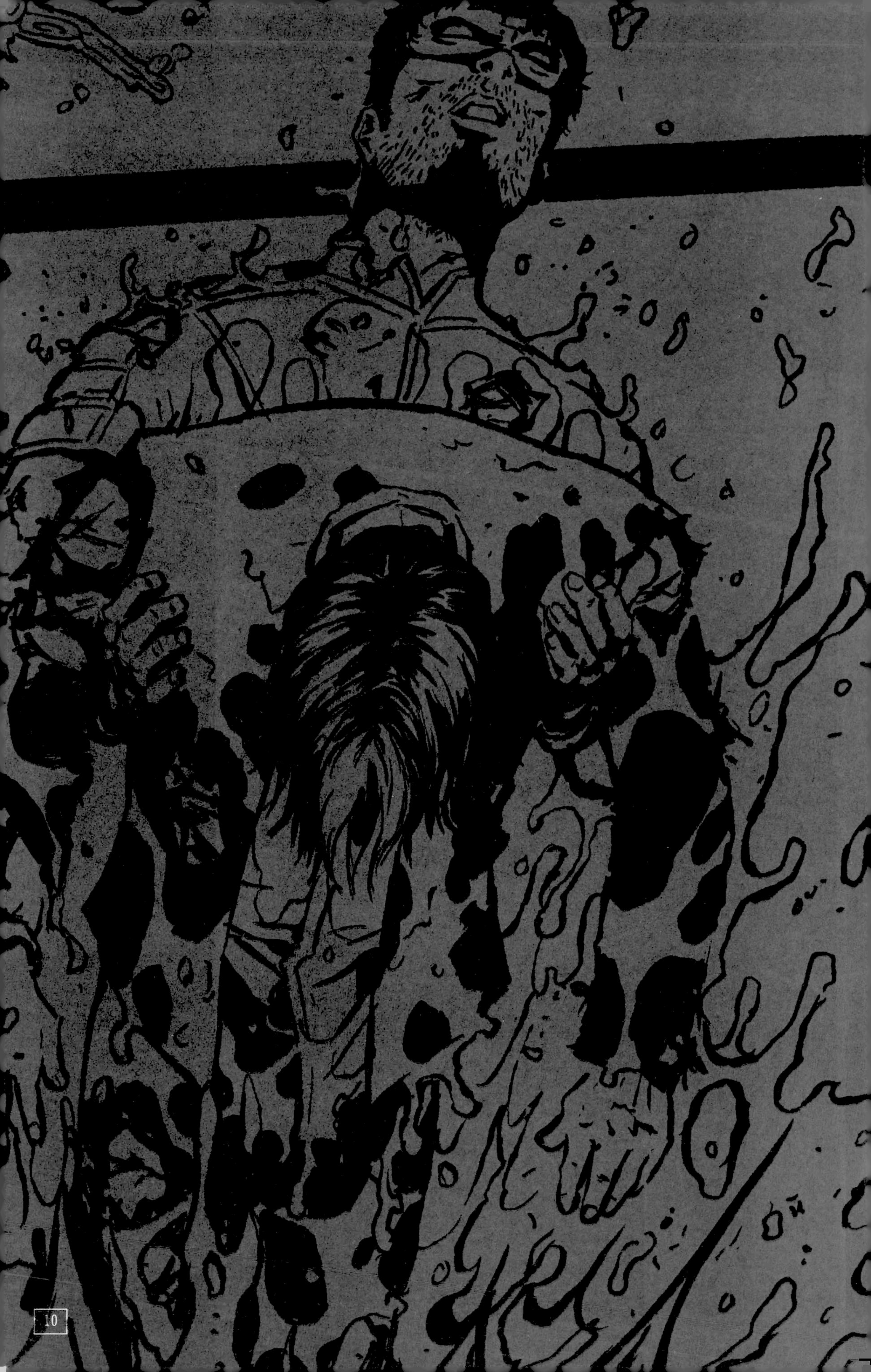

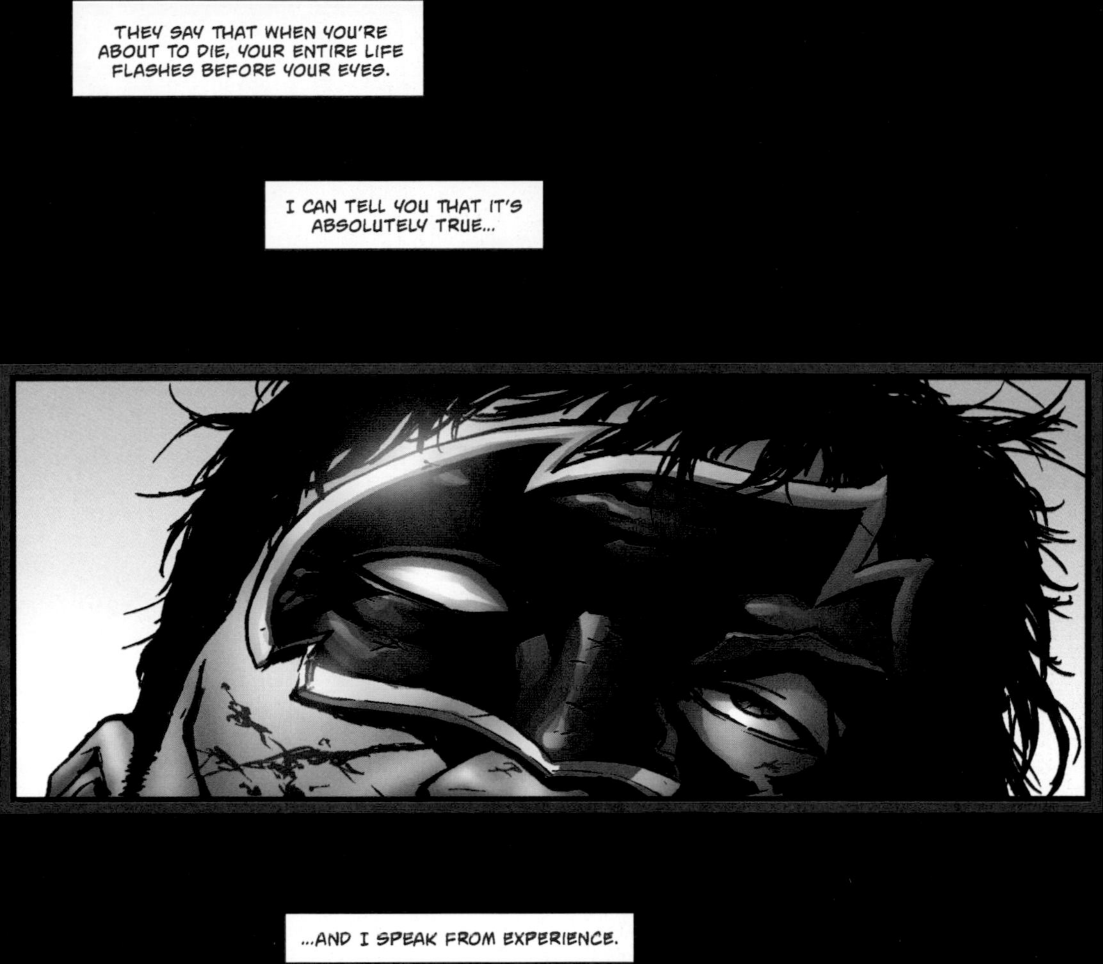
THEY SAY THAT WHEN YOU'RE ABOUT TO DIE, YOUR ENTIRE LIFE FLASHES BEFORE YOUR EYES.
I CAN TELL YOU THAT IT'S ABSOLUTELY TRUE...
...AND I SPEAK FROM EXPERIENCE.

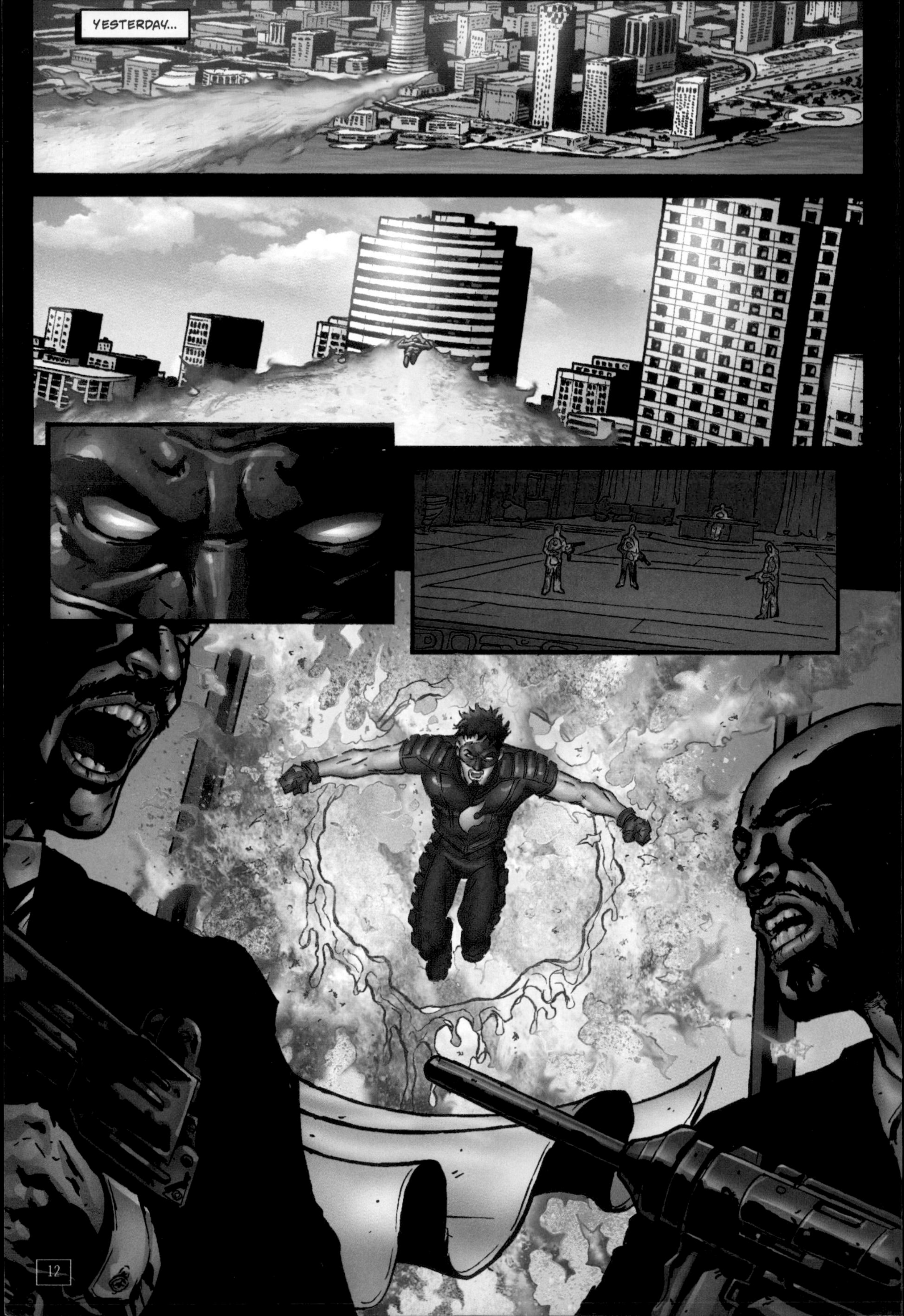
YESTERDAY...

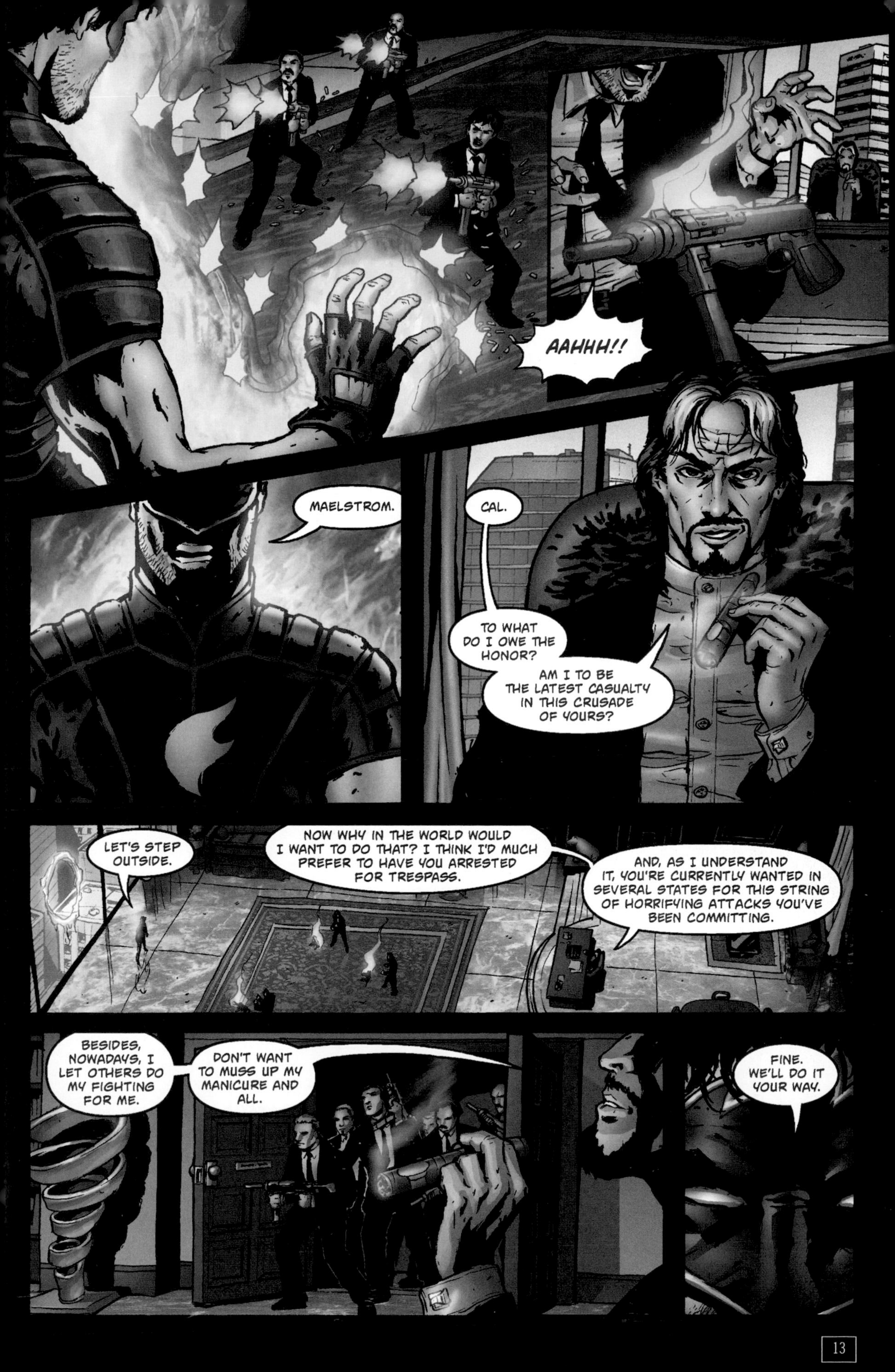
AAHHH!!
MAELSTROM.
CAL.
TO WHAT DO I OWE THE HONOR?
AM I TO BE THE LATEST CASUALTY IN THIS CRUSADE OF YOURS?
LET'S STEP OUTSIDE.
NOW WHY IN THE WORLD WOULD I WANT TO DO THAT? I THINK I'D MUCH PREFER TO HAVE YOU ARRESTED FOR TRESPASS.
AND, AS I UNDERSTAND IT, YOU'RE CURRENTLY WANTED IN SEVERAL STATES FOR THIS STRING OF HORRIFYING ATTACKS YOU'VE BEEN COMMITTING.
BESIDES, NOWADAYS, I LET OTHERS DO MY FIGHTING FOR ME.
DON'T WANT TO MUSS UP MY MANICURE AND ALL.
FINE. WE'LL DO IT YOUR WAY.

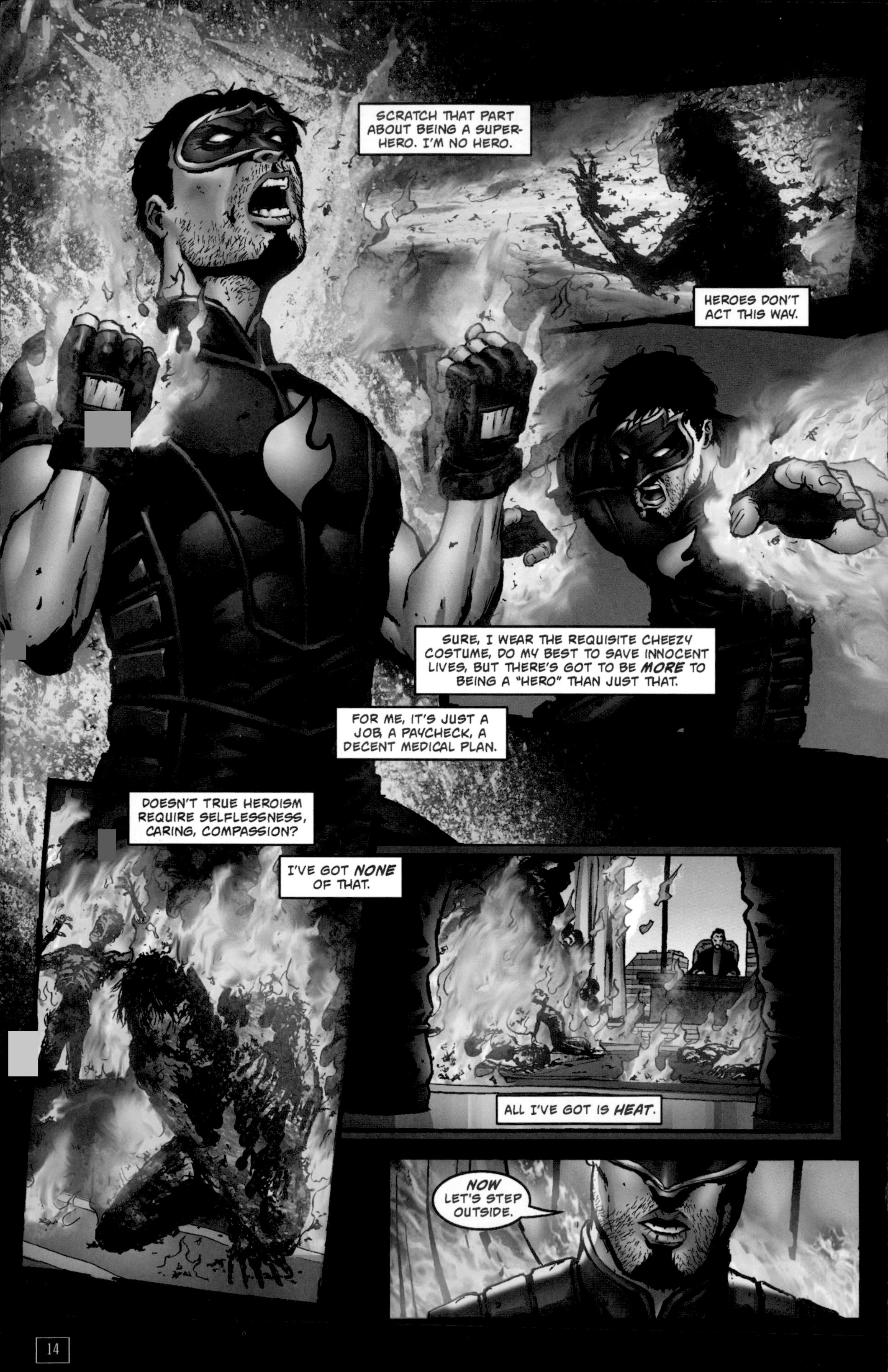
SCRATCH THAT PART ABOUT BEING A SUPER-HERO. I'M NO HERO.
HEROES DON'T ACT THIS WAY.
SURE, I WEAR THE REQUISITE CHEEZY COSTUME, DO MY BEST TO SAVE INNOCENT LIVES, BUT THERE'S GOT TO BE MORE TO BEING A "HERO" THAN JUST THAT.
FOR ME, IT'S JUST A JOB, A PAYCHECK, A DECENT MEDICAL PLAN.
DOESN'T TRUE HEROISM REQUIRE SELFLESSNESS, CARING, COMPASSION?
I'VE GOT NONE OF THAT.
ALL I'VE GOT IS HEAT.
NOW LET'S STEP OUTSIDE.

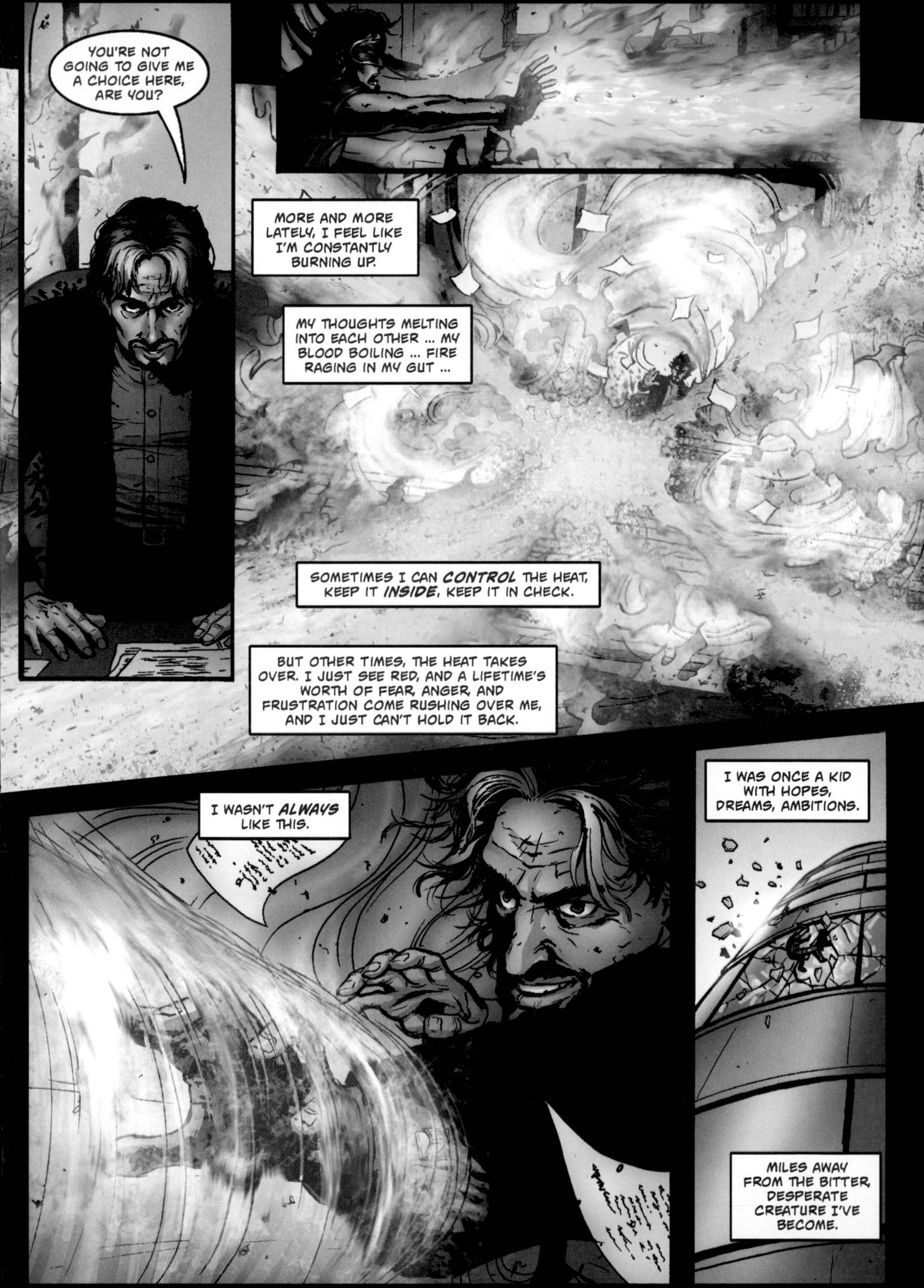
YOU'RE NOT GOING TO GIVE ME A CHOICE HERE, ARE YOU?
MORE AND MORE LATELY, I FEEL LIKE I'M CONSTANTLY BURNING UP.
MY THOUGHTS MELTING INTO EACH OTHER ... MY BLOOD BOILING ... FIRE RAGING IN MY GUT ...
SOMETIMES I CAN CONTROL THE HEAT, KEEP IT INSIDE, KEEP IT IN CHECK.
BUT OTHER TIMES, THE HEAT TAKES OVER. I JUST SEE RED, AND A LIFETIME'S WORTH OF FEAR, ANGER, AND FRUSTRATION COME RUSHING OVER ME, AND I JUST CAN'T HOLD IT BACK.
I WASN'T ALWAYS LIKE THIS.
I WAS ONCE A KID WITH HOPES, DREAMS, AMBITIONS.
MILES AWAY FROM THE BITTER, DESPERATE CREATURE I'VE BECOME.

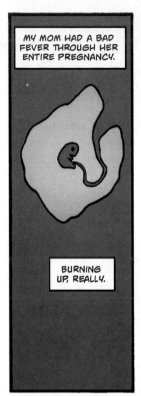

MY MOM HAD A BAD FEVER THROUGH HER ENTIRE PREGNANCY.

BURNING UP, REALLY.

A NORMAL PREGNANCY RUNS HOT AND COLD. THIS ONE WAS JUST -- *BROILING* --

-- AND I WAS BORN WITH A TEMPERATURE OF 103.7. HENCE, "CALIENTE".

THIS WAS BACK BEFORE SUPER POWERS BECAME WIDE-SPREAD. NO ONE IN VENEZUELA KNEW WHAT TO MAKE OF ME.

DOCTORS HAD NO IDEA WHY I WAS ALWAYS RUNNING A FEVER. THEY JUST THOUGHT I WAS SICKLY, A MEDICAL ODDITY WITH SOME NEW DISEASE THEY COULDN'T UNDERSTAND. THEY ALL JUST ASSUMED I'D DIE SOONER OR LATER.

BUT I DIDN'T.

INSTEAD, WHEN I WAS SIX WE MOVED FROM CARACAS TO MIAMI BEACH, LOOKING FOR BETTER DOCTORS, MORE MODERN SCIENCE.

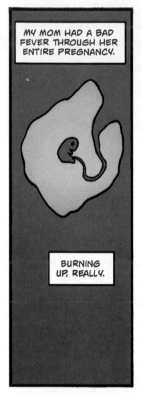

MY MOM HAD A BAD FEVER THROUGH HER ENTIRE PREGNANCY.

BURNING UP, REALLY.

A NORMAL PREGNANCY RUNS HOT AND COLD. THIS ONE WAS JUST -- *BROILING* --

-- AND I WAS BORN WITH A TEMPERATURE OF 103.7. HENCE, "CALIENTE".

THIS WAS BACK BEFORE SUPER POWERS BECAME WIDE-SPREAD. NO ONE IN VENEZUELA KNEW WHAT TO MAKE OF ME.

DOCTORS HAD NO IDEA WHY I WAS ALWAYS RUNNING A FEVER. THEY JUST THOUGHT I WAS SICKLY, A MEDICAL ODDITY WITH SOME NEW DISEASE THEY COULDN'T UNDERSTAND. THEY ALL JUST ASSUMED I'D DIE SOONER OR LATER.

BUT I DIDN'T.

INSTEAD, WHEN I WAS SIX WE MOVED FROM CARACAS TO MIAMI BEACH, LOOKING FOR BETTER DOCTORS, MORE MODERN SCIENCE.

16

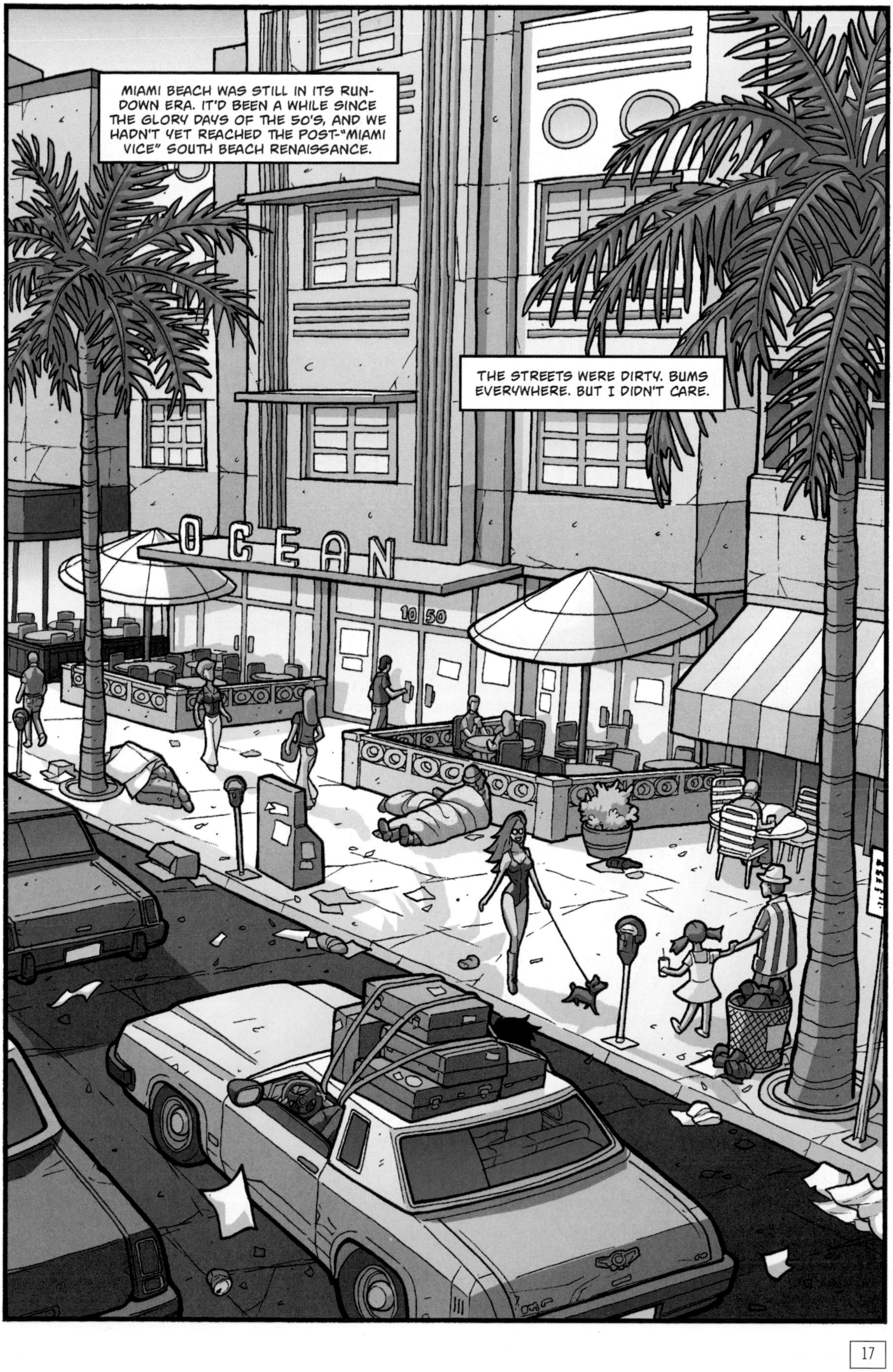
MIAMI BEACH WAS STILL IN ITS RUN-DOWN ERA. IT'D BEEN A WHILE SINCE THE GLORY DAYS OF THE 50'S, AND WE HADN'T YET REACHED THE POST-"MIAMI VICE" SOUTH BEACH RENAISSANCE.
OCEAN
1050
THE STREETS WERE DIRTY. BUMS EVERYWHERE. BUT I DIDN'T CARE.

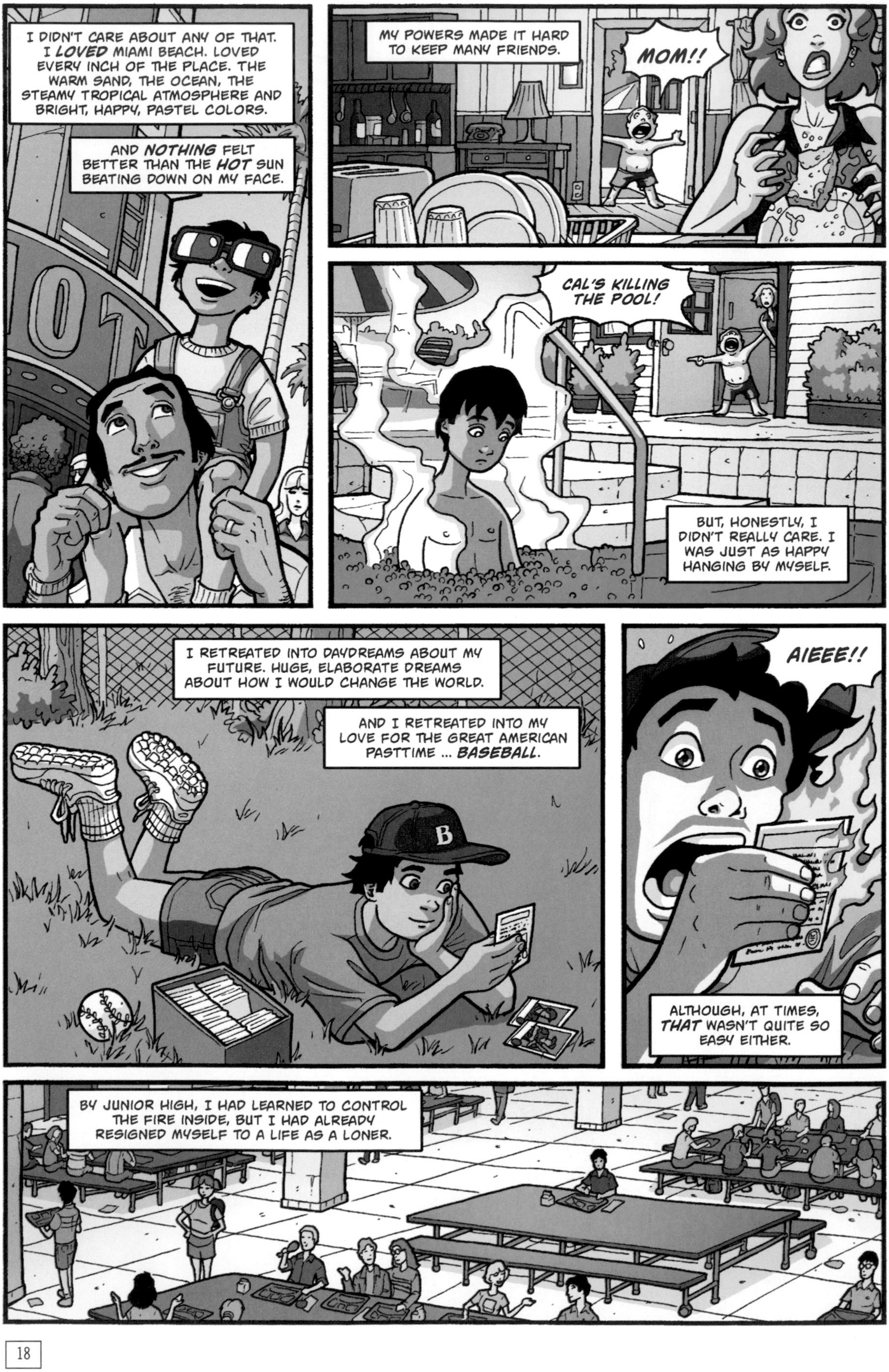
I DIDN'T CARE ABOUT ANY OF THAT. I LOVED MIAMI BEACH. LOVED EVERY INCH OF THE PLACE. THE WARM SAND, THE OCEAN, THE STEAMY TROPICAL ATMOSPHERE AND BRIGHT, HAPPY, PASTEL COLORS.
AND NOTHING FELT BETTER THAN THE HOT SUN BEATING DOWN ON MY FACE.
MY POWERS MADE IT HARD TO KEEP MANY FRIENDS.
MOM!!
CAL'S KILLING THE POOL!
BUT, HONESTLY, I DIDN'T REALLY CARE. I WAS JUST AS HAPPY HANGING BY MYSELF.
I RETREATED INTO DAYDREAMS ABOUT MY FUTURE. HUGE, ELABORATE DREAMS ABOUT HOW I WOULD CHANGE THE WORLD.
AND I RETREATED INTO MY LOVE FOR THE GREAT AMERICAN PASTTIME ... BASEBALL.
AIEEE!!
ALTHOUGH, AT TIMES, THAT WASN'T QUITE SO EASY EITHER.
BY JUNIOR HIGH, I HAD LEARNED TO CONTROL THE FIRE INSIDE, BUT I HAD ALREADY RESIGNED MYSELF TO A LIFE AS A LONER.

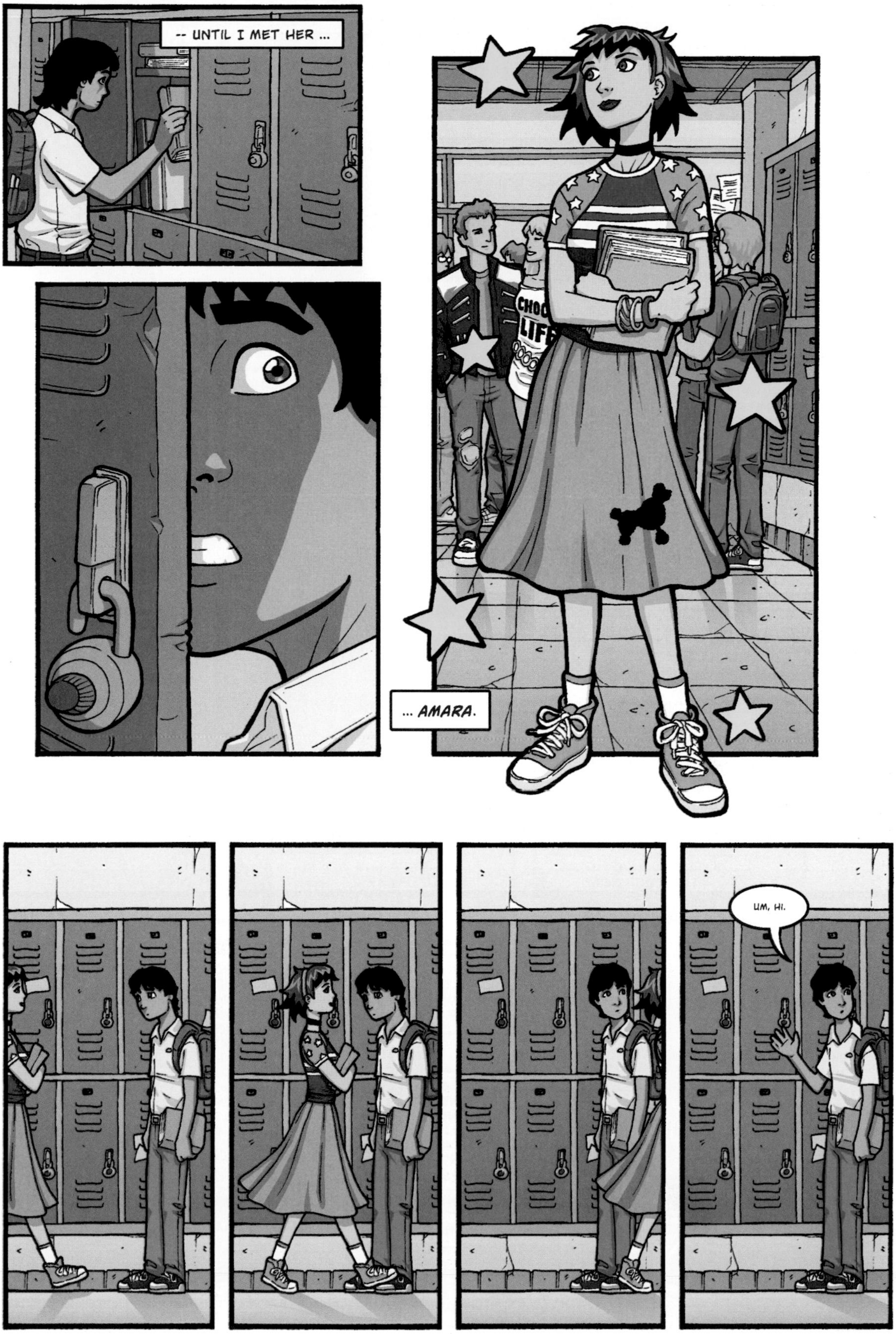
-- UNTIL I MET HER ...
... AMARA.
UM, HI.

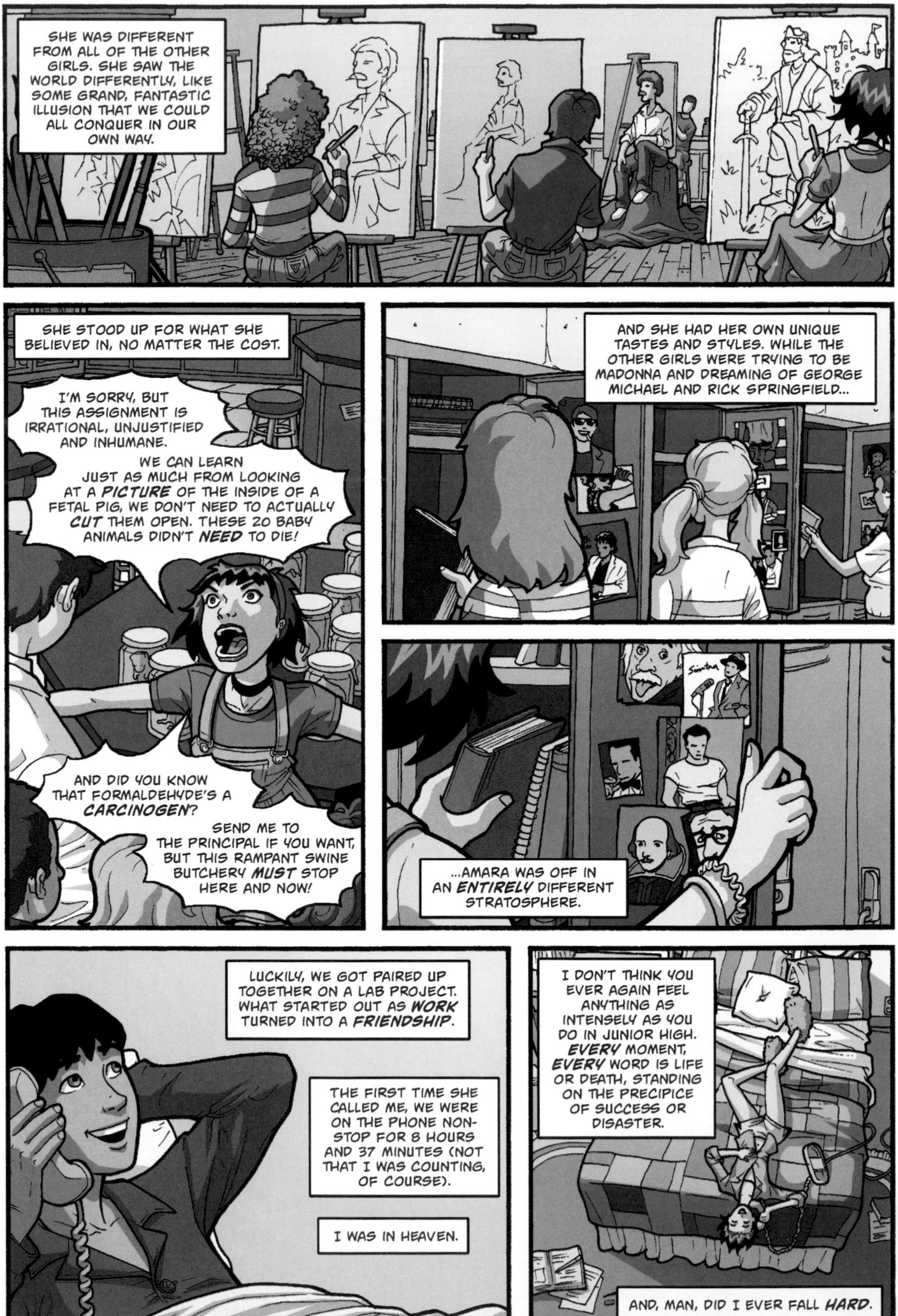
SHE WAS DIFFERENT FROM ALL OF THE OTHER GIRLS. SHE SAW THE WORLD DIFFERENTLY, LIKE SOME GRAND, FANTASTIC ILLUSION THAT WE COULD ALL CONQUER IN OUR OWN WAY.
SHE STOOD UP FOR WHAT SHE BELIEVED IN, NO MATTER THE COST.
I'M SORRY, BUT THIS ASSIGNMENT IS IRRATIONAL, UNJUSTIFIED AND INHUMANE.
WE CAN LEARN JUST AS MUCH FROM LOOKING AT A *PICTURE* OF THE INSIDE OF A FETAL PIG, WE DON'T NEED TO ACTUALLY *CUT* THEM OPEN. THESE 20 BABY ANIMALS DIDN'T *NEED* TO DIE!
AND DID YOU KNOW THAT FORMALDEHYDE'S A *CARCINOGEN*?
SEND ME TO THE PRINCIPAL IF YOU WANT, BUT THIS RAMPANT SWINE BUTCHERY *MUST* STOP HERE AND NOW!
AND SHE HAD HER OWN UNIQUE TASTES AND STYLES. WHILE THE OTHER GIRLS WERE TRYING TO BE MADONNA AND DREAMING OF GEORGE MICHAEL AND RICK SPRINGFIELD...
Sinatra
...AMARA WAS OFF IN AN *ENTIRELY* DIFFERENT STRATOSPHERE.
LUCKILY, WE GOT PAIRED UP TOGETHER ON A LAB PROJECT. WHAT STARTED OUT AS *WORK* TURNED INTO A *FRIENDSHIP*.
THE FIRST TIME SHE CALLED ME, WE WERE ON THE PHONE NON-STOP FOR 8 HOURS AND 37 MINUTES (NOT THAT I WAS COUNTING, OF COURSE).
I WAS IN HEAVEN.
I DON'T THINK YOU EVER AGAIN FEEL ANYTHING AS INTENSELY AS YOU DO IN JUNIOR HIGH. *EVERY* MOMENT, *EVERY* WORD IS LIFE OR DEATH, STANDING ON THE PRECIPICE OF SUCCESS OR DISASTER.
AND, MAN, DID I EVER FALL *HARD*.

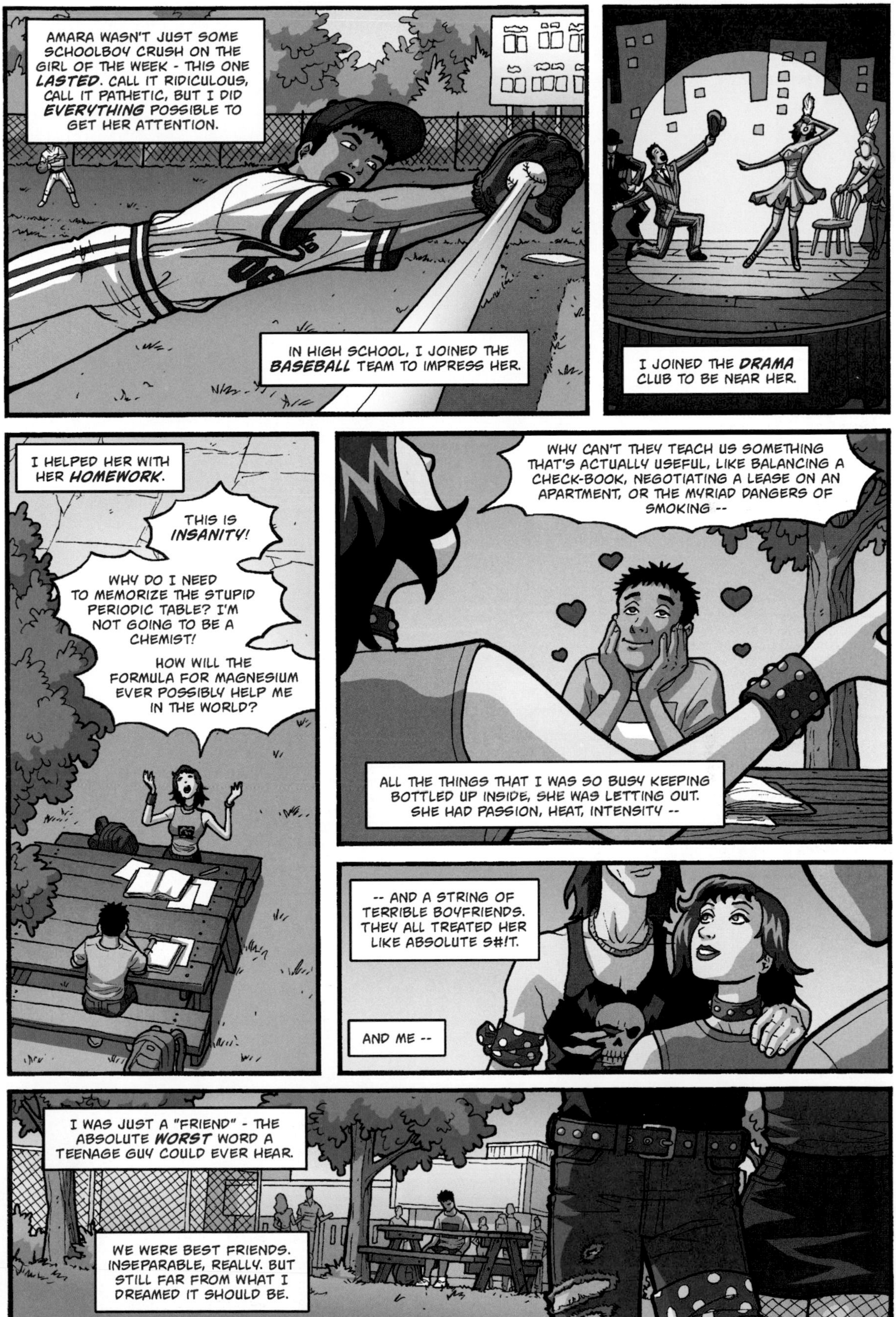
AMARA WASN'T JUST SOME SCHOOLBOY CRUSH ON THE GIRL OF THE WEEK - THIS ONE LASTED. CALL IT RIDICULOUS, CALL IT PATHETIC, BUT I DID EVERYTHING POSSIBLE TO GET HER ATTENTION.
IN HIGH SCHOOL, I JOINED THE BASEBALL TEAM TO IMPRESS HER.
I JOINED THE DRAMA CLUB TO BE NEAR HER.
I HELPED HER WITH HER HOMEWORK.
THIS IS INSANITY!
WHY DO I NEED TO MEMORIZE THE STUPID PERIODIC TABLE? I'M NOT GOING TO BE A CHEMIST!
HOW WILL THE FORMULA FOR MAGNESIUM EVER POSSIBLY HELP ME IN THE WORLD?
WHY CAN'T THEY TEACH US SOMETHING THAT'S ACTUALLY USEFUL, LIKE BALANCING A CHECK-BOOK, NEGOTIATING A LEASE ON AN APARTMENT, OR THE MYRIAD DANGERS OF SMOKING --
ALL THE THINGS THAT I WAS SO BUSY KEEPING BOTTLED UP INSIDE, SHE WAS LETTING OUT. SHE HAD PASSION, HEAT, INTENSITY --
-- AND A STRING OF TERRIBLE BOYFRIENDS. THEY ALL TREATED HER LIKE ABSOLUTE S#!T.
AND ME --
I WAS JUST A "FRIEND" - THE ABSOLUTE WORST WORD A TEENAGE GUY COULD EVER HEAR.
WE WERE BEST FRIENDS. INSEPARABLE, REALLY. BUT STILL FAR FROM WHAT I DREAMED IT SHOULD BE.

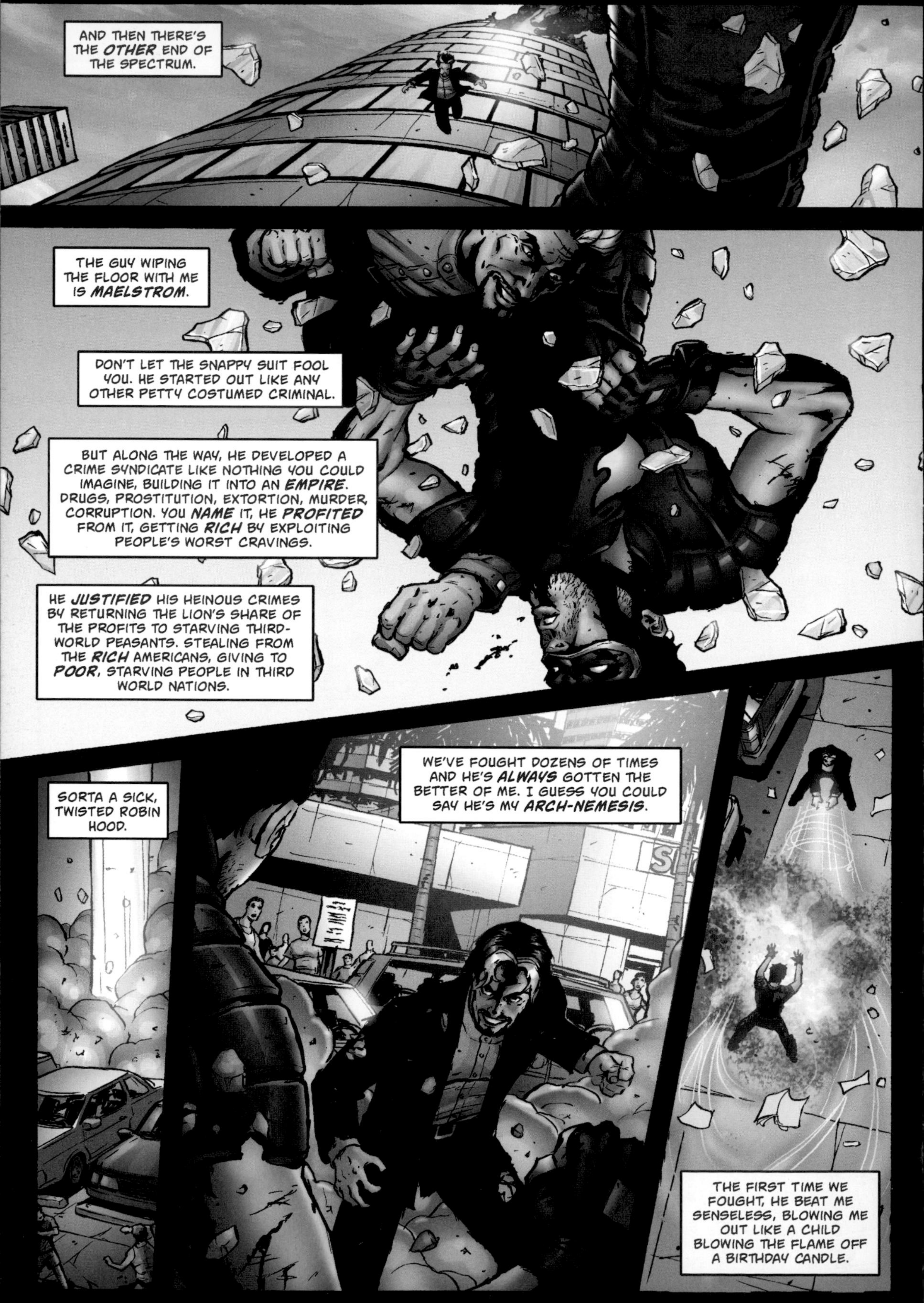
AND THEN THERE'S THE OTHER END OF THE SPECTRUM.
THE GUY WIPING THE FLOOR WITH ME IS MAELSTROM.
DON'T LET THE SNAPPY SUIT FOOL YOU. HE STARTED OUT LIKE ANY OTHER PETTY COSTUMED CRIMINAL.
BUT ALONG THE WAY, HE DEVELOPED A CRIME SYNDICATE LIKE NOTHING YOU COULD IMAGINE, BUILDING IT INTO AN EMPIRE. DRUGS, PROSTITUTION, EXTORTION, MURDER, CORRUPTION. YOU NAME IT, HE PROFITED FROM IT, GETTING RICH BY EXPLOITING PEOPLE'S WORST CRAVINGS.
HE JUSTIFIED HIS HEINOUS CRIMES BY RETURNING THE LION'S SHARE OF THE PROFITS TO STARVING THIRD-WORLD PEASANTS. STEALING FROM THE RICH AMERICANS, GIVING TO POOR, STARVING PEOPLE IN THIRD WORLD NATIONS.
SORTA A SICK, TWISTED ROBIN HOOD.
WE'VE FOUGHT DOZENS OF TIMES AND HE'S ALWAYS GOTTEN THE BETTER OF ME. I GUESS YOU COULD SAY HE'S MY ARCH-NEMESIS.
THE FIRST TIME WE FOUGHT, HE BEAT ME SENSELESS, BLOWING ME OUT LIKE A CHILD BLOWING THE FLAME OFF A BIRTHDAY CANDLE.

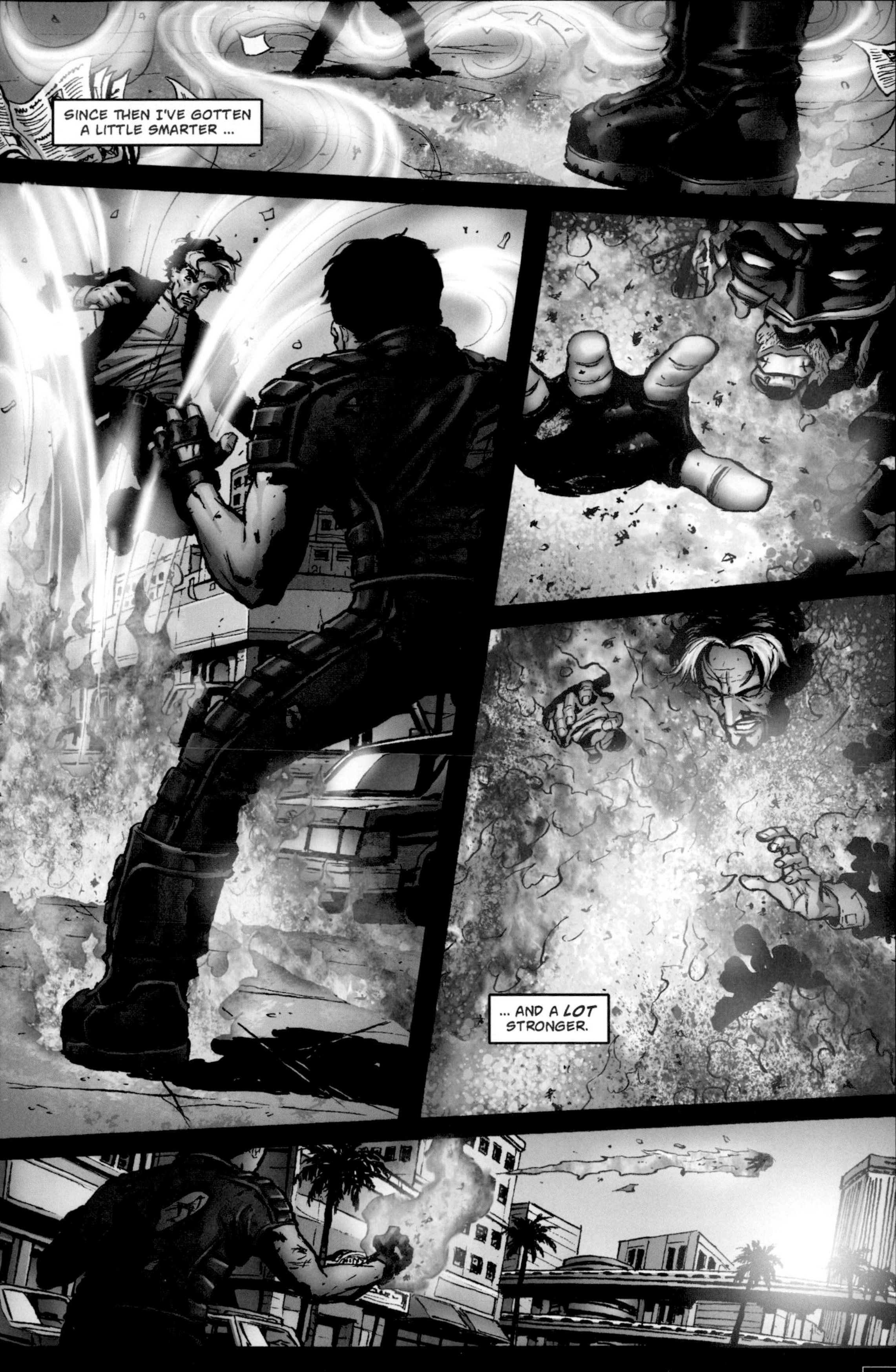
SINCE THEN I'VE GOTTEN A LITTLE SMARTER ...
... AND A LOT STRONGER.

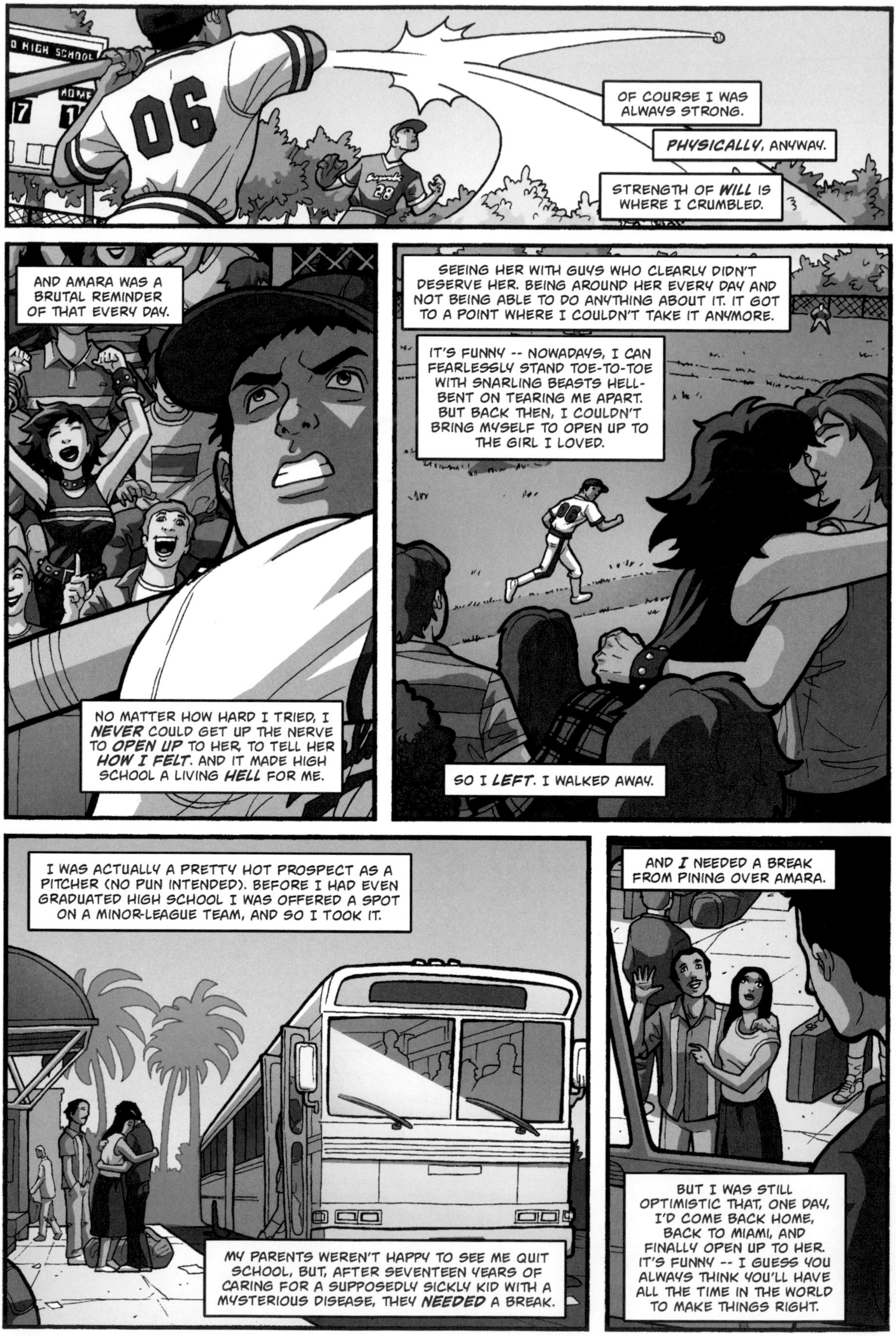
O HIGH SCHOOL
HOME
06
OF COURSE I WAS ALWAYS STRONG.
PHYSICALLY, ANYWAY.
STRENGTH OF WILL IS WHERE I CRUMBLED.
AND AMARA WAS A BRUTAL REMINDER OF THAT EVERY DAY.
NO MATTER HOW HARD I TRIED, I NEVER COULD GET UP THE NERVE TO OPEN UP TO HER, TO TELL HER HOW I FELT. AND IT MADE HIGH SCHOOL A LIVING HELL FOR ME.
SEEING HER WITH GUYS WHO CLEARLY DIDN'T DESERVE HER. BEING AROUND HER EVERY DAY AND NOT BEING ABLE TO DO ANYTHING ABOUT IT. IT GOT TO A POINT WHERE I COULDN'T TAKE IT ANYMORE.
IT'S FUNNY -- NOWADAYS, I CAN FEARLESSLY STAND TOE-TO-TOE WITH SNARLING BEASTS HELL-BENT ON TEARING ME APART. BUT BACK THEN, I COULDN'T BRING MYSELF TO OPEN UP TO THE GIRL I LOVED.
SO I LEFT. I WALKED AWAY.
I WAS ACTUALLY A PRETTY HOT PROSPECT AS A PITCHER (NO PUN INTENDED). BEFORE I HAD EVEN GRADUATED HIGH SCHOOL I WAS OFFERED A SPOT ON A MINOR-LEAGUE TEAM, AND SO I TOOK IT.
MY PARENTS WEREN'T HAPPY TO SEE ME QUIT SCHOOL, BUT, AFTER SEVENTEEN YEARS OF CARING FOR A SUPPOSEDLY SICKLY KID WITH A MYSTERIOUS DISEASE, THEY NEEDED A BREAK.
AND I NEEDED A BREAK FROM PINING OVER AMARA.
BUT I WAS STILL OPTIMISTIC THAT, ONE DAY, I'D COME BACK HOME, BACK TO MIAMI, AND FINALLY OPEN UP TO HER. IT'S FUNNY -- I GUESS YOU ALWAYS THINK YOU'LL HAVE ALL THE TIME IN THE WORLD TO MAKE THINGS RIGHT.

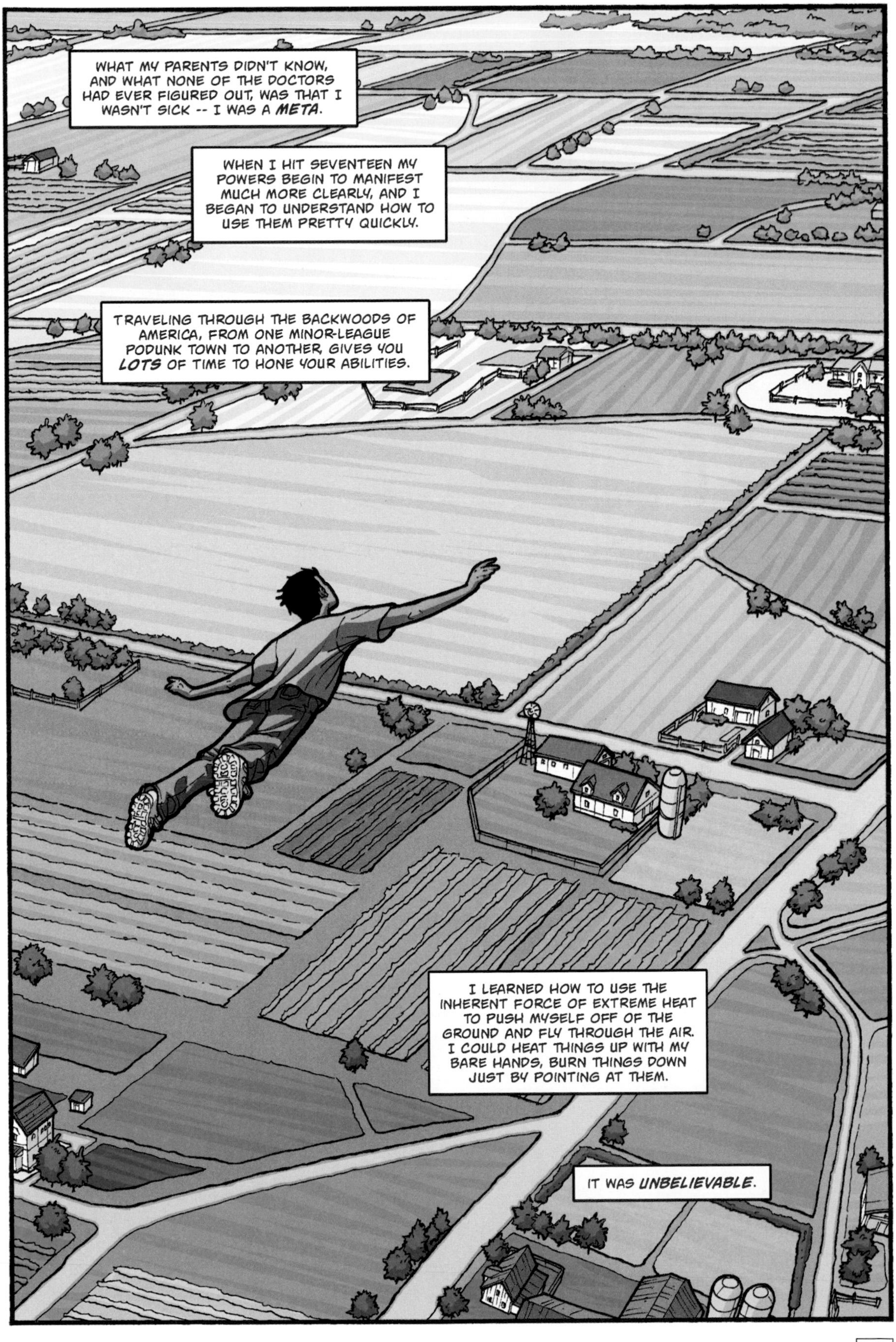
WHAT MY PARENTS DIDN'T KNOW, AND WHAT NONE OF THE DOCTORS HAD EVER FIGURED OUT, WAS THAT I WASN'T SICK -- I WAS A *META*.
WHEN I HIT SEVENTEEN MY POWERS BEGIN TO MANIFEST MUCH MORE CLEARLY, AND I BEGAN TO UNDERSTAND HOW TO USE THEM PRETTY QUICKLY.
TRAVELING THROUGH THE BACKWOODS OF AMERICA, FROM ONE MINOR-LEAGUE PODUNK TOWN TO ANOTHER, GIVES YOU *LOTS* OF TIME TO HONE YOUR ABILITIES.
I LEARNED HOW TO USE THE INHERENT FORCE OF EXTREME HEAT TO PUSH MYSELF OFF OF THE GROUND AND FLY THROUGH THE AIR. I COULD HEAT THINGS UP WITH MY BARE HANDS, BURN THINGS DOWN JUST BY POINTING AT THEM.
IT WAS *UNBELIEVABLE*.

I WAS HAVING A *BLAST*. WE WERE WINNING, I WAS GETTING TONS OF ATTENTION. I WAS YOUNG, FREE, A *SUPERSTAR* IN THE MAKING.

I ACTUALLY MADE FRIENDS. I MET A TON OF WOMEN --

BUT NONE OF THEM COULD COMPARE TO *AMARA*.

I STARTED DREAMING OF DAYS IN THE BIG LEAGUES, FANS SCREAMING MY NAME, MORE MONEY THAN GOD - AND I WAS WELL ON MY WAY TO MAKING ALL OF IT COME TRUE.

AND, RIGHT AS I WAS ABOUT TO GET THE CALL-UP TO THE MAJORS, THAT'S WHERE MY LIFE BEGAN TO FALL APART.

The Podunk Gazette

Theda fea thasoef ritp efw nmjpma aw

Topeka Tigers Have Super-Powered Pitcher
Putting TOO MUCH Heat on the Ball?

MY *POWERS* WERE DISCOVERED.

EVEN THOUGH I WOULD NEVER *DREAM* OF INTENTIONALLY USING THEM IN A GAME, THE LEAGUE DIDN'T CARE.

SO I GOT THE BOOT. THE *ONE* GOOD THING I HAD IN MY LIFE AND I HAD IT *RIPPED* FROM ME BECAUSE OF MY STUPID SUPER POWERS.

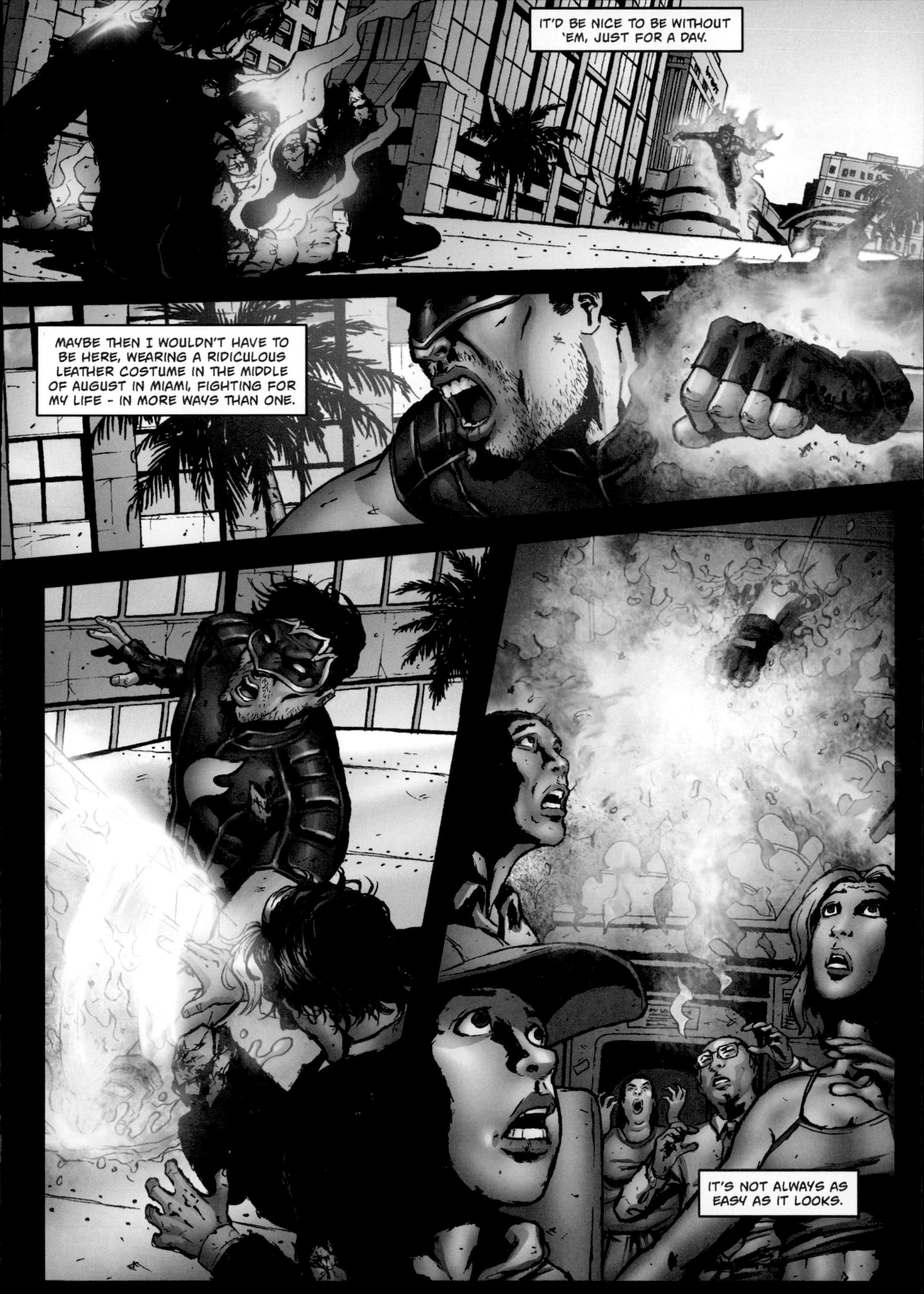
IT'D BE NICE TO BE WITHOUT 'EM, JUST FOR A DAY.
MAYBE THEN I WOULDN'T HAVE TO BE HERE, WEARING A RIDICULOUS LEATHER COSTUME IN THE MIDDLE OF AUGUST IN MIAMI, FIGHTING FOR MY LIFE - IN MORE WAYS THAN ONE.
IT'S NOT ALWAYS AS EASY AS IT LOOKS.

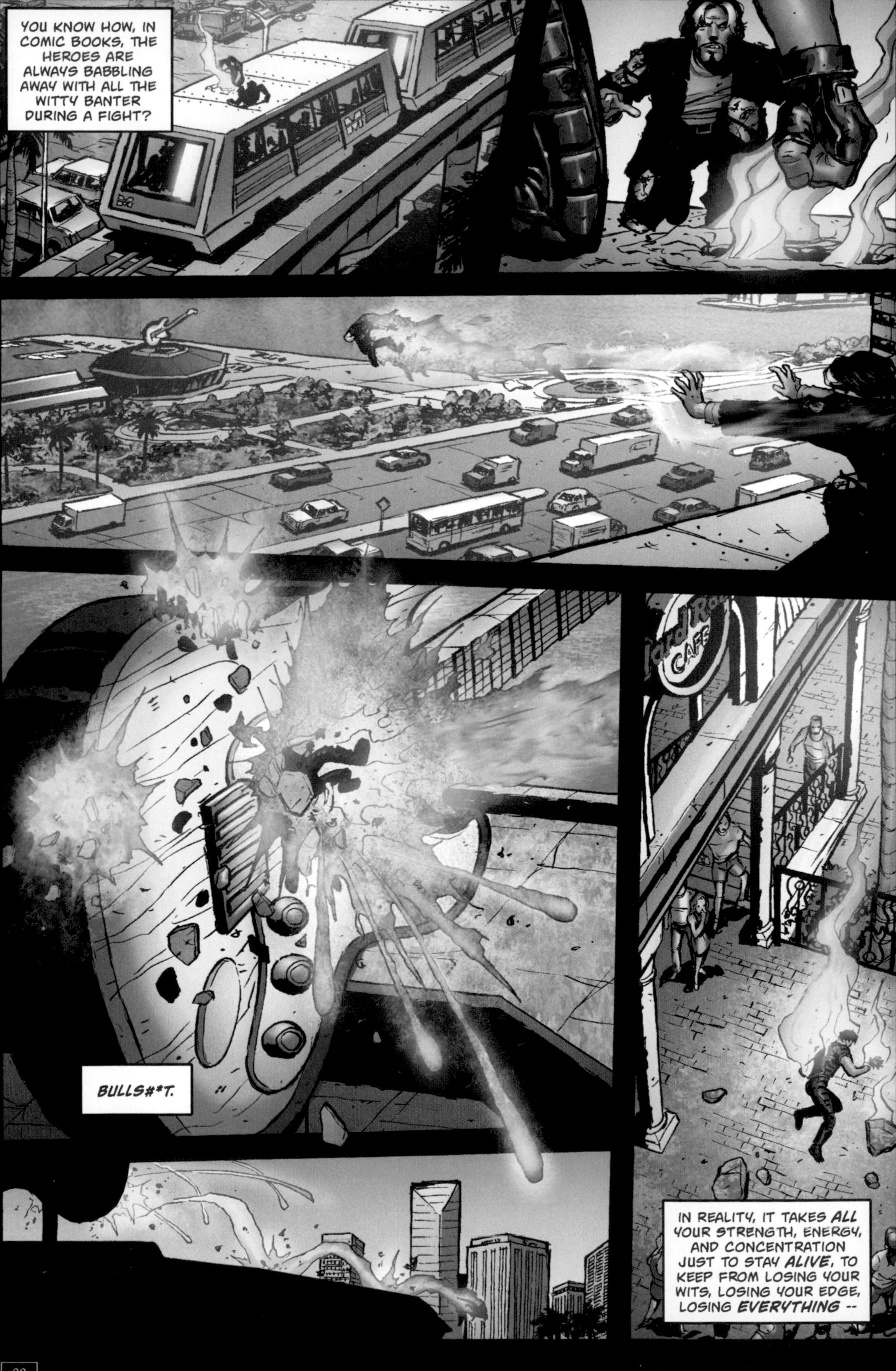
YOU KNOW HOW, IN COMIC BOOKS, THE HEROES ARE ALWAYS BABBLING AWAY WITH ALL THE WITTY BANTER DURING A FIGHT?
BULLS#*T.
IN REALITY, IT TAKES ALL YOUR STRENGTH, ENERGY, AND CONCENTRATION JUST TO STAY ALIVE, TO KEEP FROM LOSING YOUR WITS, LOSING YOUR EDGE, LOSING EVERYTHING --

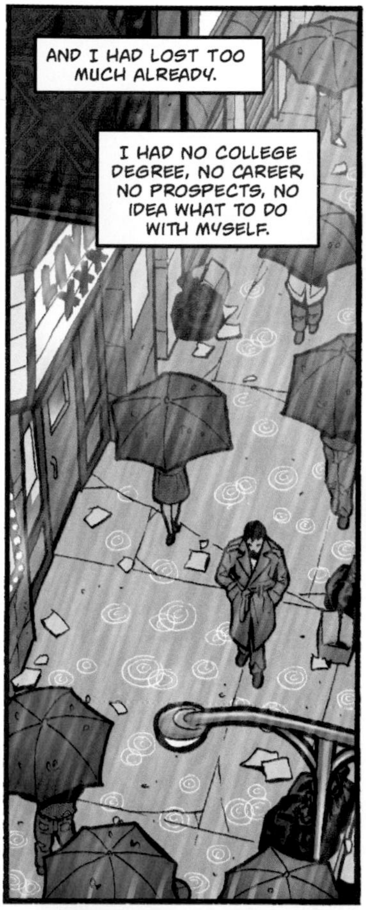
AND I HAD LOST TOO MUCH ALREADY.
I HAD NO COLLEGE DEGREE, NO CAREER, NO PROSPECTS, NO IDEA WHAT TO DO WITH MYSELF.

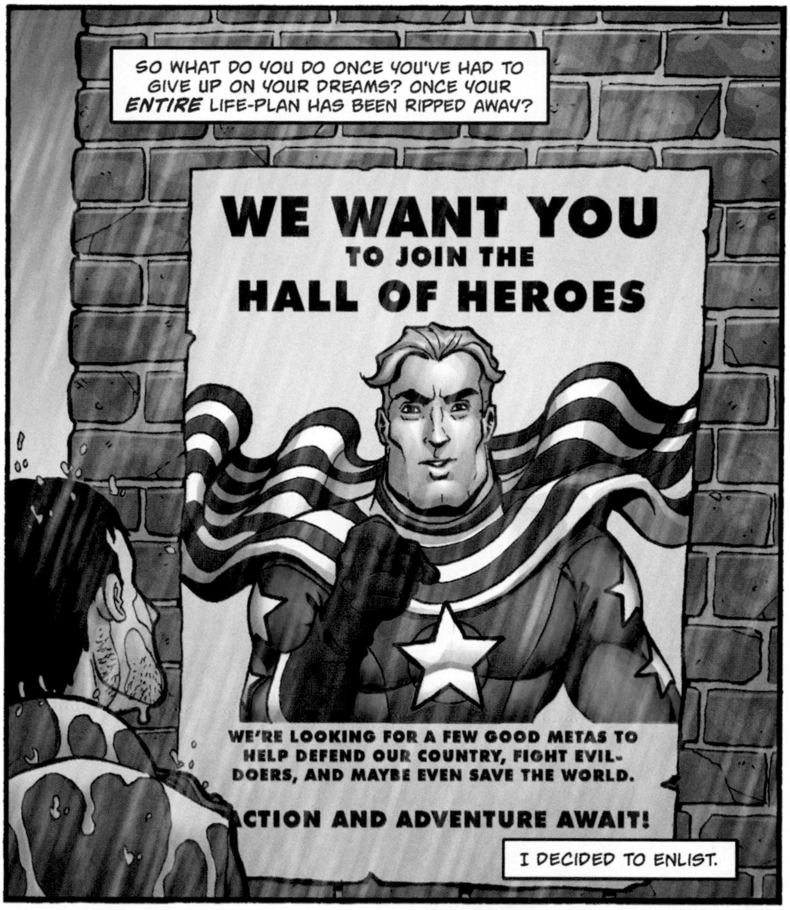
SO WHAT DO YOU DO ONCE YOU'VE HAD TO GIVE UP ON YOUR DREAMS? ONCE YOUR ENTIRE LIFE-PLAN HAS BEEN RIPPED AWAY?
WE WANT YOU
TO JOIN THE
HALL OF HEROES
WE'RE LOOKING FOR A FEW GOOD METAS TO HELP DEFEND OUR COUNTRY, FIGHT EVIL-DOERS, AND MAYBE EVEN SAVE THE WORLD.
ACTION AND ADVENTURE AWAIT!
I DECIDED TO ENLIST.

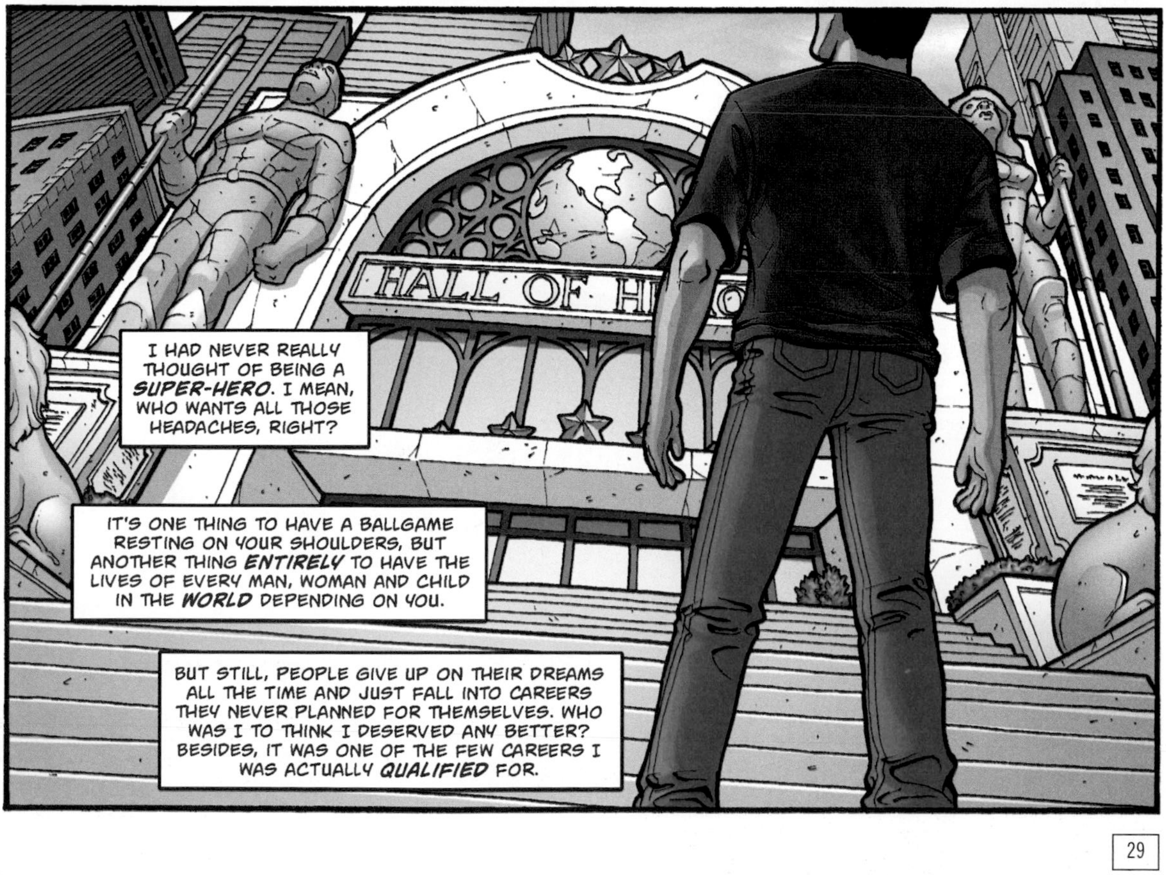
HALL OF HE
I HAD NEVER REALLY THOUGHT OF BEING A SUPER-HERO. I MEAN, WHO WANTS ALL THOSE HEADACHES, RIGHT?
IT'S ONE THING TO HAVE A BALLGAME RESTING ON YOUR SHOULDERS, BUT ANOTHER THING ENTIRELY TO HAVE THE LIVES OF EVERY MAN, WOMAN AND CHILD IN THE WORLD DEPENDING ON YOU.
BUT STILL, PEOPLE GIVE UP ON THEIR DREAMS ALL THE TIME AND JUST FALL INTO CAREERS THEY NEVER PLANNED FOR THEMSELVES. WHO WAS I TO THINK I DESERVED ANY BETTER? BESIDES, IT WAS ONE OF THE FEW CAREERS I WAS ACTUALLY QUALIFIED FOR.

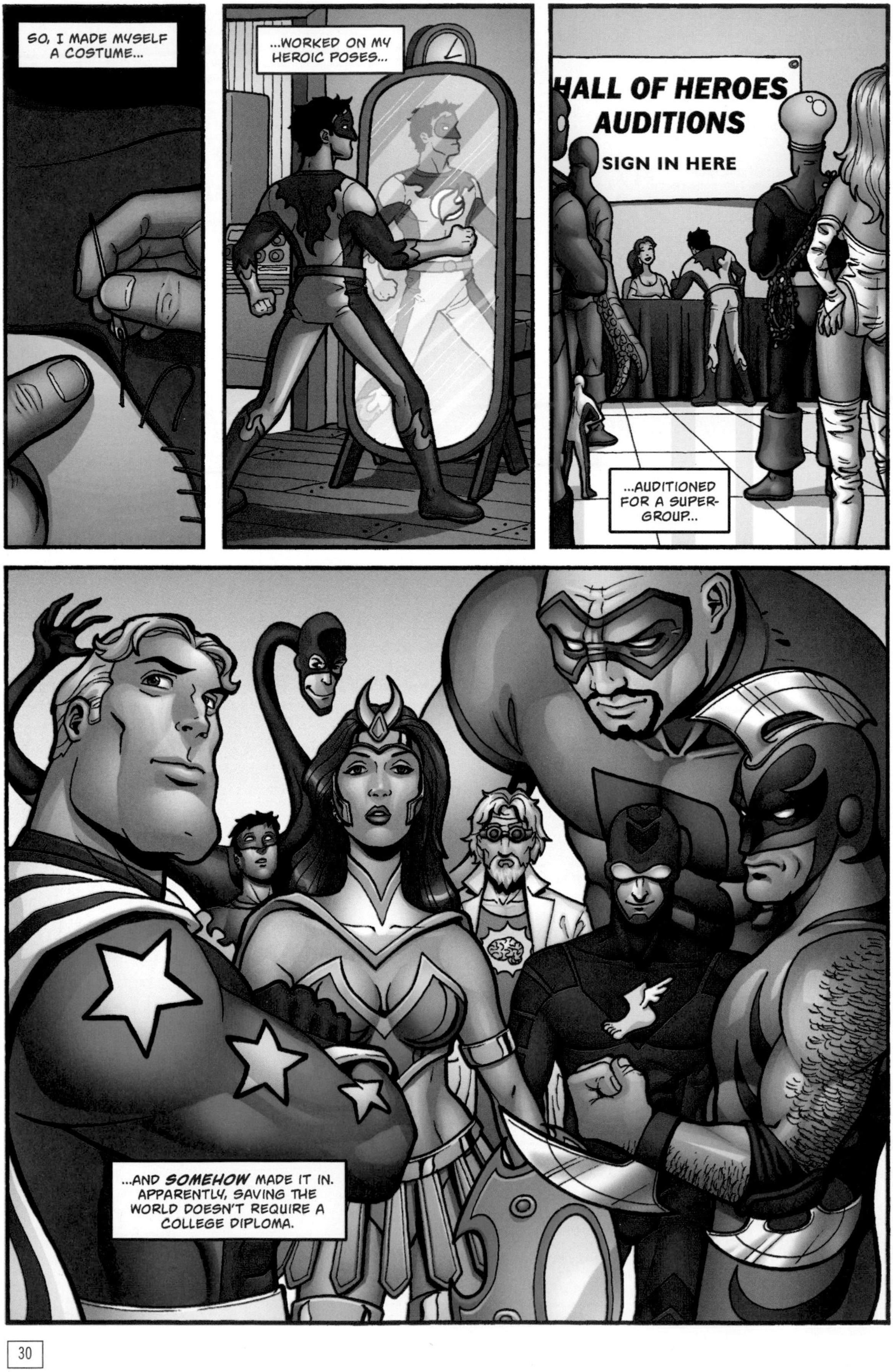
SO, I MADE MYSELF A COSTUME...
...WORKED ON MY HEROIC POSES...
HALL OF HEROES AUDITIONS
SIGN IN HERE
...AUDITIONED FOR A SUPER-GROUP...
...AND SOMEHOW MADE IT IN. APPARENTLY, SAVING THE WORLD DOESN'T REQUIRE A COLLEGE DIPLOMA.

I WAS A PART OF THE MOST RENOWNED SUPER-GROUP IN THE WORLD --

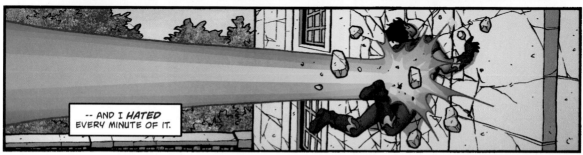

-- AND I *HATED* EVERY MINUTE OF IT.

SURE, THE JOB WAS NEVER DULL - BUT AS THE NEW GUY, AND THE TOKEN MINORITY, I DID ALL THE GRUNT-WORK, WHILE THE MORE ESTABLISHED HEROES HOUNDED ALL THE GLORY.

AND THERE WAS *NO* MONEY. WE WERE GOVERNMENT FUNDED, SO THE PAY *SUCKED*.

SURE, DOWN THE LINE I COULD GO SOLO, RAKE IN SOME ENDORSEMENT MONEY AND MERCHANDISING DEALS. BUT FOR NOW, I WAS BUSTING MY ASS EVERY DAY, AND COMING HOME TO A DISGUSTING APARTMENT AND A PACKET OF SPICY SHRIMP FLAVORED INSTANT NOODLES.

(WELL, I ACTUALLY KINDA *LIKED* THE INSTANT NOODLES.)

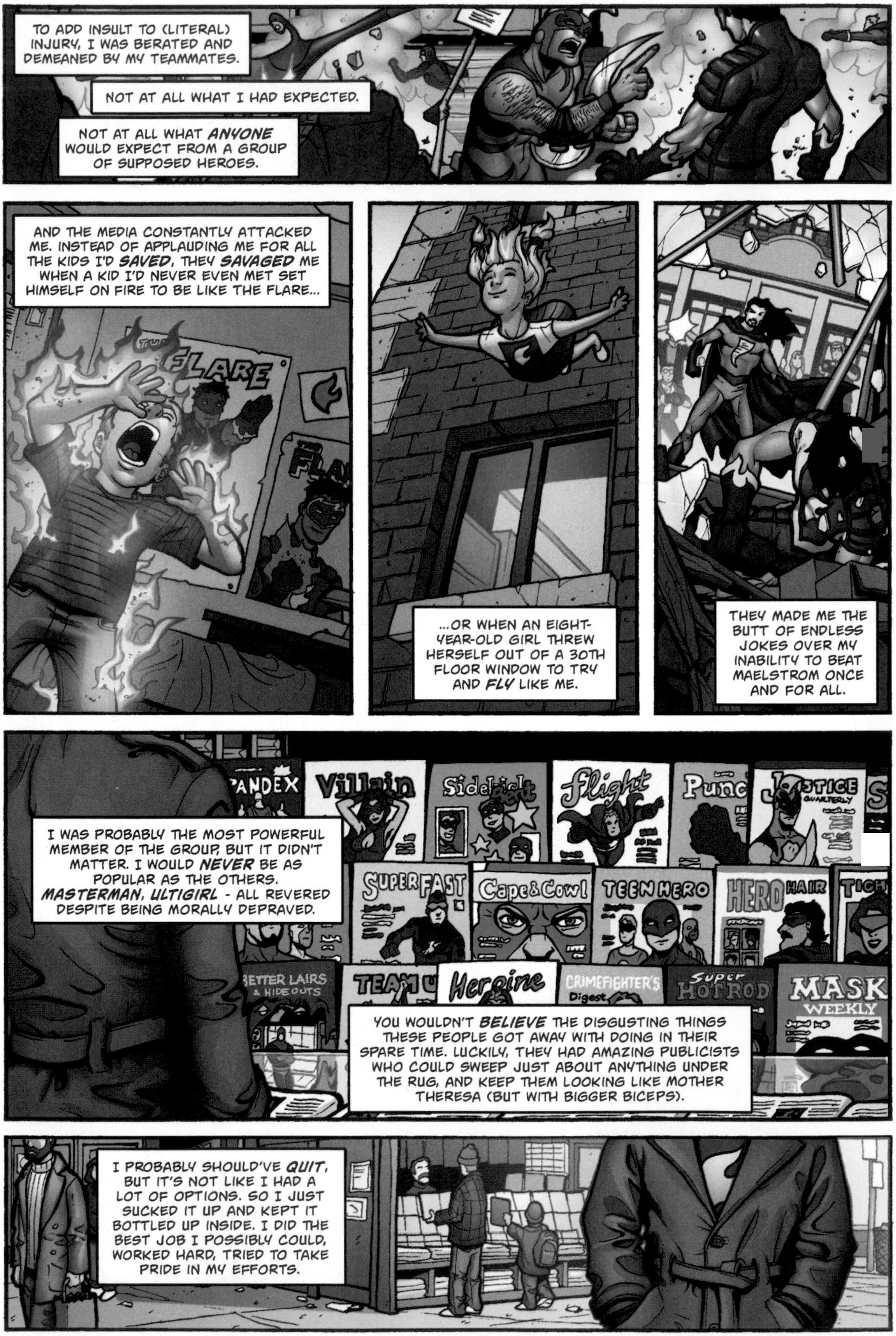
TO ADD INSULT TO (LITERAL) INJURY, I WAS BERATED AND DEMEANED BY MY TEAMMATES.
NOT AT ALL WHAT I HAD EXPECTED.
NOT AT ALL WHAT ANYONE WOULD EXPECT FROM A GROUP OF SUPPOSED HEROES.
AND THE MEDIA CONSTANTLY ATTACKED ME. INSTEAD OF APPLAUDING ME FOR ALL THE KIDS I'D SAVED, THEY SAVAGED ME WHEN A KID I'D NEVER EVEN MET SET HIMSELF ON FIRE TO BE LIKE THE FLARE...
FLARE
...OR WHEN AN EIGHT-YEAR-OLD GIRL THREW HERSELF OUT OF A 30TH FLOOR WINDOW TO TRY AND FLY LIKE ME.
THEY MADE ME THE BUTT OF ENDLESS JOKES OVER MY INABILITY TO BEAT MAELSTROM ONCE AND FOR ALL.
Villain
flight
QUARTERLY
I WAS PROBABLY THE MOST POWERFUL MEMBER OF THE GROUP, BUT IT DIDN'T MATTER. I WOULD NEVER BE AS POPULAR AS THE OTHERS. MASTERMAN, ULTIGIRL - ALL REVERED DESPITE BEING MORALLY DEPRAVED.
SUPERFAST
Cape&Cowl
TEENHERO
HERO HAIR
BETTER LAIRS & HIDEOUTS
Heroine
CRIMEFIGHTER'S Digest
Super HOTROD
MASK WEEKLY
YOU WOULDN'T BELIEVE THE DISGUSTING THINGS THESE PEOPLE GOT AWAY WITH DOING IN THEIR SPARE TIME. LUCKILY, THEY HAD AMAZING PUBLICISTS WHO COULD SWEEP JUST ABOUT ANYTHING UNDER THE RUG, AND KEEP THEM LOOKING LIKE MOTHER THERESA (BUT WITH BIGGER BICEPS).
I PROBABLY SHOULD'VE QUIT, BUT IT'S NOT LIKE I HAD A LOT OF OPTIONS. SO I JUST SUCKED IT UP AND KEPT IT BOTTLED UP INSIDE. I DID THE BEST JOB I POSSIBLY COULD, WORKED HARD, TRIED TO TAKE PRIDE IN MY EFFORTS.

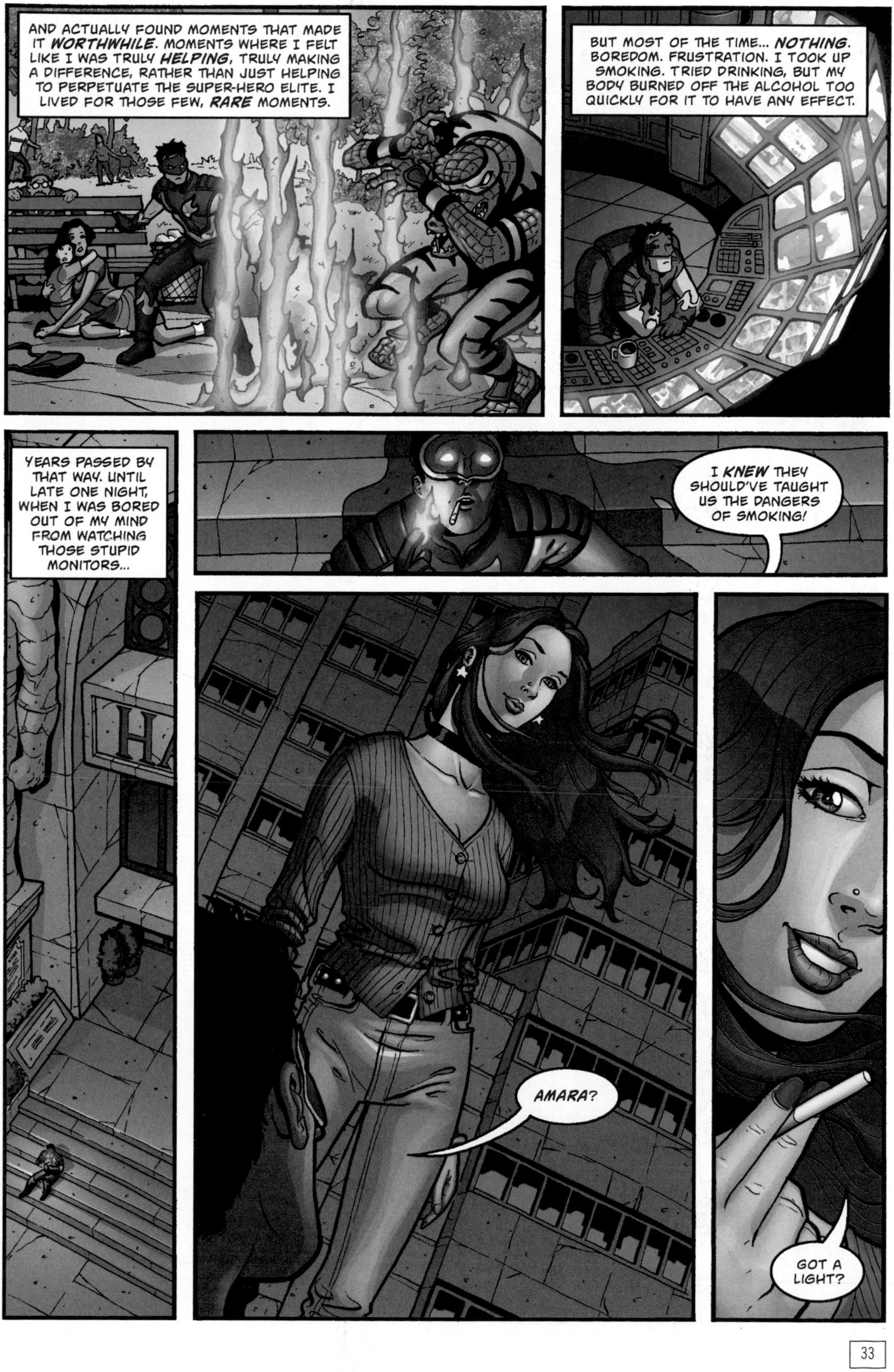
AND ACTUALLY FOUND MOMENTS THAT MADE IT ***WORTHWHILE***. MOMENTS WHERE I FELT LIKE I WAS TRULY ***HELPING***, TRULY MAKING A DIFFERENCE, RATHER THAN JUST HELPING TO PERPETUATE THE SUPER-HERO ELITE. I LIVED FOR THOSE FEW, ***RARE*** MOMENTS.
BUT MOST OF THE TIME... ***NOTHING***. BOREDOM. FRUSTRATION. I TOOK UP SMOKING. TRIED DRINKING, BUT MY BODY BURNED OFF THE ALCOHOL TOO QUICKLY FOR IT TO HAVE ANY EFFECT.
YEARS PASSED BY THAT WAY. UNTIL LATE ONE NIGHT, WHEN I WAS BORED OUT OF MY MIND FROM WATCHING THOSE STUPID MONITORS...
I ***KNEW*** THEY SHOULD'VE TAUGHT US THE DANGERS OF SMOKING!
H
AMARA?
GOT A LIGHT?

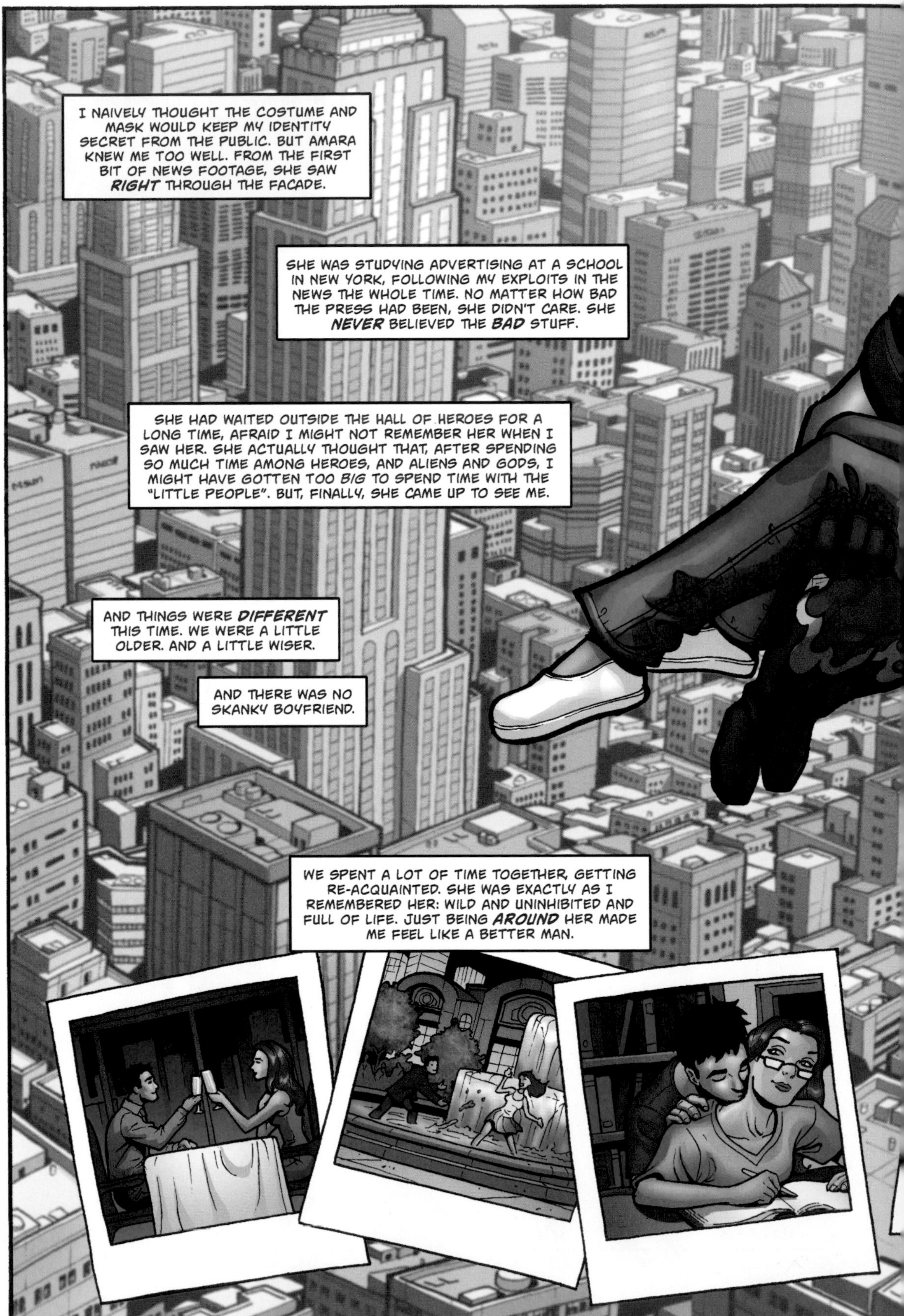
I NAIVELY THOUGHT THE COSTUME AND MASK WOULD KEEP MY IDENTITY SECRET FROM THE PUBLIC. BUT AMARA KNEW ME TOO WELL. FROM THE FIRST BIT OF NEWS FOOTAGE, SHE SAW *RIGHT* THROUGH THE FACADE.
SHE WAS STUDYING ADVERTISING AT A SCHOOL IN NEW YORK, FOLLOWING MY EXPLOITS IN THE NEWS THE WHOLE TIME. NO MATTER HOW BAD THE PRESS HAD BEEN, SHE DIDN'T CARE. SHE *NEVER* BELIEVED THE *BAD* STUFF.
SHE HAD WAITED OUTSIDE THE HALL OF HEROES FOR A LONG TIME, AFRAID I MIGHT NOT REMEMBER HER WHEN I SAW HER. SHE ACTUALLY THOUGHT THAT, AFTER SPENDING SO MUCH TIME AMONG HEROES, AND ALIENS AND GODS, I MIGHT HAVE GOTTEN TOO *BIG* TO SPEND TIME WITH THE "LITTLE PEOPLE". BUT, FINALLY, SHE CAME UP TO SEE ME.
AND THINGS WERE *DIFFERENT* THIS TIME. WE WERE A LITTLE OLDER. AND A LITTLE WISER.
AND THERE WAS NO SKANKY BOYFRIEND.
WE SPENT A LOT OF TIME TOGETHER, GETTING RE-ACQUAINTED. SHE WAS EXACTLY AS I REMEMBERED HER: WILD AND UNINHIBITED AND FULL OF LIFE. JUST BEING *AROUND* HER MADE ME FEEL LIKE A BETTER MAN.

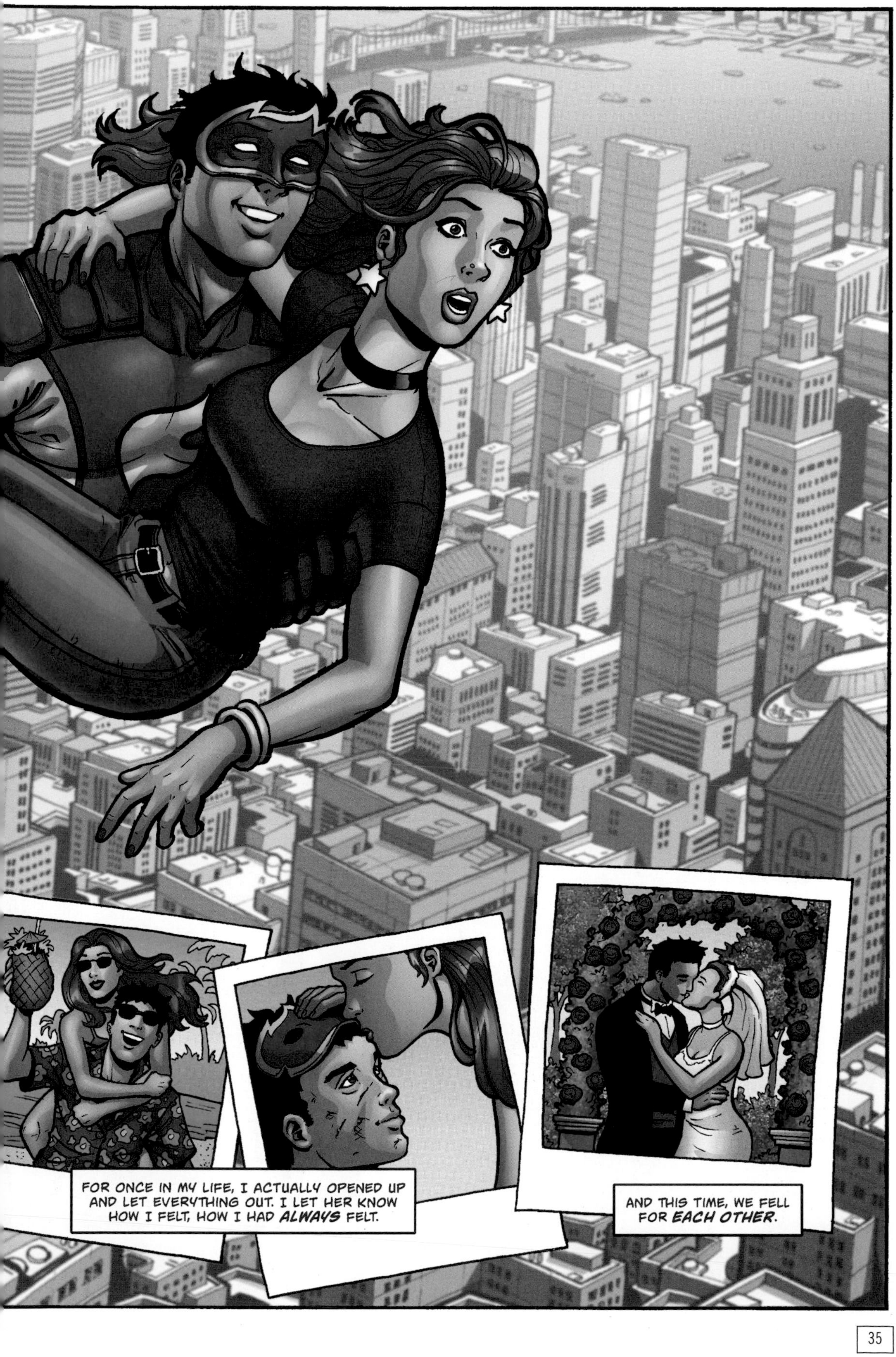
FOR ONCE IN MY LIFE, I ACTUALLY OPENED UP AND LET EVERYTHING OUT. I LET HER KNOW HOW I FELT, HOW I HAD *ALWAYS* FELT.
AND THIS TIME, WE FELL FOR *EACH OTHER*.

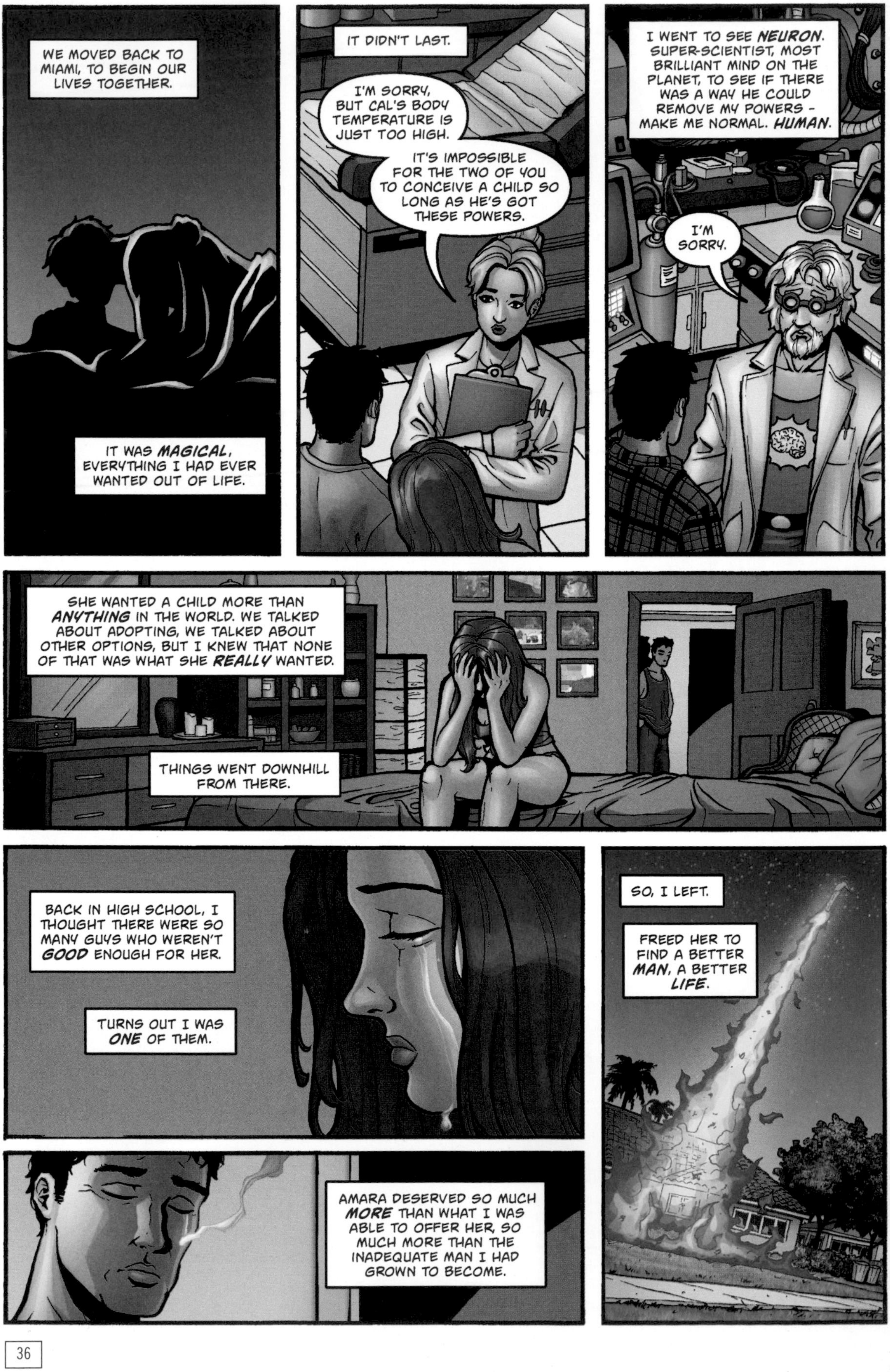
WE MOVED BACK TO MIAMI, TO BEGIN OUR LIVES TOGETHER.
IT WAS MAGICAL, EVERYTHING I HAD EVER WANTED OUT OF LIFE.
IT DIDN'T LAST.
I'M SORRY, BUT CAL'S BODY TEMPERATURE IS JUST TOO HIGH.
IT'S IMPOSSIBLE FOR THE TWO OF YOU TO CONCEIVE A CHILD SO LONG AS HE'S GOT THESE POWERS.
I WENT TO SEE NEURON. SUPER-SCIENTIST, MOST BRILLIANT MIND ON THE PLANET, TO SEE IF THERE WAS A WAY HE COULD REMOVE MY POWERS - MAKE ME NORMAL. HUMAN.
I'M SORRY.
SHE WANTED A CHILD MORE THAN ANYTHING IN THE WORLD. WE TALKED ABOUT ADOPTING, WE TALKED ABOUT OTHER OPTIONS, BUT I KNEW THAT NONE OF THAT WAS WHAT SHE REALLY WANTED.
THINGS WENT DOWNHILL FROM THERE.
BACK IN HIGH SCHOOL, I THOUGHT THERE WERE SO MANY GUYS WHO WEREN'T GOOD ENOUGH FOR HER.
TURNS OUT I WAS ONE OF THEM.
AMARA DESERVED SO MUCH MORE THAN WHAT I WAS ABLE TO OFFER HER, SO MUCH MORE THAN THE INADEQUATE MAN I HAD GROWN TO BECOME.
SO, I LEFT.
FREED HER TO FIND A BETTER MAN, A BETTER LIFE.

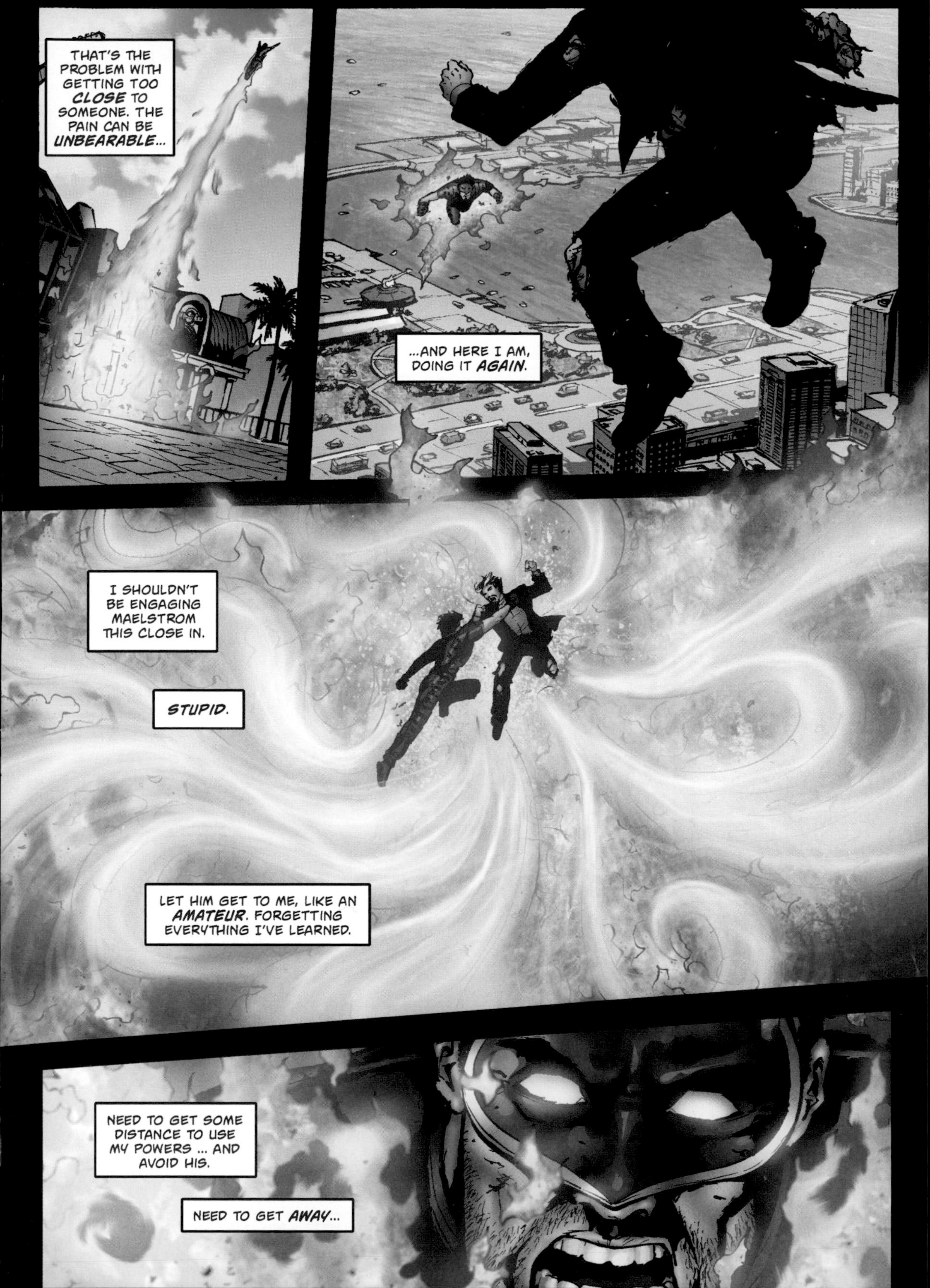
THAT'S THE PROBLEM WITH GETTING TOO CLOSE TO SOMEONE. THE PAIN CAN BE UNBEARABLE...
...AND HERE I AM, DOING IT AGAIN.
I SHOULDN'T BE ENGAGING MAELSTROM THIS CLOSE IN.
STUPID.
LET HIM GET TO ME, LIKE AN AMATEUR. FORGETTING EVERYTHING I'VE LEARNED.
NEED TO GET SOME DISTANCE TO USE MY POWERS ... AND AVOID HIS.
NEED TO GET AWAY...

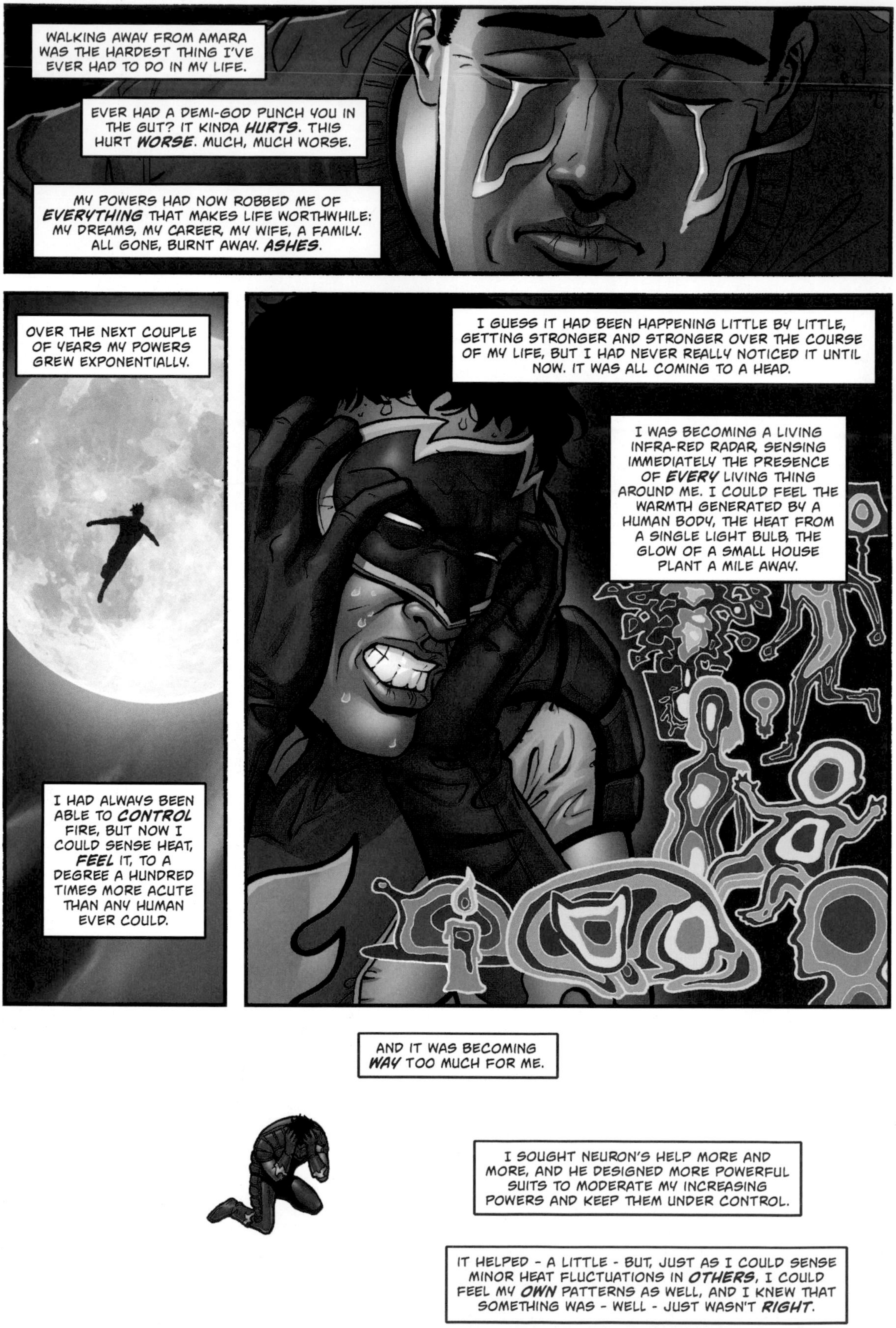
WALKING AWAY FROM AMARA WAS THE HARDEST THING I'VE EVER HAD TO DO IN MY LIFE.
EVER HAD A DEMI-GOD PUNCH YOU IN THE GUT? IT KINDA HURTS. THIS HURT WORSE. MUCH, MUCH WORSE.
MY POWERS HAD NOW ROBBED ME OF EVERYTHING THAT MAKES LIFE WORTHWHILE: MY DREAMS, MY CAREER, MY WIFE, A FAMILY. ALL GONE, BURNT AWAY. ASHES.
OVER THE NEXT COUPLE OF YEARS MY POWERS GREW EXPONENTIALLY.
I HAD ALWAYS BEEN ABLE TO CONTROL FIRE, BUT NOW I COULD SENSE HEAT, FEEL IT, TO A DEGREE A HUNDRED TIMES MORE ACUTE THAN ANY HUMAN EVER COULD.
I GUESS IT HAD BEEN HAPPENING LITTLE BY LITTLE, GETTING STRONGER AND STRONGER OVER THE COURSE OF MY LIFE, BUT I HAD NEVER REALLY NOTICED IT UNTIL NOW. IT WAS ALL COMING TO A HEAD.
I WAS BECOMING A LIVING INFRA-RED RADAR, SENSING IMMEDIATELY THE PRESENCE OF EVERY LIVING THING AROUND ME. I COULD FEEL THE WARMTH GENERATED BY A HUMAN BODY, THE HEAT FROM A SINGLE LIGHT BULB, THE GLOW OF A SMALL HOUSE PLANT A MILE AWAY.
AND IT WAS BECOMING WAY TOO MUCH FOR ME.
I SOUGHT NEURON'S HELP MORE AND MORE, AND HE DESIGNED MORE POWERFUL SUITS TO MODERATE MY INCREASING POWERS AND KEEP THEM UNDER CONTROL.
IT HELPED - A LITTLE - BUT, JUST AS I COULD SENSE MINOR HEAT FLUCTUATIONS IN OTHERS, I COULD FEEL MY OWN PATTERNS AS WELL, AND I KNEW THAT SOMETHING WAS - WELL - JUST WASN'T RIGHT.

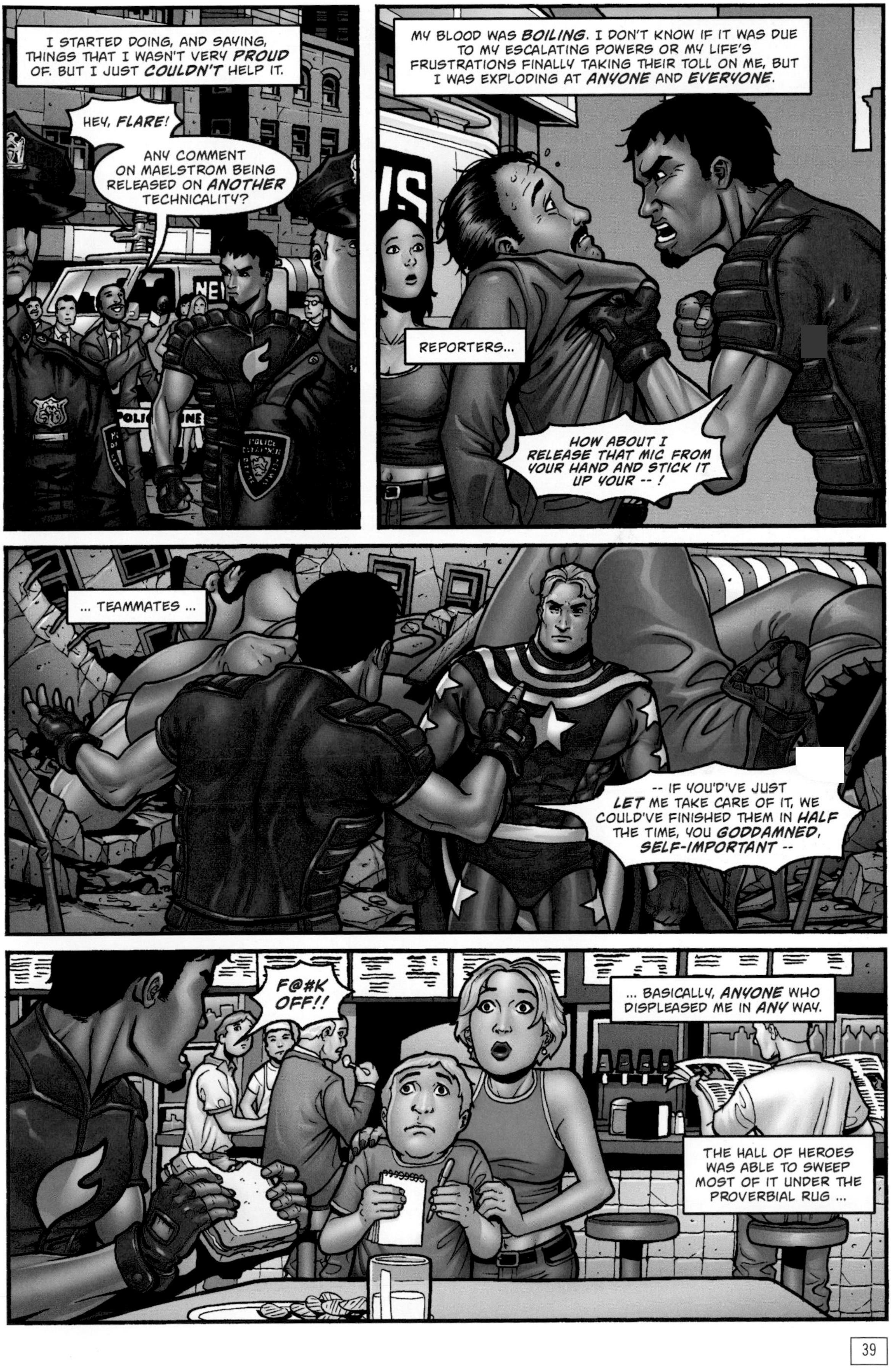

I STARTED DOING, AND SAYING, THINGS THAT I WASN'T VERY *PROUD* OF. BUT I JUST *COULDN'T* HELP IT.
HEY, *FLARE!*
ANY COMMENT ON MAELSTROM BEING RELEASED ON *ANOTHER* TECHNICALITY?
MY BLOOD WAS *BOILING*. I DON'T KNOW IF IT WAS DUE TO MY ESCALATING POWERS OR MY LIFE'S FRUSTRATIONS FINALLY TAKING THEIR TOLL ON ME, BUT I WAS EXPLODING AT *ANYONE* AND *EVERYONE*.
REPORTERS...
HOW ABOUT I RELEASE THAT MIC FROM YOUR HAND AND STICK IT UP YOUR -- !
... TEAMMATES ...
-- IF YOU'D'VE JUST *LET* ME TAKE CARE OF IT, WE COULD'VE FINISHED THEM IN *HALF* THE TIME, YOU *GODDAMNED, SELF-IMPORTANT* --
F@#K OFF!!
... BASICALLY, *ANYONE* WHO DISPLEASED ME IN *ANY* WAY.
THE HALL OF HEROES WAS ABLE TO SWEEP MOST OF IT UNDER THE PROVERBIAL RUG ...

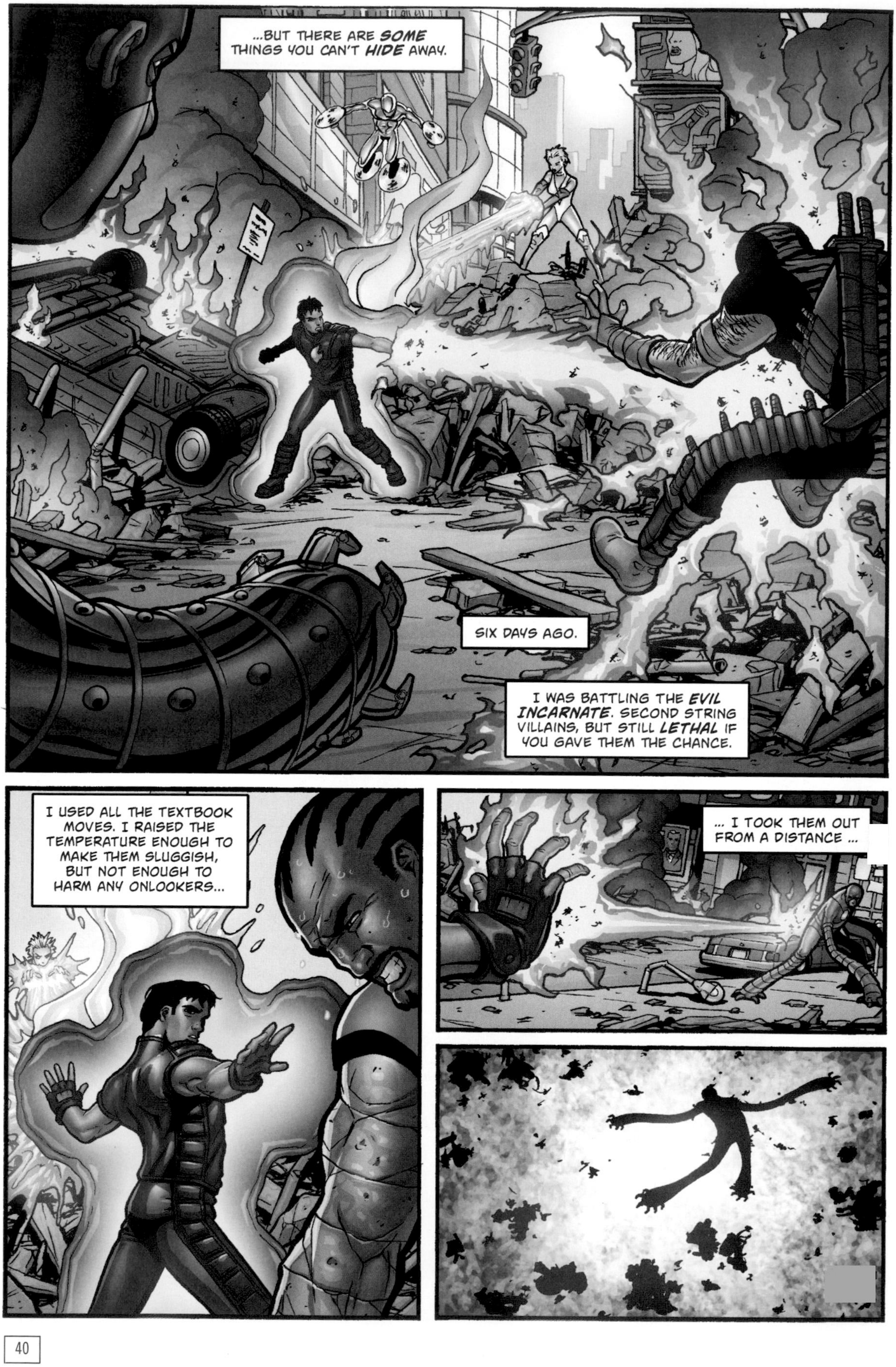
...BUT THERE ARE SOME THINGS YOU CAN'T HIDE AWAY.
SIX DAYS AGO.
I WAS BATTLING THE EVIL INCARNATE. SECOND STRING VILLAINS, BUT STILL LETHAL IF YOU GAVE THEM THE CHANCE.
I USED ALL THE TEXTBOOK MOVES. I RAISED THE TEMPERATURE ENOUGH TO MAKE THEM SLUGGISH, BUT NOT ENOUGH TO HARM ANY ONLOOKERS...
... I TOOK THEM OUT FROM A DISTANCE ...

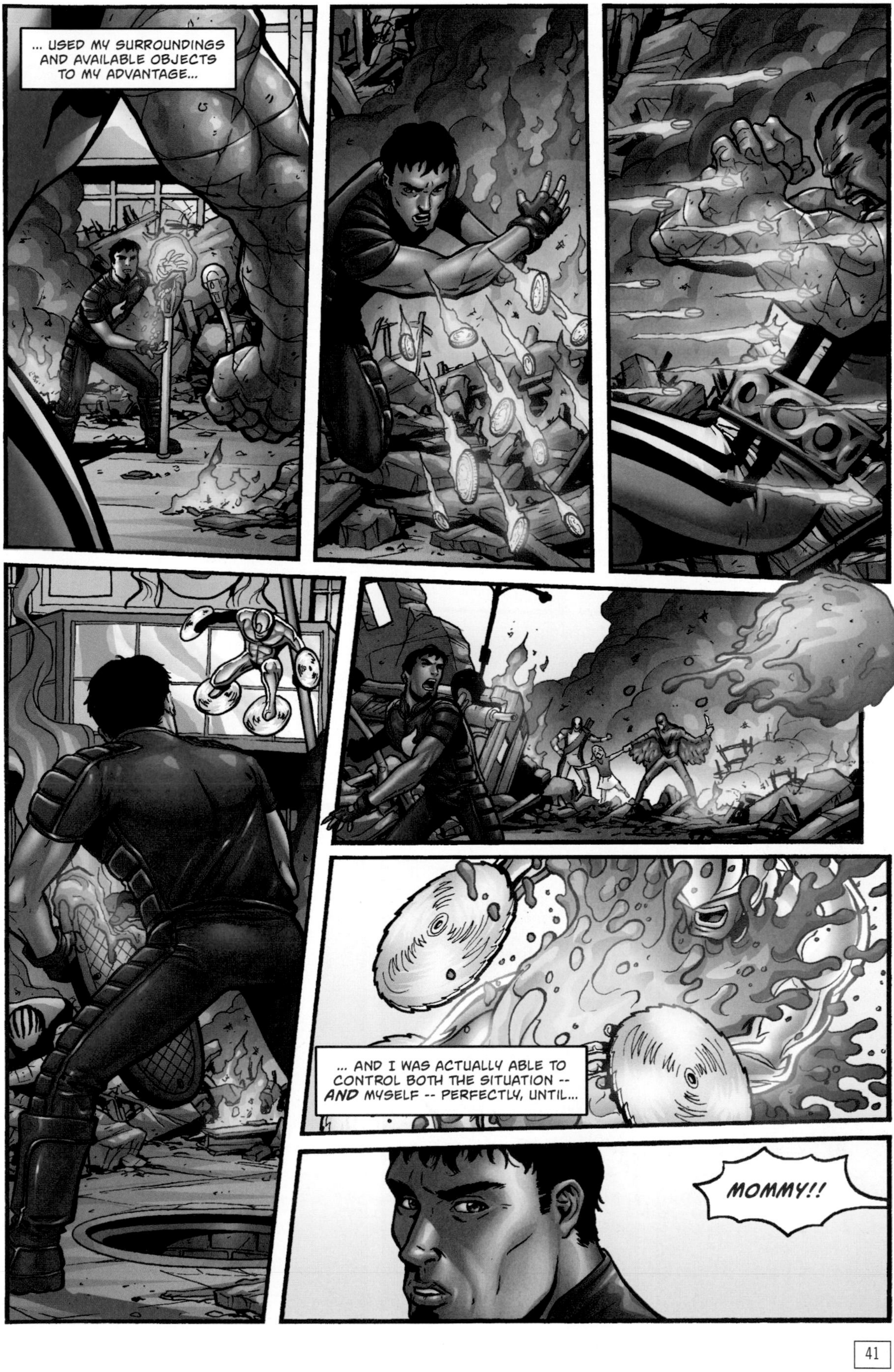
... USED MY SURROUNDINGS
AND AVAILABLE OBJECTS
TO MY ADVANTAGE...
... AND I WAS ACTUALLY ABLE TO
CONTROL BOTH THE SITUATION --
AND MYSELF -- PERFECTLY, UNTIL...
MOMMY!!

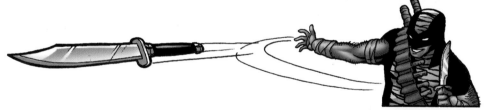

STOP F@#KING AROUND!

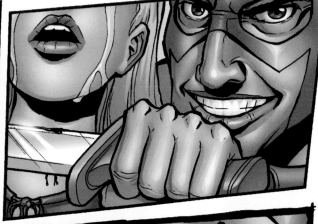

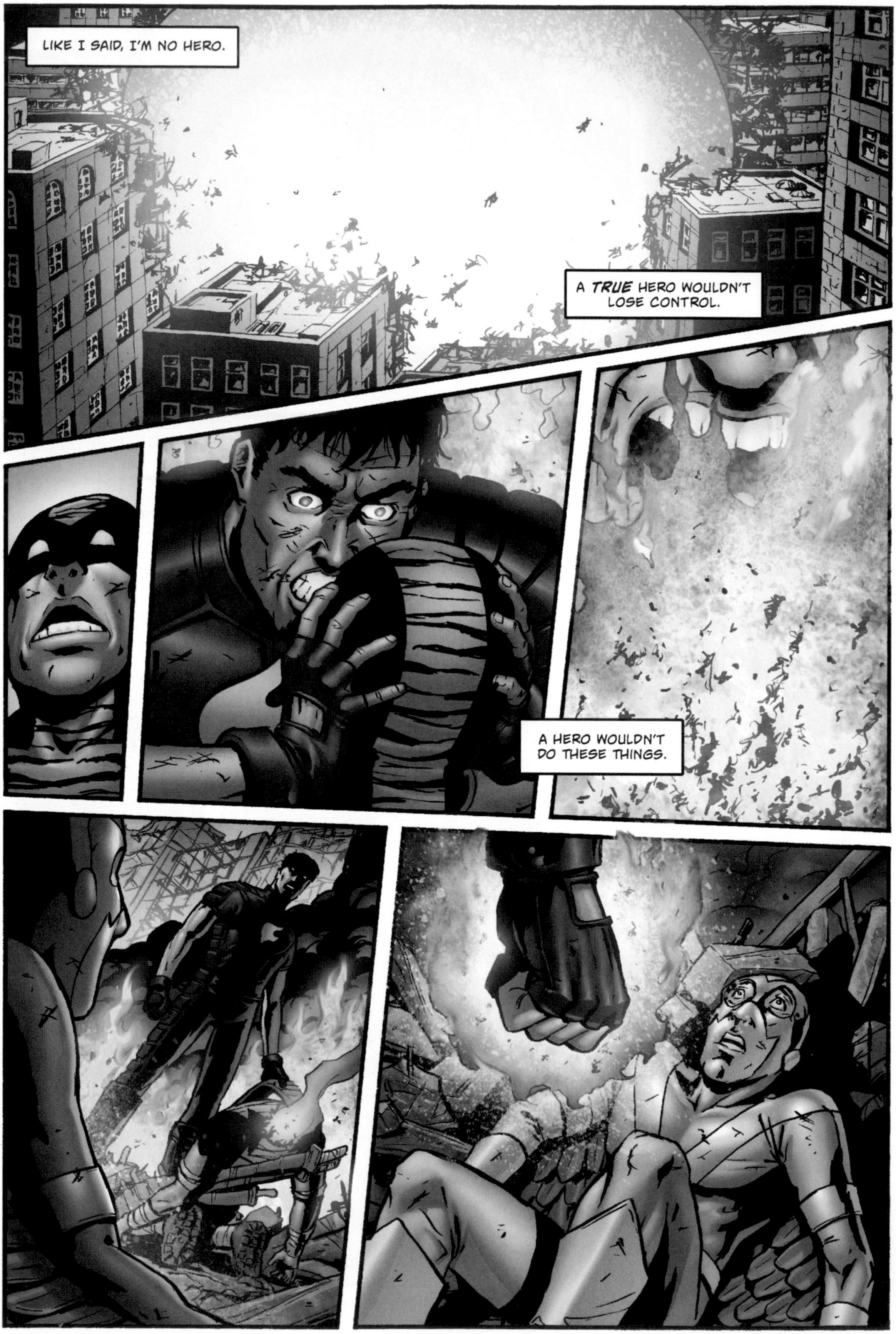
LIKE I SAID, I'M NO HERO.
A *TRUE* HERO WOULDN'T LOSE CONTROL.
A HERO WOULDN'T DO THESE THINGS.

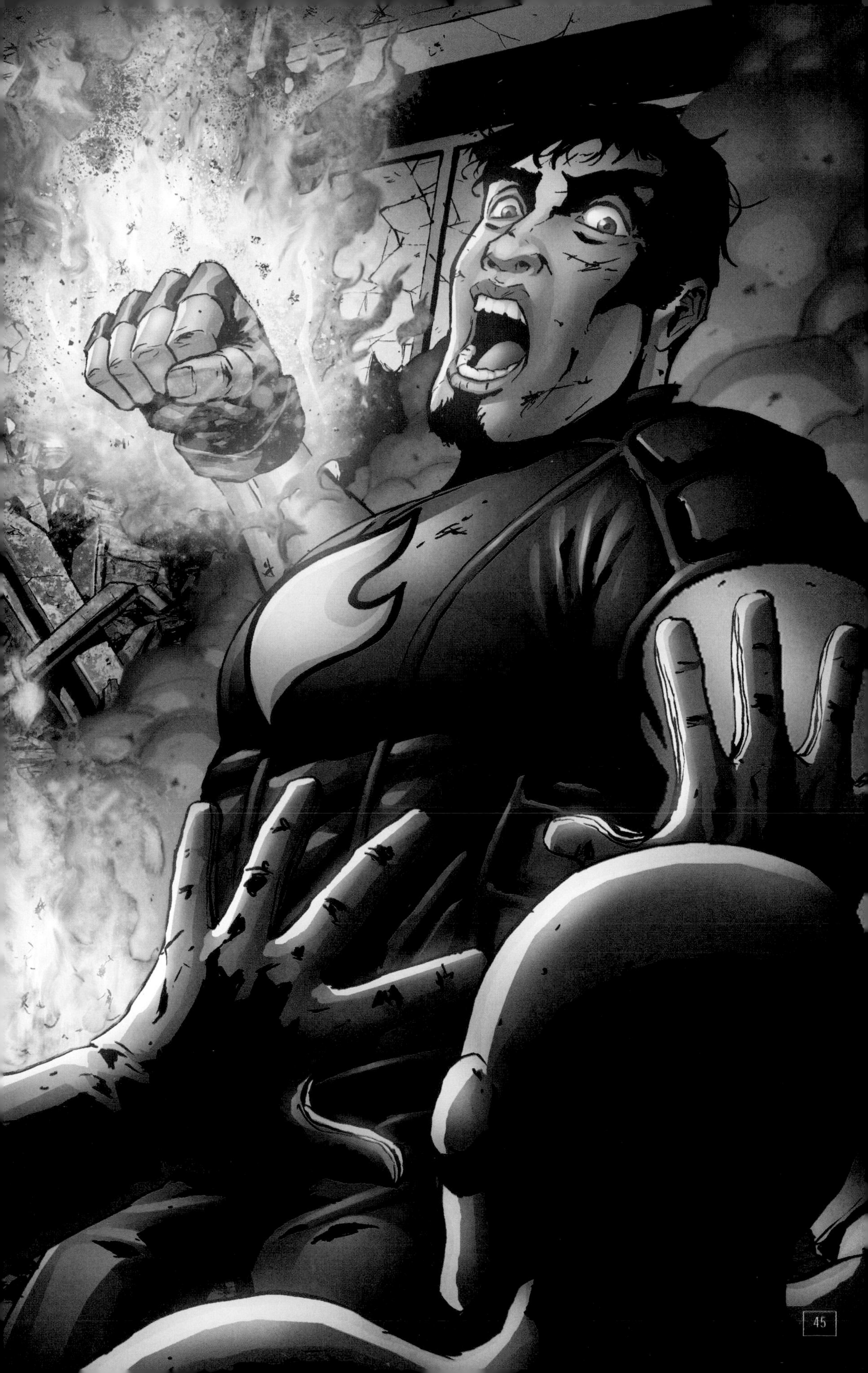

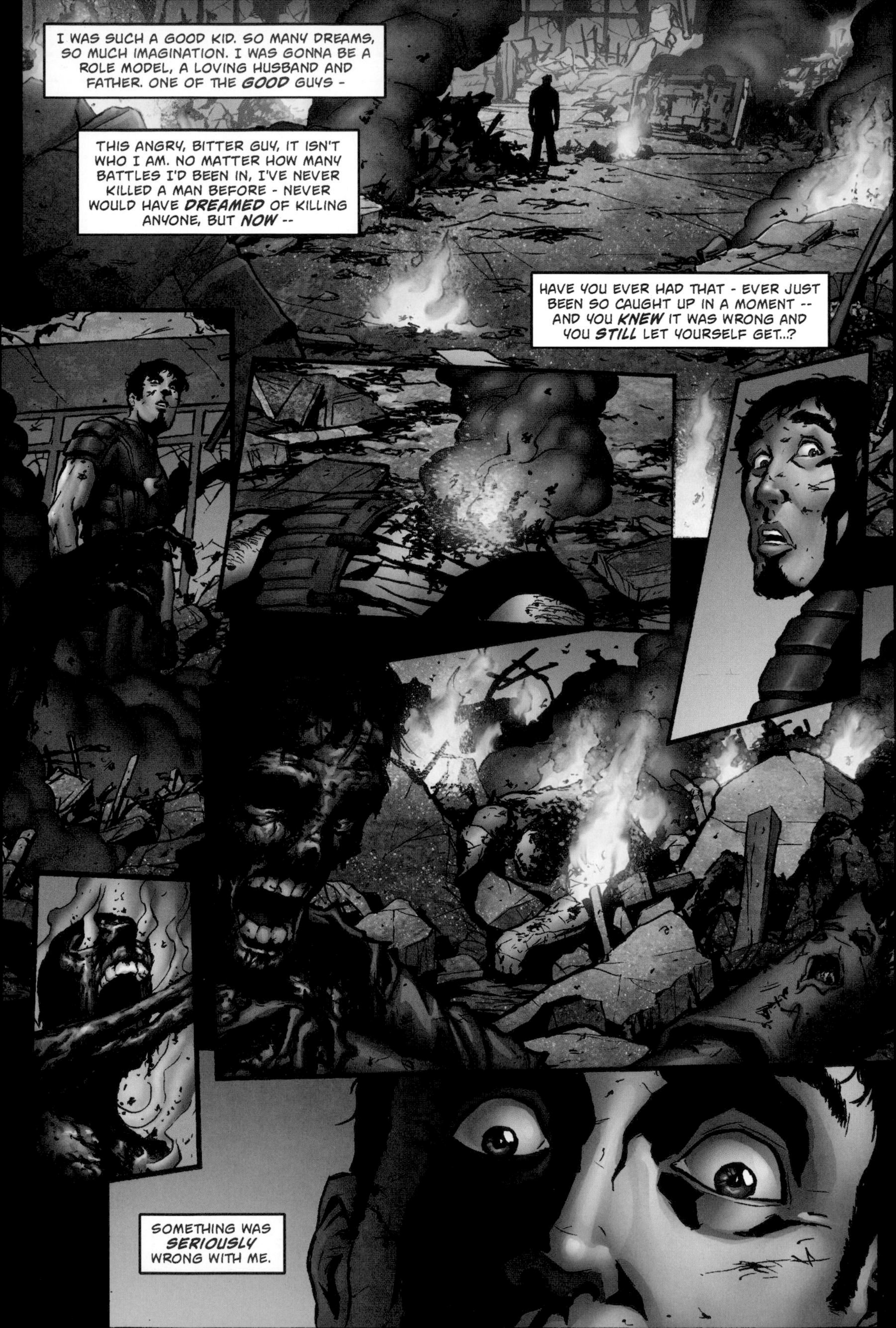
I WAS SUCH A GOOD KID. SO MANY DREAMS, SO MUCH IMAGINATION. I WAS GONNA BE A ROLE MODEL, A LOVING HUSBAND AND FATHER. ONE OF THE GOOD GUYS -
THIS ANGRY, BITTER GUY, IT ISN'T WHO I AM. NO MATTER HOW MANY BATTLES I'D BEEN IN, I'VE NEVER KILLED A MAN BEFORE - NEVER WOULD HAVE DREAMED OF KILLING ANYONE, BUT NOW --
HAVE YOU EVER HAD THAT - EVER JUST BEEN SO CAUGHT UP IN A MOMENT -- AND YOU KNEW IT WAS WRONG AND YOU STILL LET YOURSELF GET...?
SOMETHING WAS SERIOUSLY WRONG WITH ME.

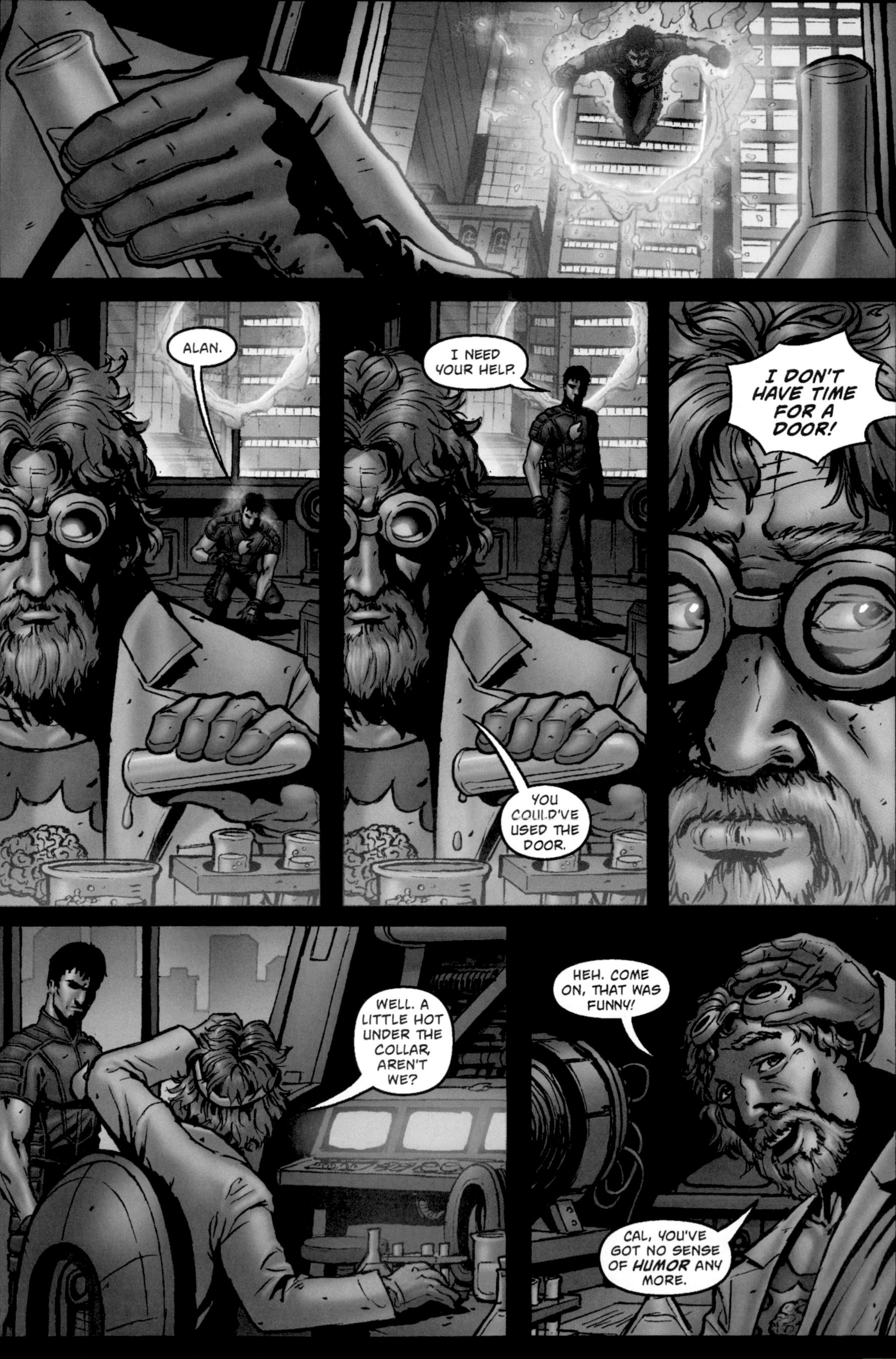
ALAN.
I NEED YOUR HELP.
YOU COULD'VE USED THE DOOR.
I DON'T HAVE TIME FOR A DOOR!
WELL. A LITTLE HOT UNDER THE COLLAR, AREN'T WE?
HEH. COME ON, THAT WAS FUNNY!
CAL, YOU'VE GOT NO SENSE OF HUMOR ANY MORE.

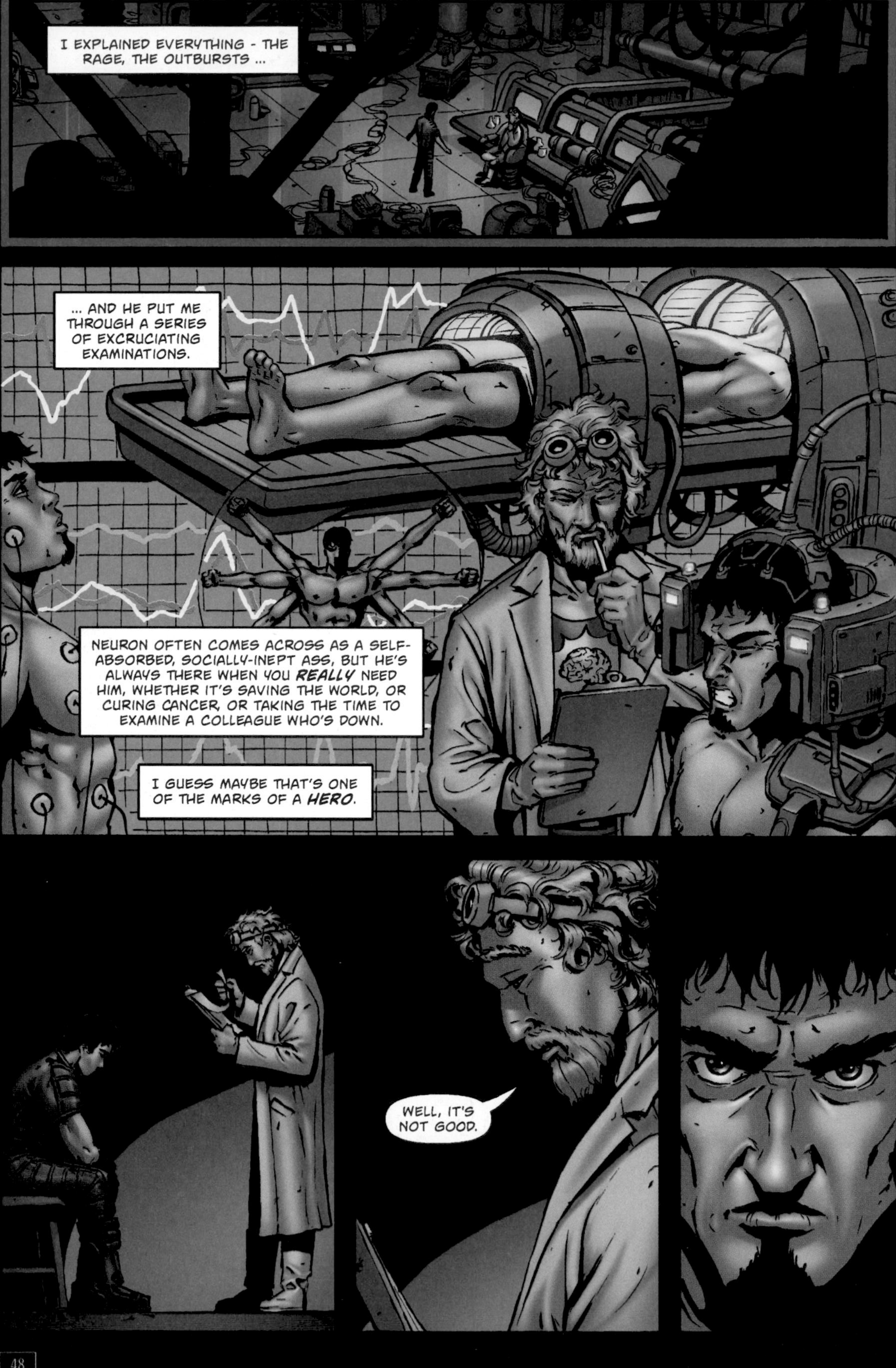
I EXPLAINED EVERYTHING - THE RAGE, THE OUTBURSTS ...
... AND HE PUT ME THROUGH A SERIES OF EXCRUCIATING EXAMINATIONS.
NEURON OFTEN COMES ACROSS AS A SELF-ABSORBED, SOCIALLY-INEPT ASS, BUT HE'S ALWAYS THERE WHEN YOU REALLY NEED HIM, WHETHER IT'S SAVING THE WORLD, OR CURING CANCER, OR TAKING THE TIME TO EXAMINE A COLLEAGUE WHO'S DOWN.
I GUESS MAYBE THAT'S ONE OF THE MARKS OF A HERO.
WELL, IT'S NOT GOOD.

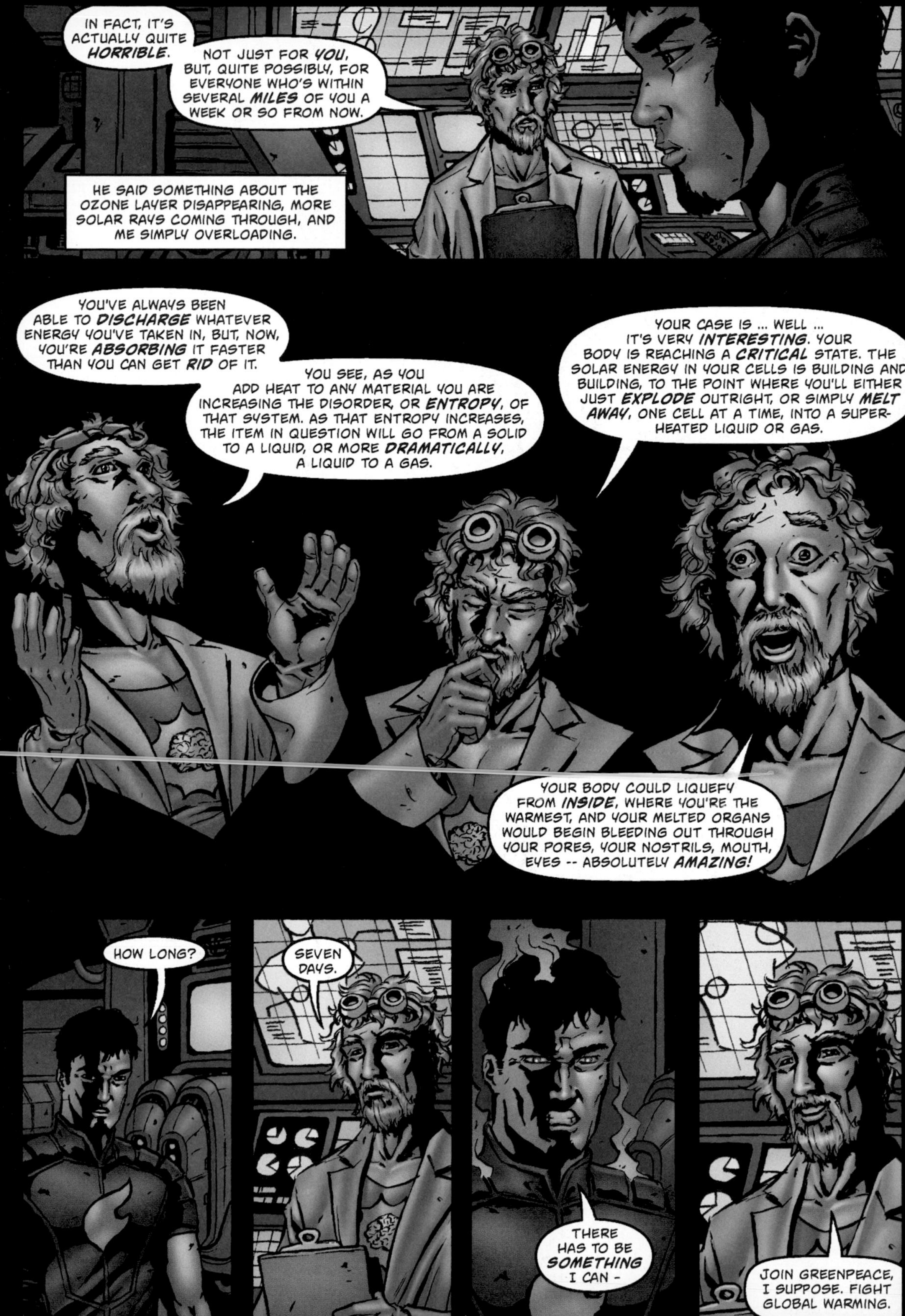

IN FACT, IT'S ACTUALLY QUITE *HORRIBLE*.
NOT JUST FOR *YOU*, BUT, QUITE POSSIBLY, FOR EVERYONE WHO'S WITHIN SEVERAL *MILES* OF YOU A WEEK OR SO FROM NOW.
HE SAID SOMETHING ABOUT THE OZONE LAYER DISAPPEARING, MORE SOLAR RAYS COMING THROUGH, AND ME SIMPLY OVERLOADING.
YOU'VE ALWAYS BEEN ABLE TO *DISCHARGE* WHATEVER ENERGY YOU'VE TAKEN IN, BUT, NOW, YOU'RE *ABSORBING* IT FASTER THAN YOU CAN GET *RID* OF IT.
YOU SEE, AS YOU ADD HEAT TO ANY MATERIAL YOU ARE INCREASING THE DISORDER, OR *ENTROPY*, OF THAT SYSTEM. AS THAT ENTROPY INCREASES, THE ITEM IN QUESTION WILL GO FROM A SOLID TO A LIQUID, OR MORE *DRAMATICALLY*, A LIQUID TO A GAS.
YOUR CASE IS ... WELL ... IT'S VERY *INTERESTING*. YOUR BODY IS REACHING A *CRITICAL* STATE. THE SOLAR ENERGY IN YOUR CELLS IS BUILDING AND BUILDING, TO THE POINT WHERE YOU'LL EITHER JUST *EXPLODE* OUTRIGHT, OR SIMPLY *MELT AWAY*, ONE CELL AT A TIME, INTO A SUPER-HEATED LIQUID OR GAS.
YOUR BODY COULD LIQUEFY FROM *INSIDE*, WHERE YOU'RE THE WARMEST, AND YOUR MELTED ORGANS WOULD BEGIN BLEEDING OUT THROUGH YOUR PORES, YOUR NOSTRILS, MOUTH, EYES -- ABSOLUTELY *AMAZING!*
HOW LONG?
SEVEN DAYS.
THERE HAS TO BE *SOMETHING* I CAN -
JOIN GREENPEACE, I SUPPOSE. FIGHT GLOBAL WARMING.

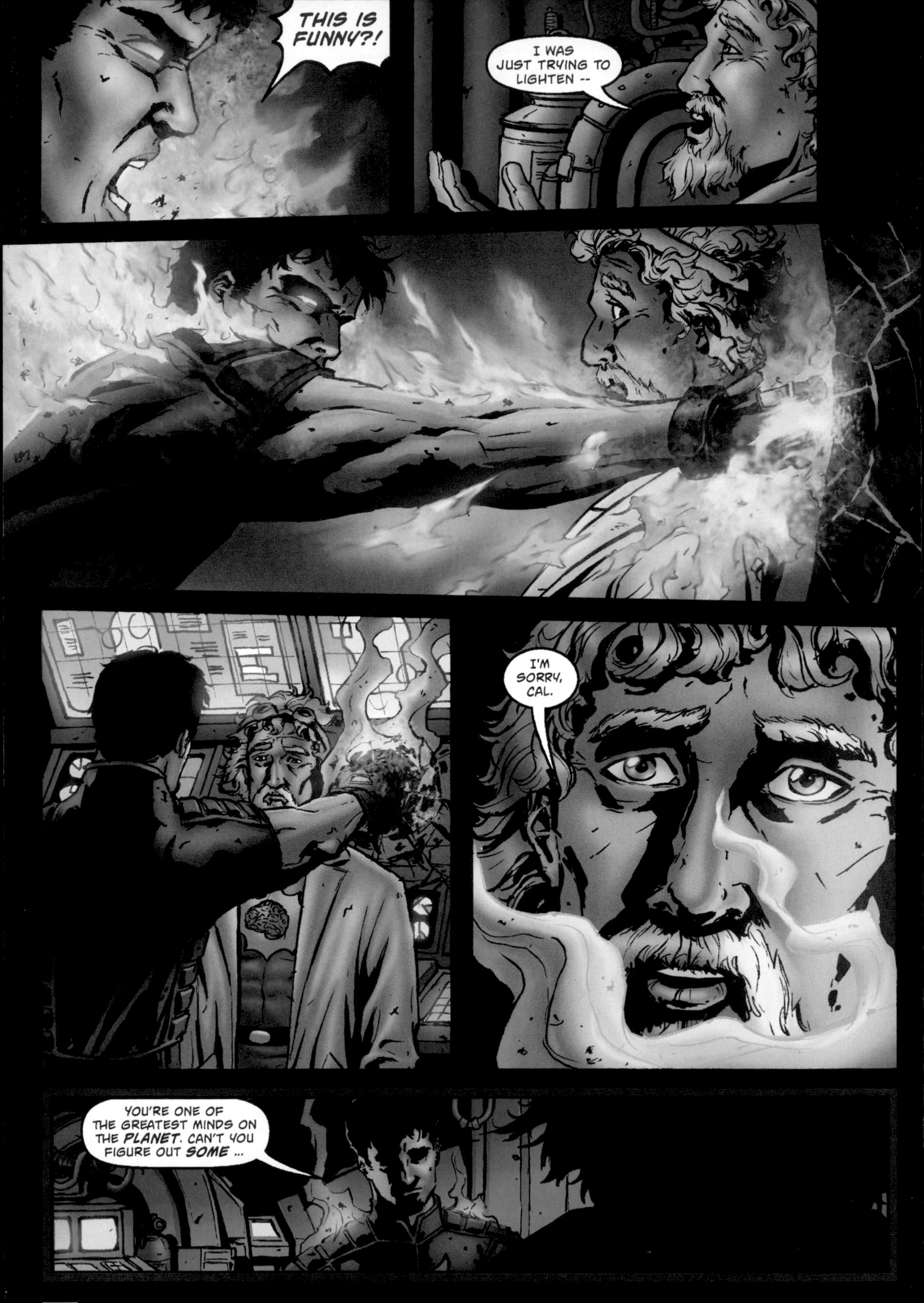
THIS IS FUNNY?!
I WAS JUST TRYING TO LIGHTEN --
I'M SORRY, CAL.
YOU'RE ONE OF THE GREATEST MINDS ON THE PLANET. CAN'T YOU FIGURE OUT SOME ...

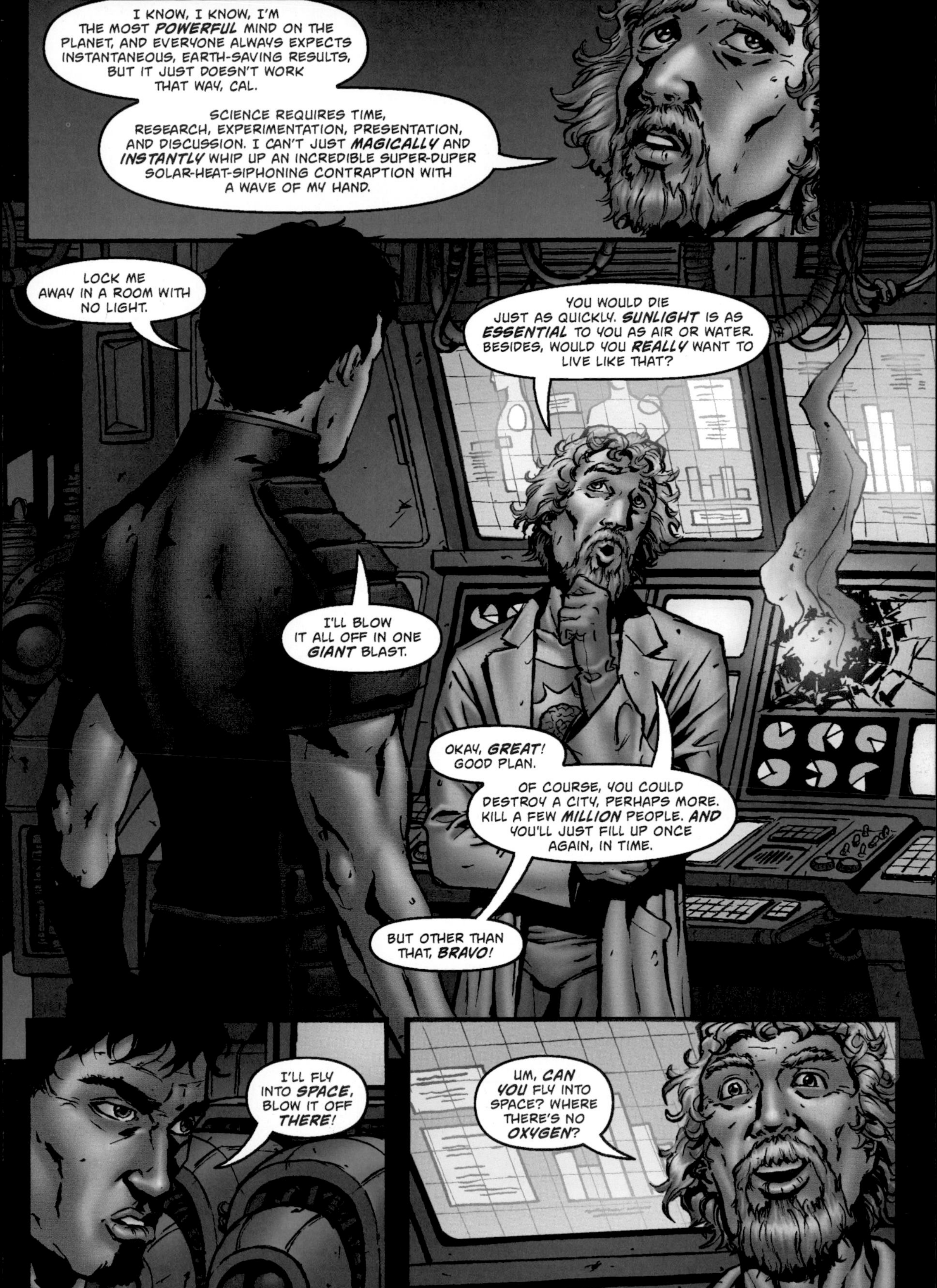

I KNOW, I KNOW, I'M THE MOST POWERFUL MIND ON THE PLANET, AND EVERYONE ALWAYS EXPECTS INSTANTANEOUS, EARTH-SAVING RESULTS, BUT IT JUST DOESN'T WORK THAT WAY, CAL.
SCIENCE REQUIRES TIME, RESEARCH, EXPERIMENTATION, PRESENTATION, AND DISCUSSION. I CAN'T JUST MAGICALLY AND INSTANTLY WHIP UP AN INCREDIBLE SUPER-DUPER SOLAR-HEAT-SIPHONING CONTRAPTION WITH A WAVE OF MY HAND.
LOCK ME AWAY IN A ROOM WITH NO LIGHT.
YOU WOULD DIE JUST AS QUICKLY. SUNLIGHT IS AS ESSENTIAL TO YOU AS AIR OR WATER. BESIDES, WOULD YOU REALLY WANT TO LIVE LIKE THAT?
I'LL BLOW IT ALL OFF IN ONE GIANT BLAST.
OKAY, GREAT! GOOD PLAN.
OF COURSE, YOU COULD DESTROY A CITY, PERHAPS MORE. KILL A FEW MILLION PEOPLE. AND YOU'LL JUST FILL UP ONCE AGAIN, IN TIME.
BUT OTHER THAN THAT, BRAVO!
I'LL FLY INTO SPACE, BLOW IT OFF THERE!
UM, CAN YOU FLY INTO SPACE? WHERE THERE'S NO OXYGEN?

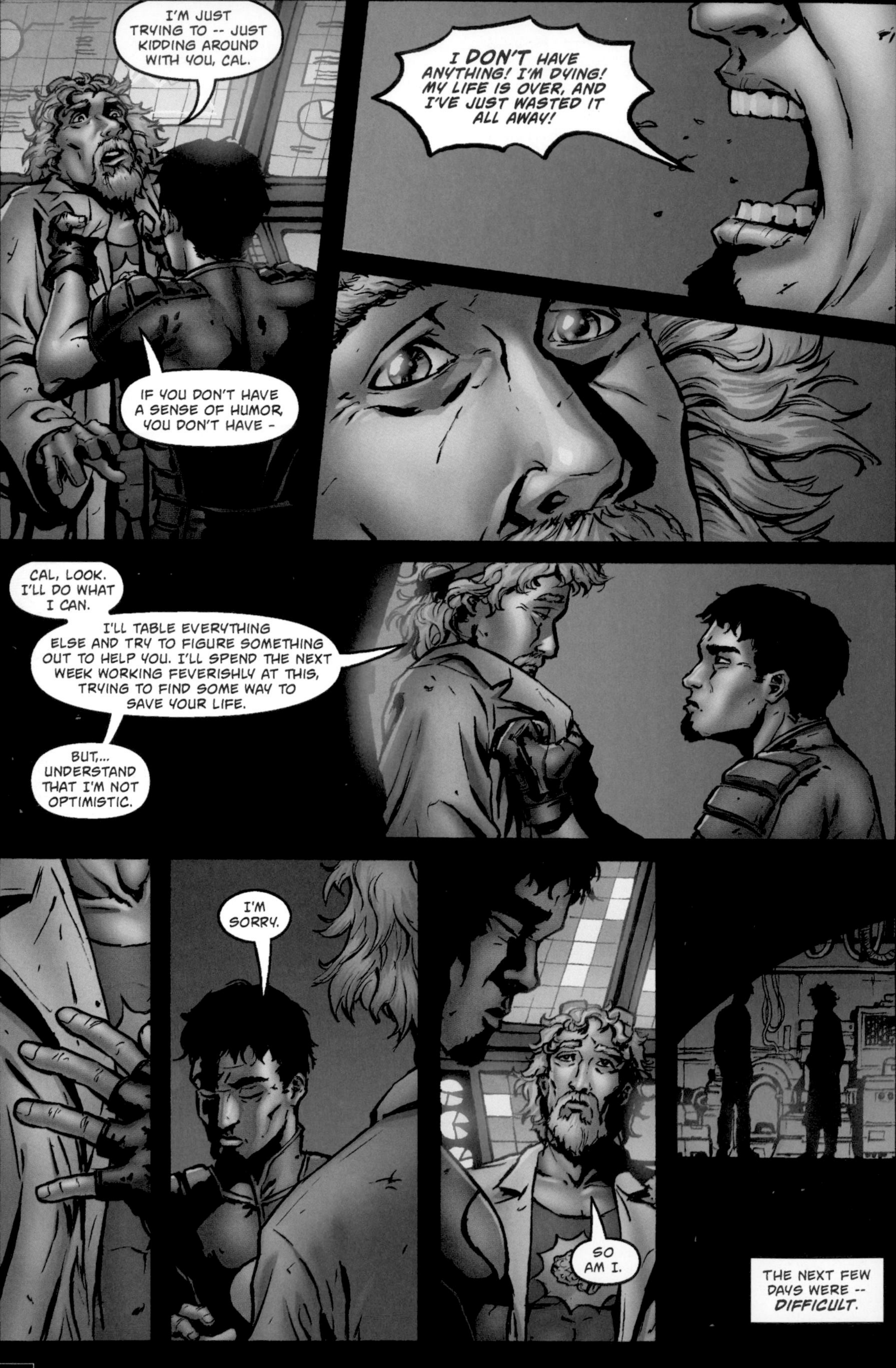

I'M JUST TRYING TO -- JUST KIDDING AROUND WITH YOU, CAL.
IF YOU DON'T HAVE A SENSE OF HUMOR, YOU DON'T HAVE -
I DON'T HAVE ANYTHING! I'M DYING! MY LIFE IS OVER, AND I'VE JUST WASTED IT ALL AWAY!
CAL, LOOK. I'LL DO WHAT I CAN.
I'LL TABLE EVERYTHING ELSE AND TRY TO FIGURE SOMETHING OUT TO HELP YOU. I'LL SPEND THE NEXT WEEK WORKING FEVERISHLY AT THIS, TRYING TO FIND SOME WAY TO SAVE YOUR LIFE.
BUT,... UNDERSTAND THAT I'M NOT OPTIMISTIC.
I'M SORRY.
SO AM I.
THE NEXT FEW DAYS WERE -- DIFFICULT.

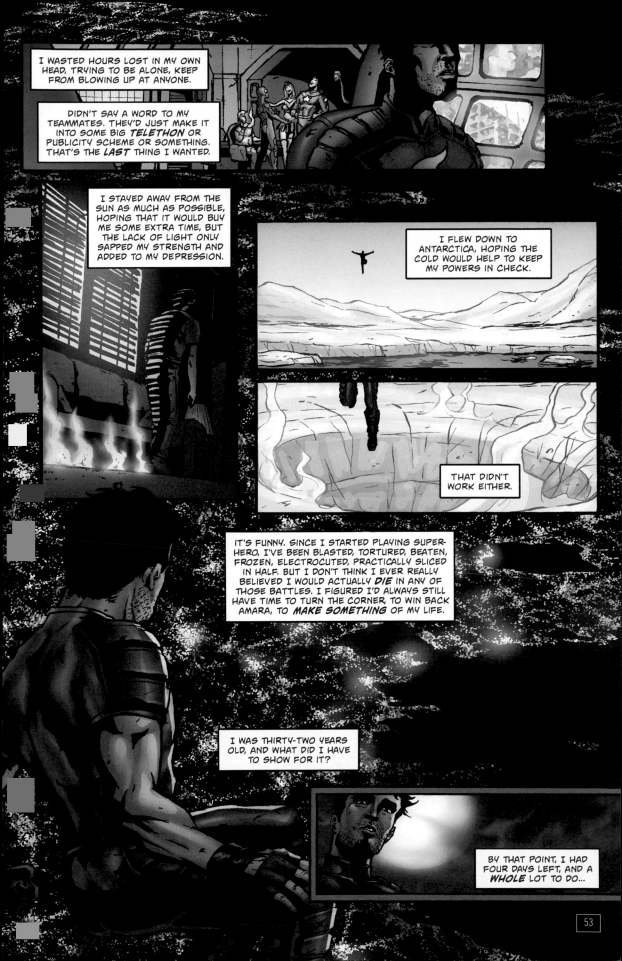

I WASTED HOURS LOST IN MY OWN HEAD, TRYING TO BE ALONE, KEEP FROM BLOWING UP AT ANYONE.

DIDN'T SAY A WORD TO MY TEAMMATES. THEY'D JUST MAKE IT INTO SOME BIG *TELETHON* OR PUBLICITY SCHEME OR SOMETHING. THAT'S THE *LAST* THING I WANTED.

I STAYED AWAY FROM THE SUN AS MUCH AS POSSIBLE, HOPING THAT IT WOULD BUY ME SOME EXTRA TIME, BUT THE LACK OF LIGHT ONLY SAPPED MY STRENGTH AND ADDED TO MY DEPRESSION.

I FLEW DOWN TO ANTARCTICA, HOPING THE COLD WOULD HELP TO KEEP MY POWERS IN CHECK.

THAT DIDN'T WORK EITHER.

IT'S FUNNY. SINCE I STARTED PLAYING SUPER-HERO, I'VE BEEN BLASTED, TORTURED, BEATEN, FROZEN, ELECTROCUTED, PRACTICALLY SLICED IN HALF. BUT I DON'T THINK I EVER REALLY BELIEVED I WOULD ACTUALLY *DIE* IN ANY OF THOSE BATTLES. I FIGURED I'D ALWAYS STILL HAVE TIME TO TURN THE CORNER, TO WIN BACK AMARA, TO *MAKE SOMETHING* OF MY LIFE.

I WAS THIRTY-TWO YEARS OLD, AND WHAT DID I HAVE TO SHOW FOR IT?

BY THAT POINT, I HAD FOUR DAYS LEFT, AND A *WHOLE* LOT TO DO...

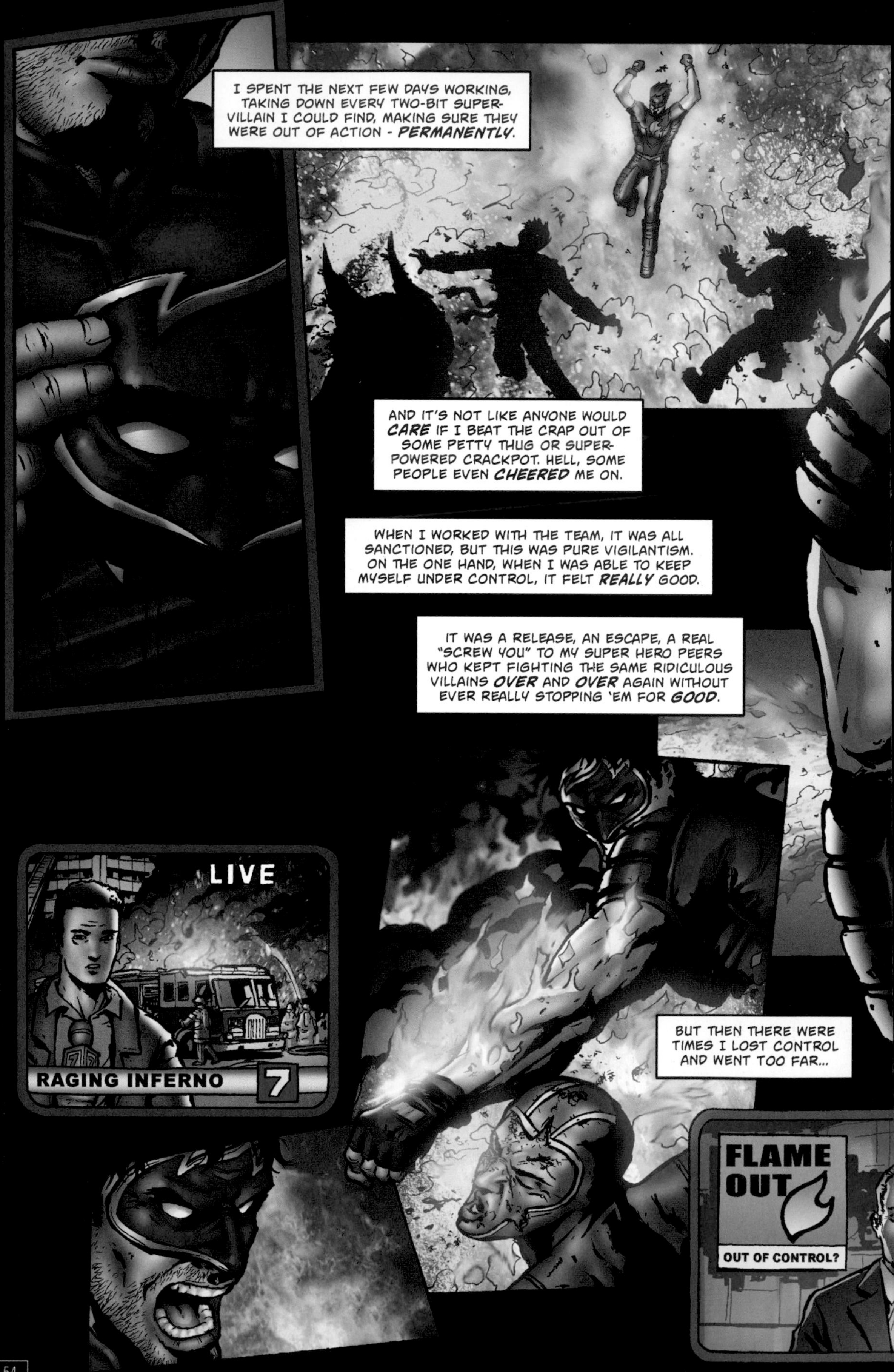

I SPENT THE NEXT FEW DAYS WORKING, TAKING DOWN EVERY TWO-BIT SUPER-VILLAIN I COULD FIND, MAKING SURE THEY WERE OUT OF ACTION - *PERMANENTLY*.
AND IT'S NOT LIKE ANYONE WOULD *CARE* IF I BEAT THE CRAP OUT OF SOME PETTY THUG OR SUPER-POWERED CRACKPOT. HELL, SOME PEOPLE EVEN *CHEERED* ME ON.
WHEN I WORKED WITH THE TEAM, IT WAS ALL SANCTIONED, BUT THIS WAS PURE VIGILANTISM. ON THE ONE HAND, WHEN I WAS ABLE TO KEEP MYSELF UNDER CONTROL, IT FELT *REALLY* GOOD.
IT WAS A RELEASE, AN ESCAPE, A REAL "SCREW YOU" TO MY SUPER HERO PEERS WHO KEPT FIGHTING THE SAME RIDICULOUS VILLAINS *OVER* AND *OVER* AGAIN WITHOUT EVER REALLY STOPPING 'EM FOR *GOOD*.
LIVE
RAGING INFERNO
7
BUT THEN THERE WERE TIMES I LOST CONTROL AND WENT TOO FAR...
FLAME OUT
OUT OF CONTROL?

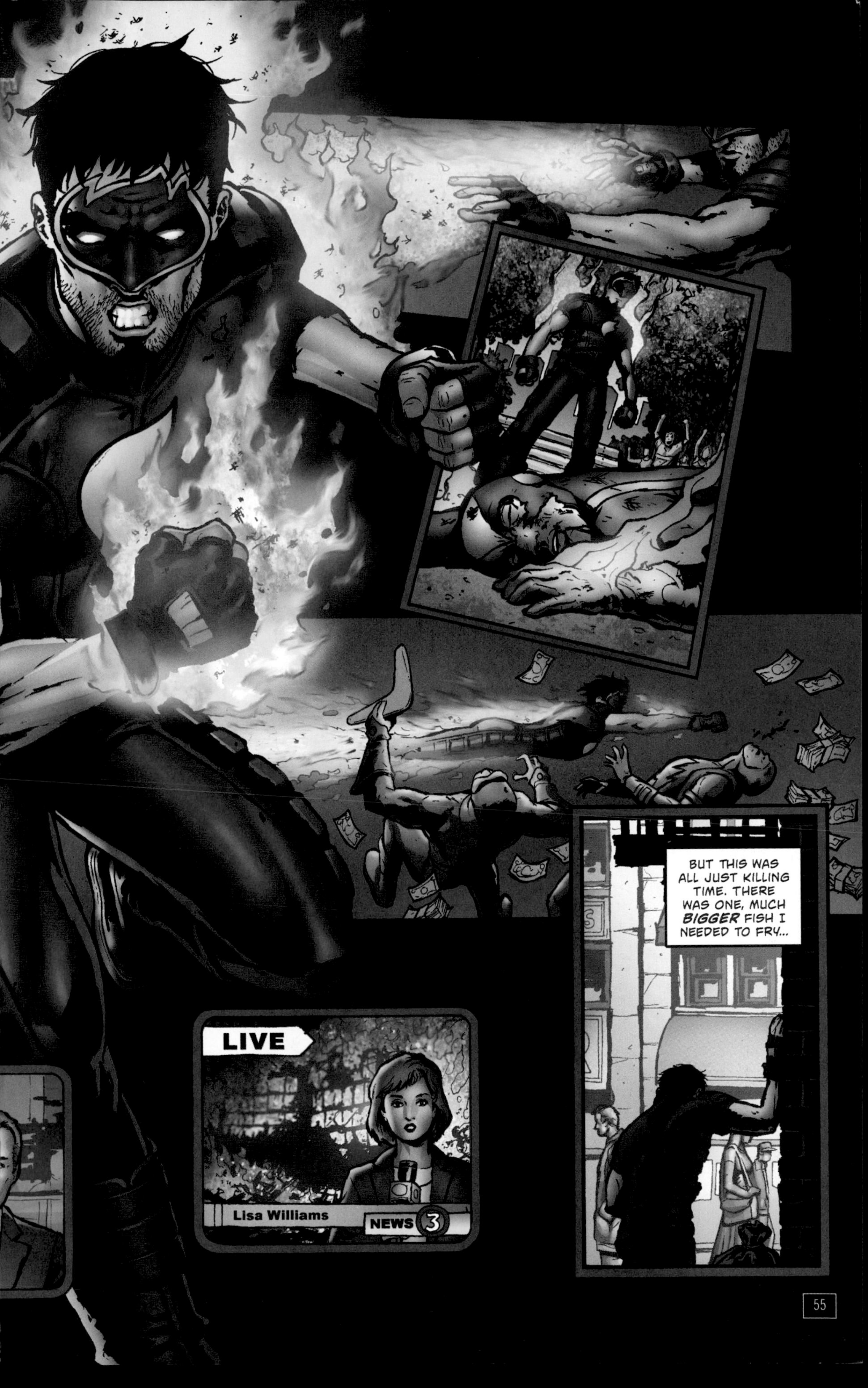
BUT THIS WAS ALL JUST KILLING TIME. THERE WAS ONE, MUCH BIGGER FISH I NEEDED TO FRY...
LIVE
Lisa Williams
NEWS 3

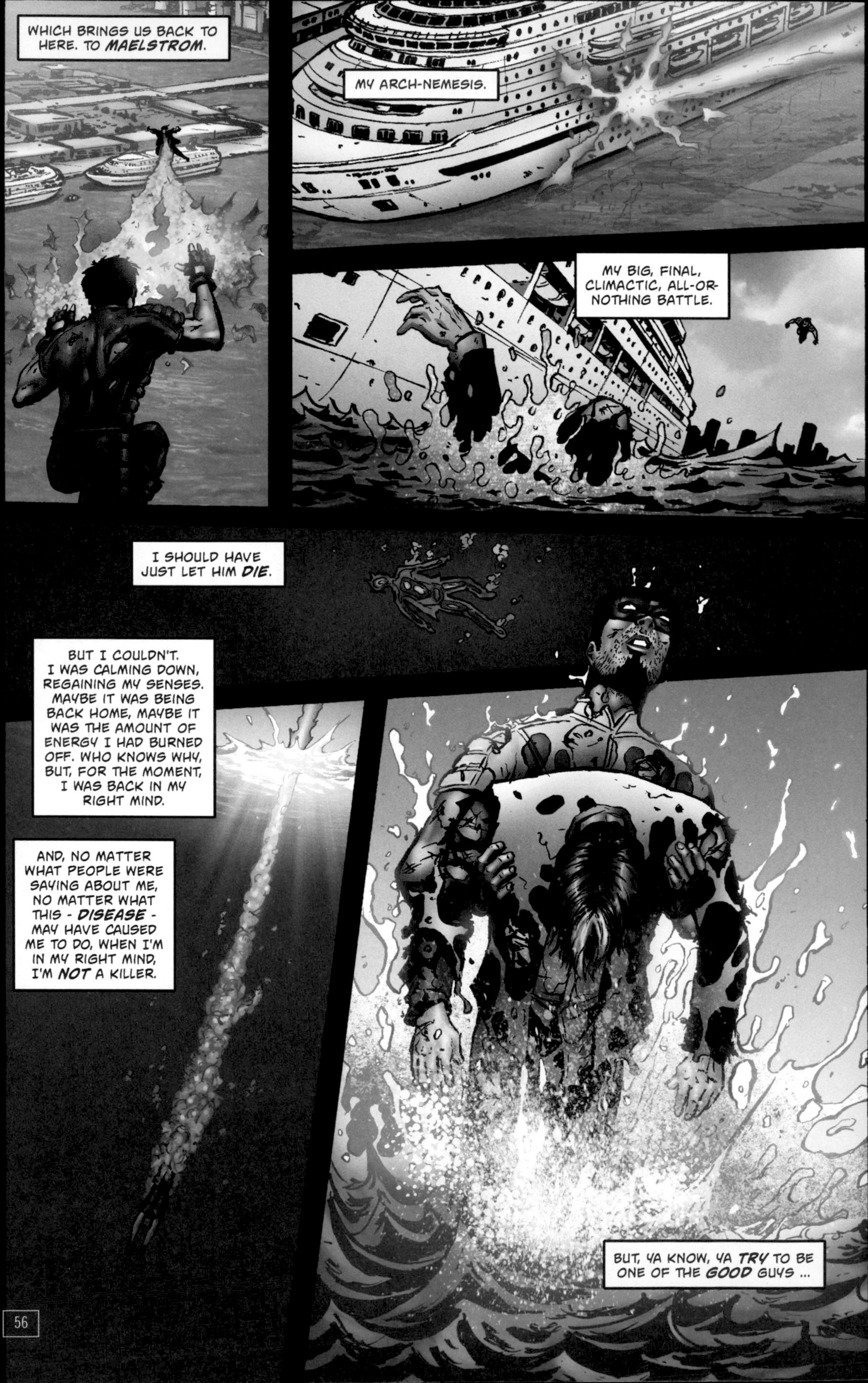
WHICH BRINGS US BACK TO HERE. TO MAELSTROM.
MY ARCH-NEMESIS.
MY BIG, FINAL, CLIMACTIC, ALL-OR-NOTHING BATTLE.
I SHOULD HAVE JUST LET HIM DIE.
BUT I COULDN'T. I WAS CALMING DOWN, REGAINING MY SENSES. MAYBE IT WAS BEING BACK HOME, MAYBE IT WAS THE AMOUNT OF ENERGY I HAD BURNED OFF. WHO KNOWS WHY, BUT, FOR THE MOMENT, I WAS BACK IN MY RIGHT MIND.
AND, NO MATTER WHAT PEOPLE WERE SAYING ABOUT ME, NO MATTER WHAT THIS - DISEASE - MAY HAVE CAUSED ME TO DO, WHEN I'M IN MY RIGHT MIND, I'M NOT A KILLER.
BUT, YA KNOW, YA TRY TO BE ONE OF THE GOOD GUYS ...

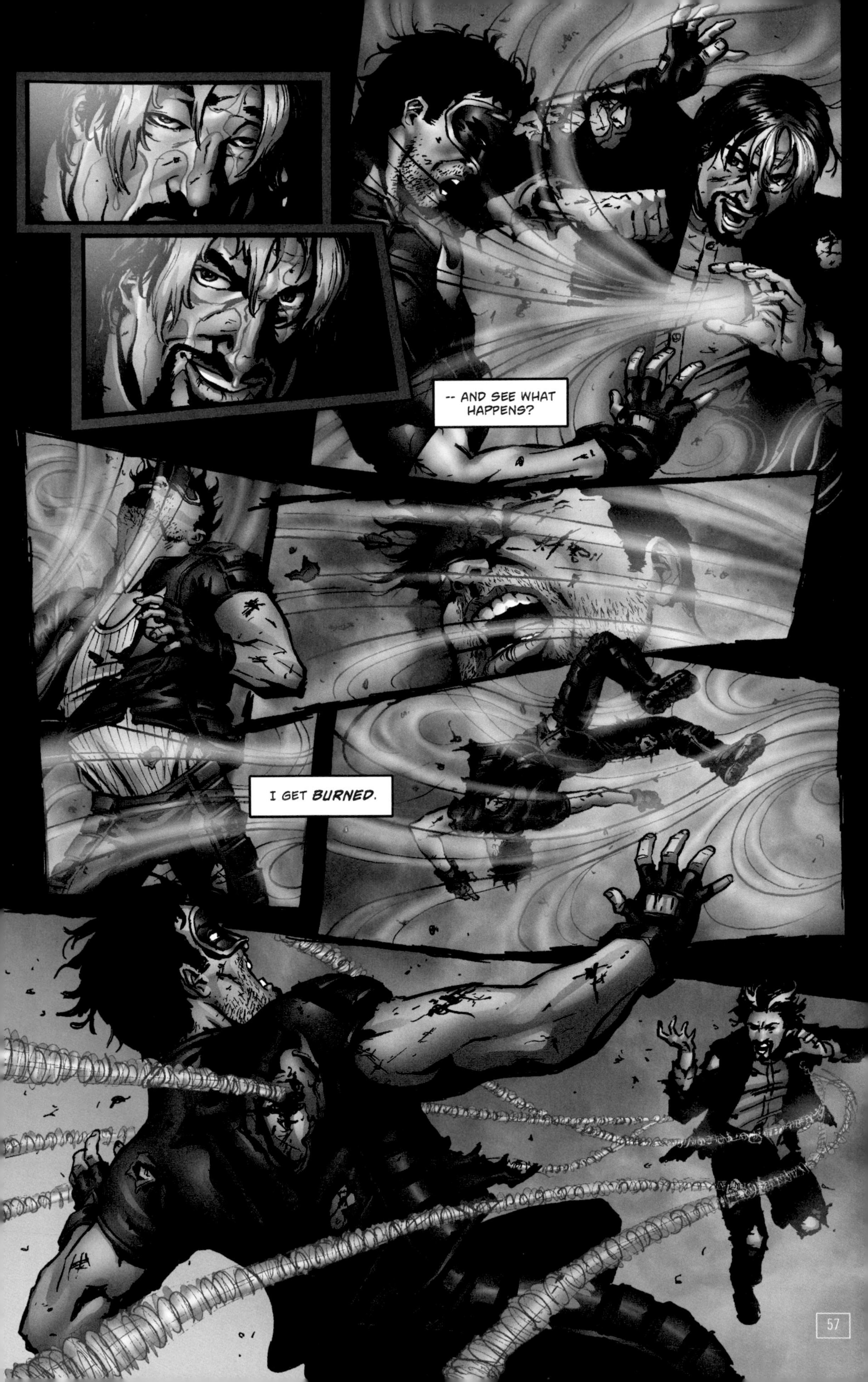

-- AND SEE WHAT HAPPENS?
I GET BURNED.

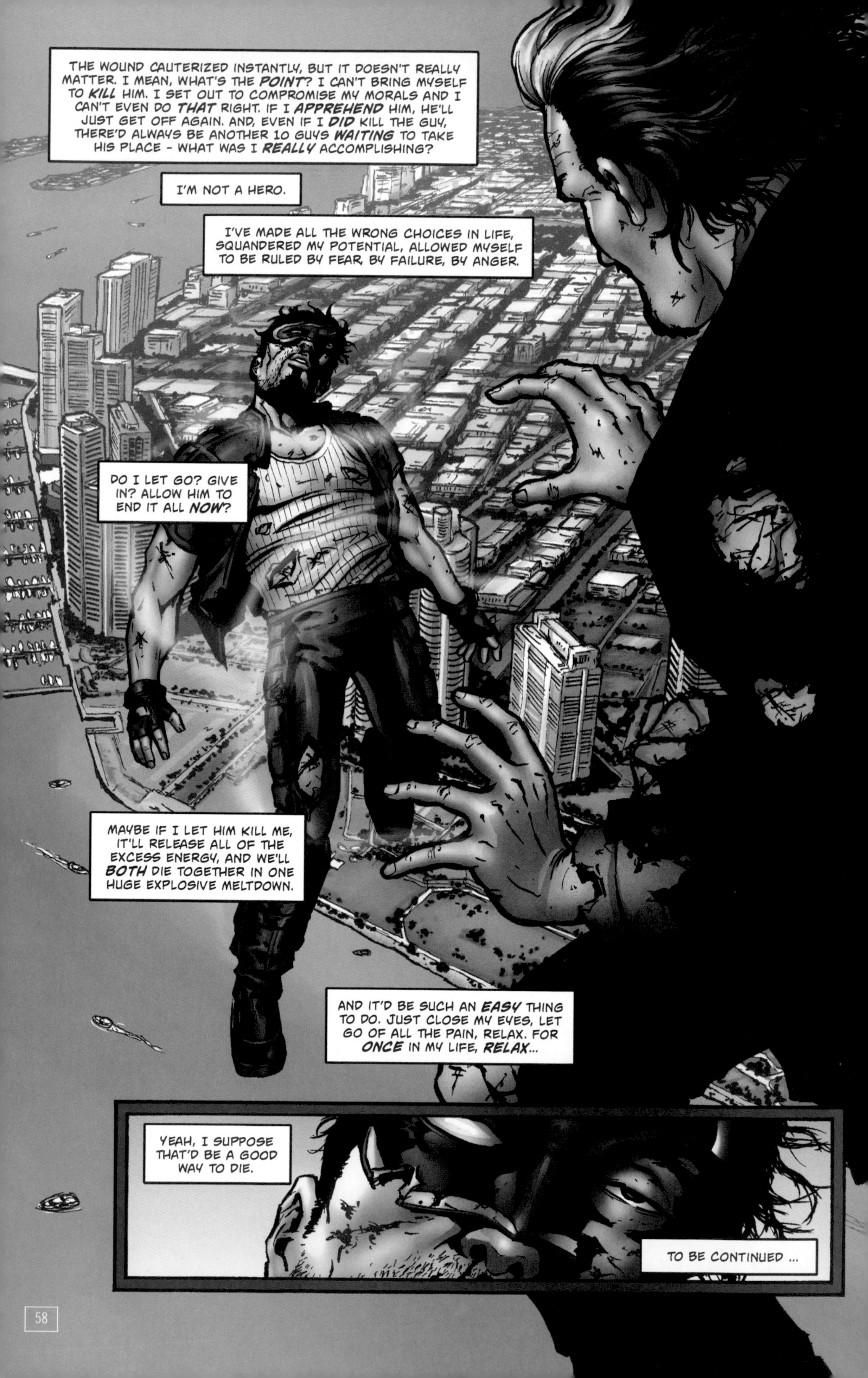
THE WOUND CAUTERIZED INSTANTLY, BUT IT DOESN'T REALLY MATTER. I MEAN, WHAT'S THE POINT? I CAN'T BRING MYSELF TO KILL HIM. I SET OUT TO COMPROMISE MY MORALS AND I CAN'T EVEN DO THAT RIGHT. IF I APPREHEND HIM, HE'LL JUST GET OFF AGAIN. AND, EVEN IF I DID KILL THE GUY, THERE'D ALWAYS BE ANOTHER 10 GUYS WAITING TO TAKE HIS PLACE - WHAT WAS I REALLY ACCOMPLISHING?
I'M NOT A HERO.
I'VE MADE ALL THE WRONG CHOICES IN LIFE, SQUANDERED MY POTENTIAL, ALLOWED MYSELF TO BE RULED BY FEAR, BY FAILURE, BY ANGER.
DO I LET GO? GIVE IN? ALLOW HIM TO END IT ALL NOW?
MAYBE IF I LET HIM KILL ME, IT'LL RELEASE ALL OF THE EXCESS ENERGY, AND WE'LL BOTH DIE TOGETHER IN ONE HUGE EXPLOSIVE MELTDOWN.
AND IT'D BE SUCH AN EASY THING TO DO. JUST CLOSE MY EYES, LET GO OF ALL THE PAIN, RELAX. FOR ONCE IN MY LIFE, RELAX...
YEAH, I SUPPOSE THAT'D BE A GOOD WAY TO DIE.
TO BE CONTINUED ...

MELTDOWN

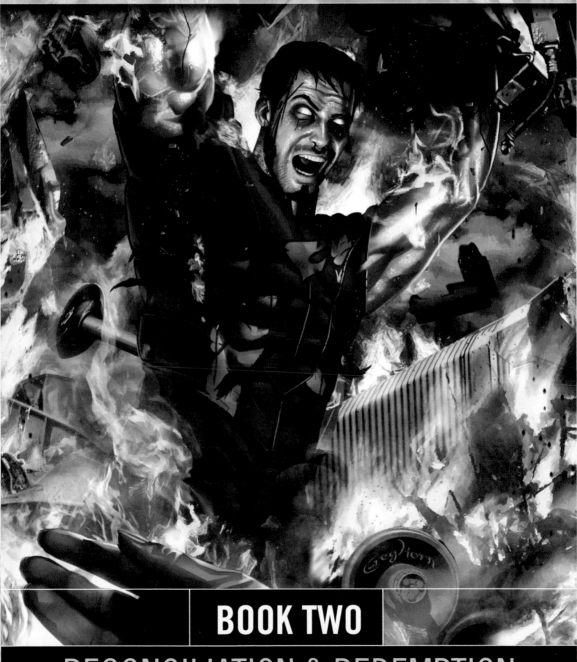

BOOK TWO
RECONCILIATION & REDEMPTION

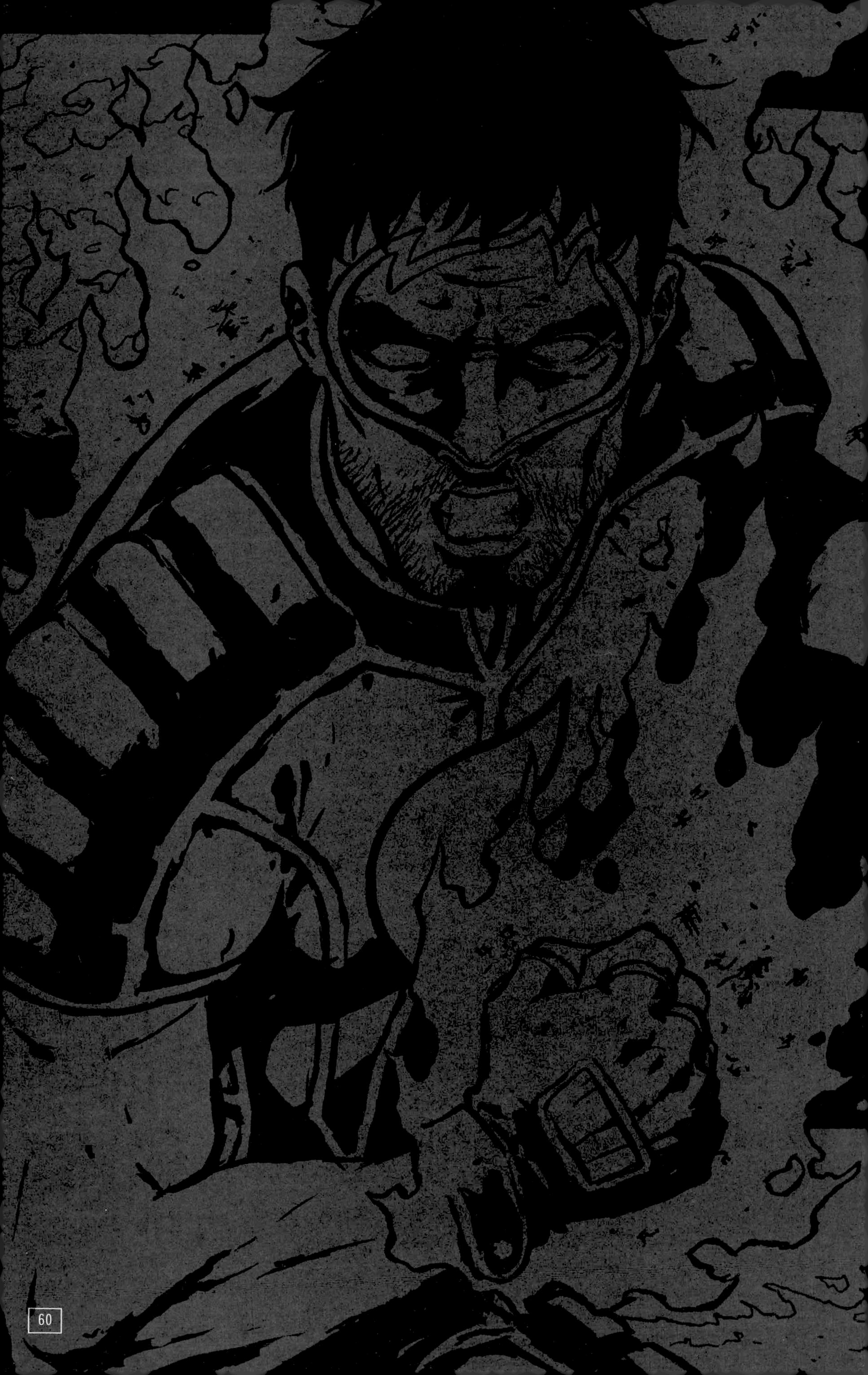

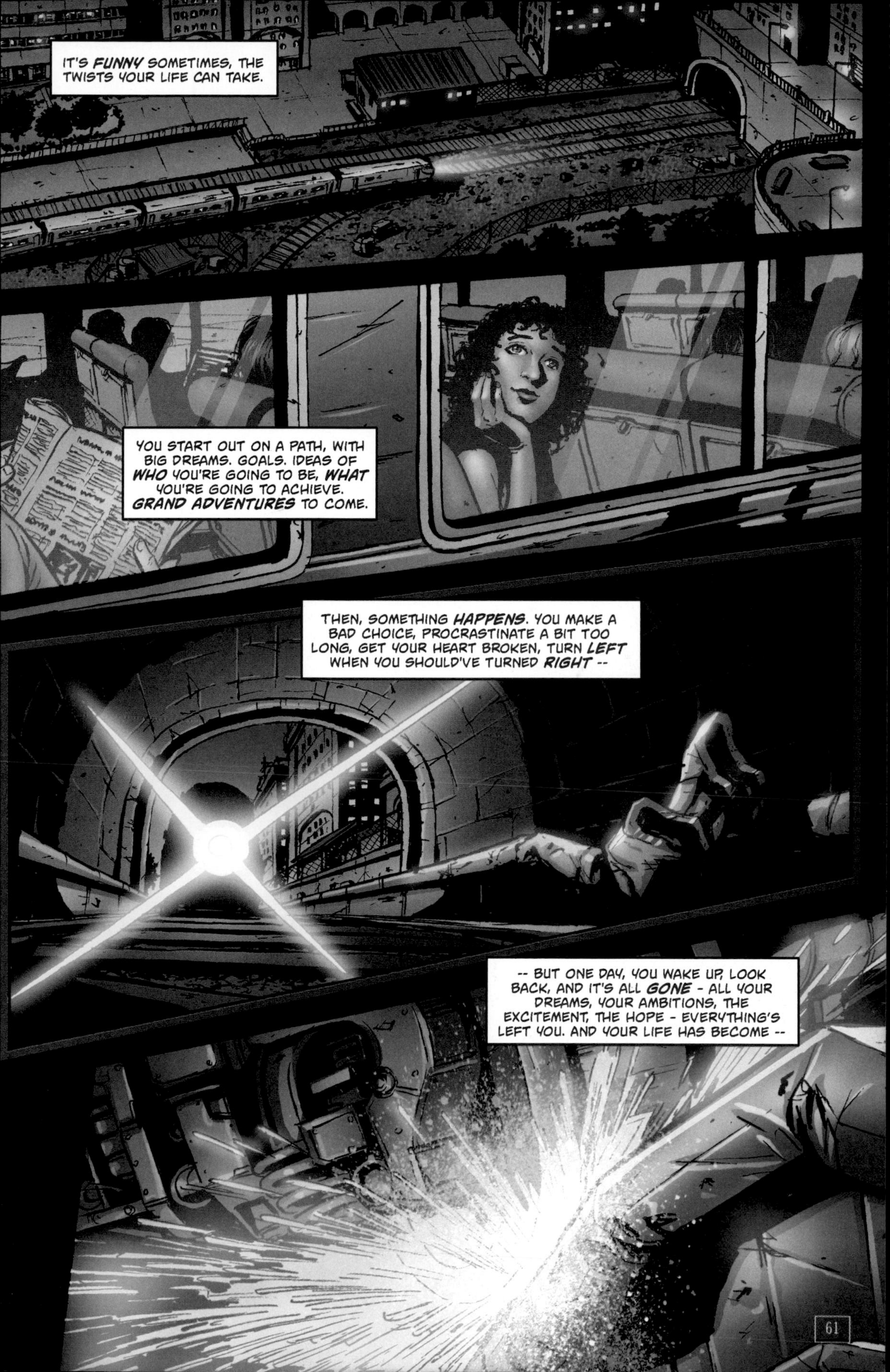
IT'S FUNNY SOMETIMES, THE TWISTS YOUR LIFE CAN TAKE.
YOU START OUT ON A PATH, WITH BIG DREAMS. GOALS. IDEAS OF WHO YOU'RE GOING TO BE, WHAT YOU'RE GOING TO ACHIEVE. GRAND ADVENTURES TO COME.
THEN, SOMETHING HAPPENS. YOU MAKE A BAD CHOICE, PROCRASTINATE A BIT TOO LONG, GET YOUR HEART BROKEN, TURN LEFT WHEN YOU SHOULD'VE TURNED RIGHT --
-- BUT ONE DAY, YOU WAKE UP, LOOK BACK, AND IT'S ALL GONE - ALL YOUR DREAMS, YOUR AMBITIONS, THE EXCITEMENT, THE HOPE - EVERYTHING'S LEFT YOU. AND YOUR LIFE HAS BECOME --

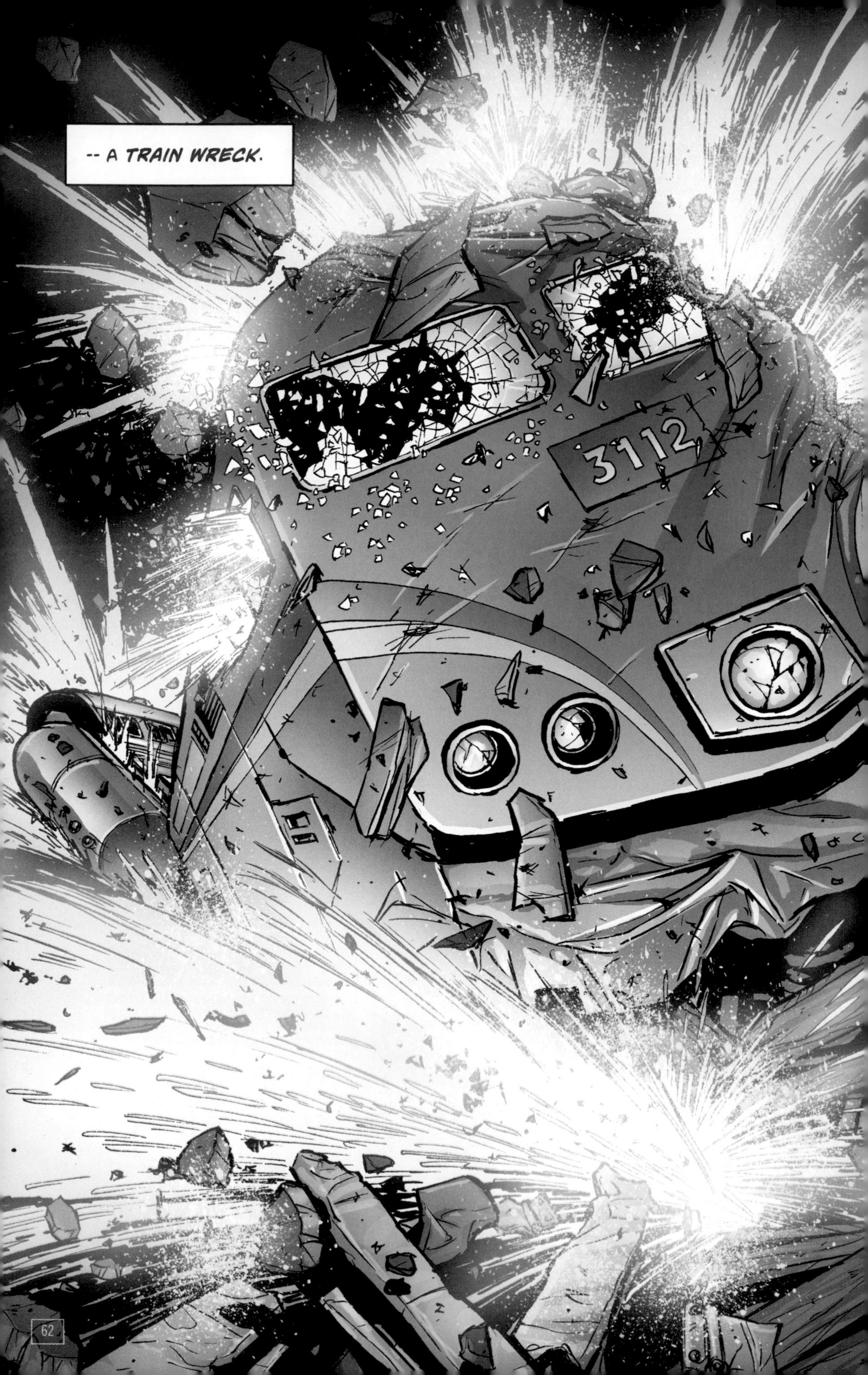
-- A TRAIN WRECK.
3112

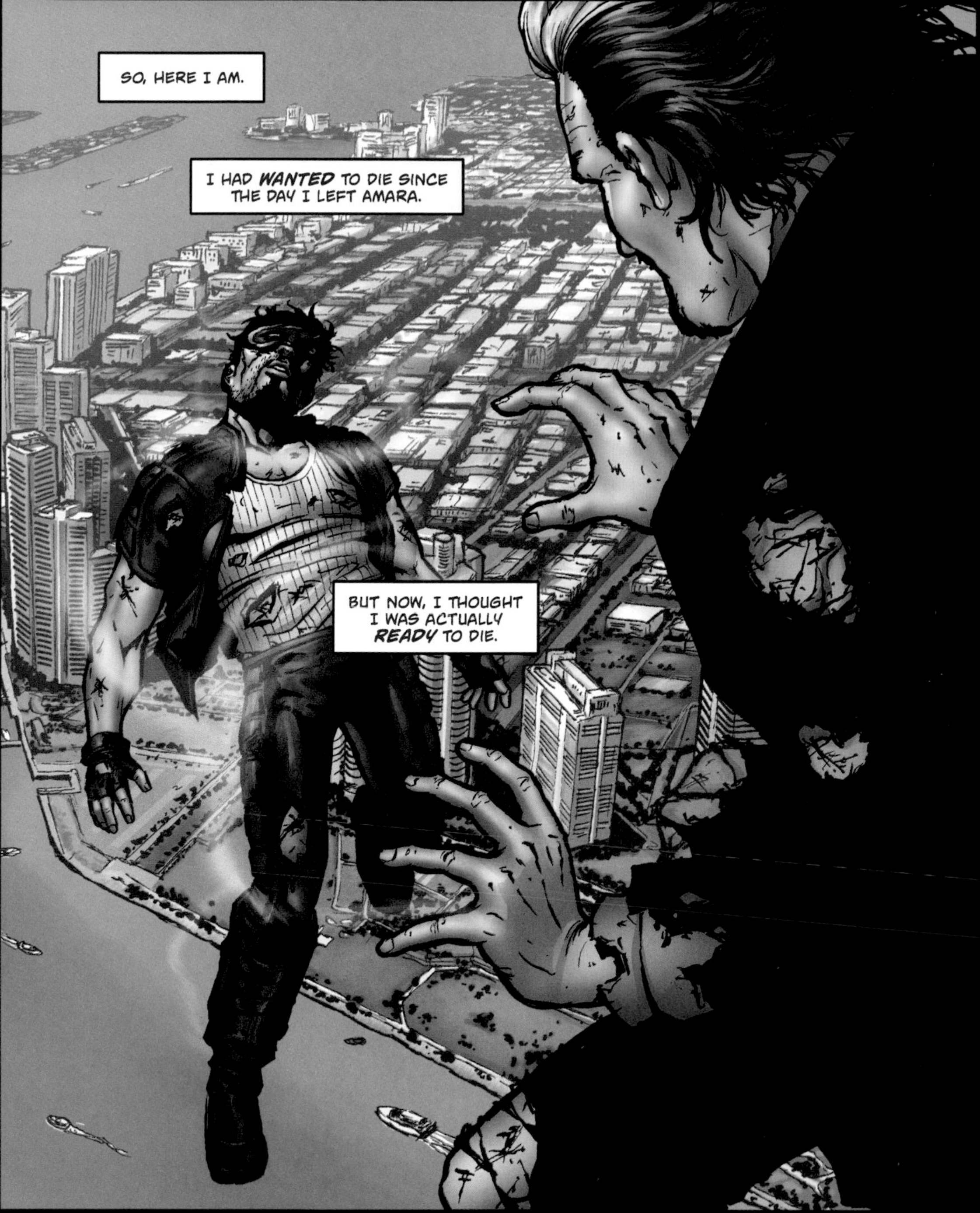
SO, HERE I AM.
I HAD WANTED TO DIE SINCE THE DAY I LEFT AMARA.
BUT NOW, I THOUGHT I WAS ACTUALLY READY TO DIE.
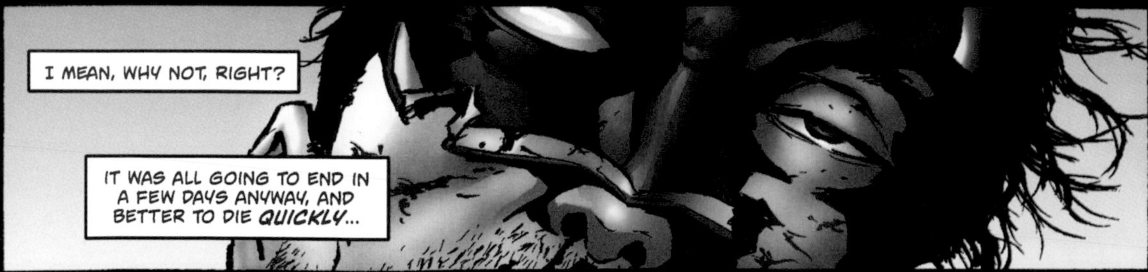
I MEAN, WHY NOT, RIGHT?
IT WAS ALL GOING TO END IN A FEW DAYS ANYWAY, AND BETTER TO DIE QUICKLY...

...THAN TO SUFFER A LONGER, *AGONIZING* DEATH.

IS HE GONNA BE OKAY?

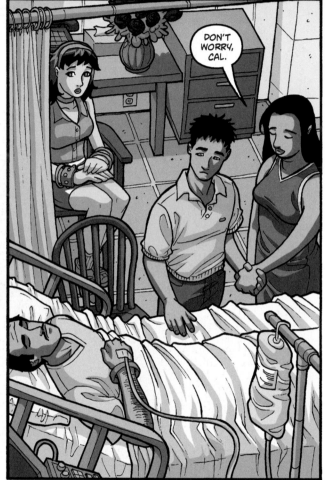

DON'T WORRY, CAL.

HE'LL BE FINE. HE'LL *BEAT* THIS.

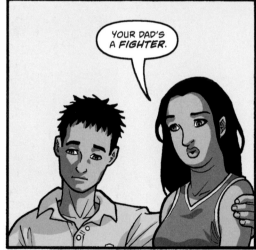

YOUR DAD'S A *FIGHTER*.

HE WON'T GIVE UP.

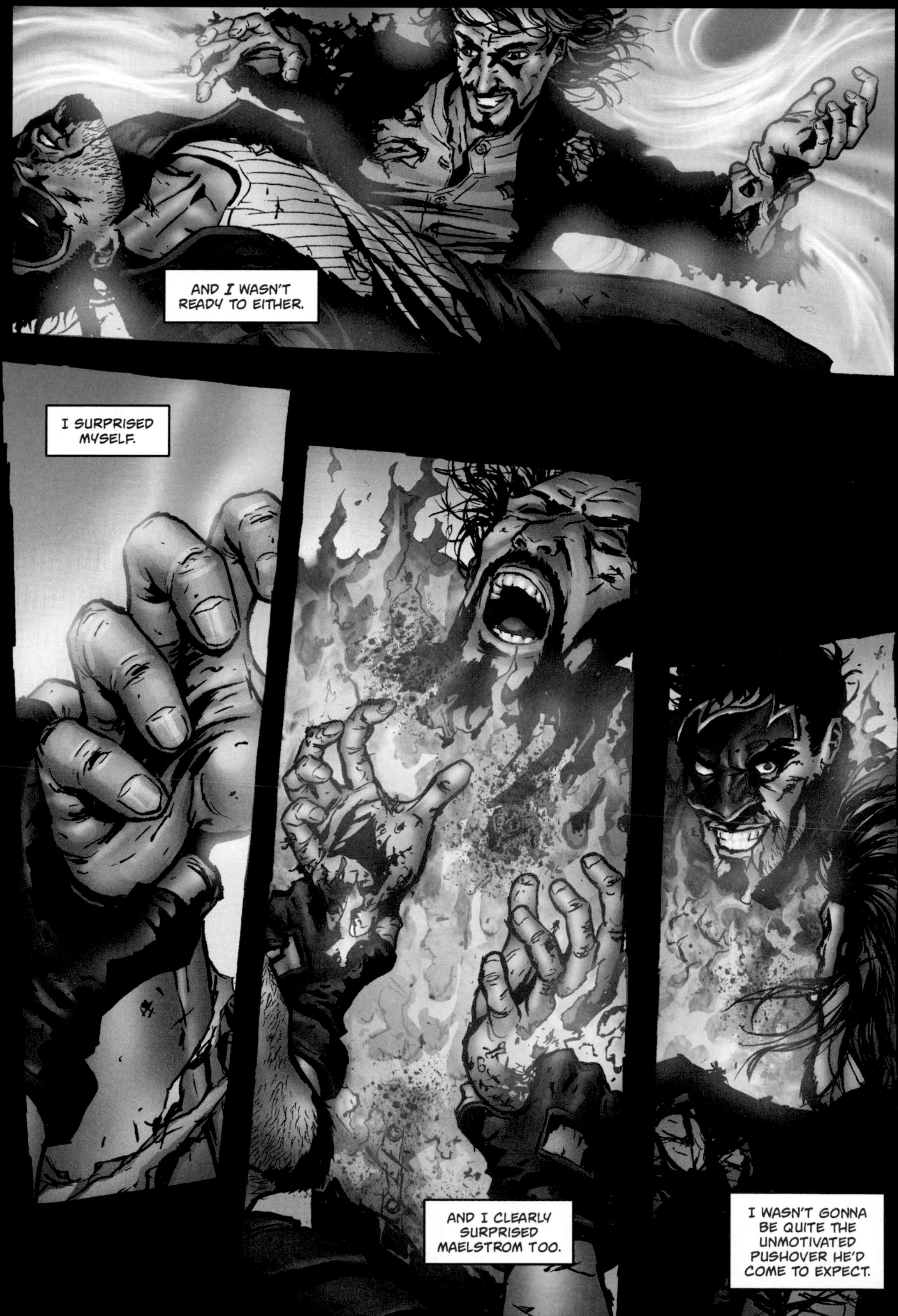
AND I WASN'T READY TO EITHER.
I SURPRISED MYSELF.
AND I CLEARLY SURPRISED MAELSTROM TOO.
I WASN'T GONNA BE QUITE THE UNMOTIVATED PUSHOVER HE'D COME TO EXPECT.

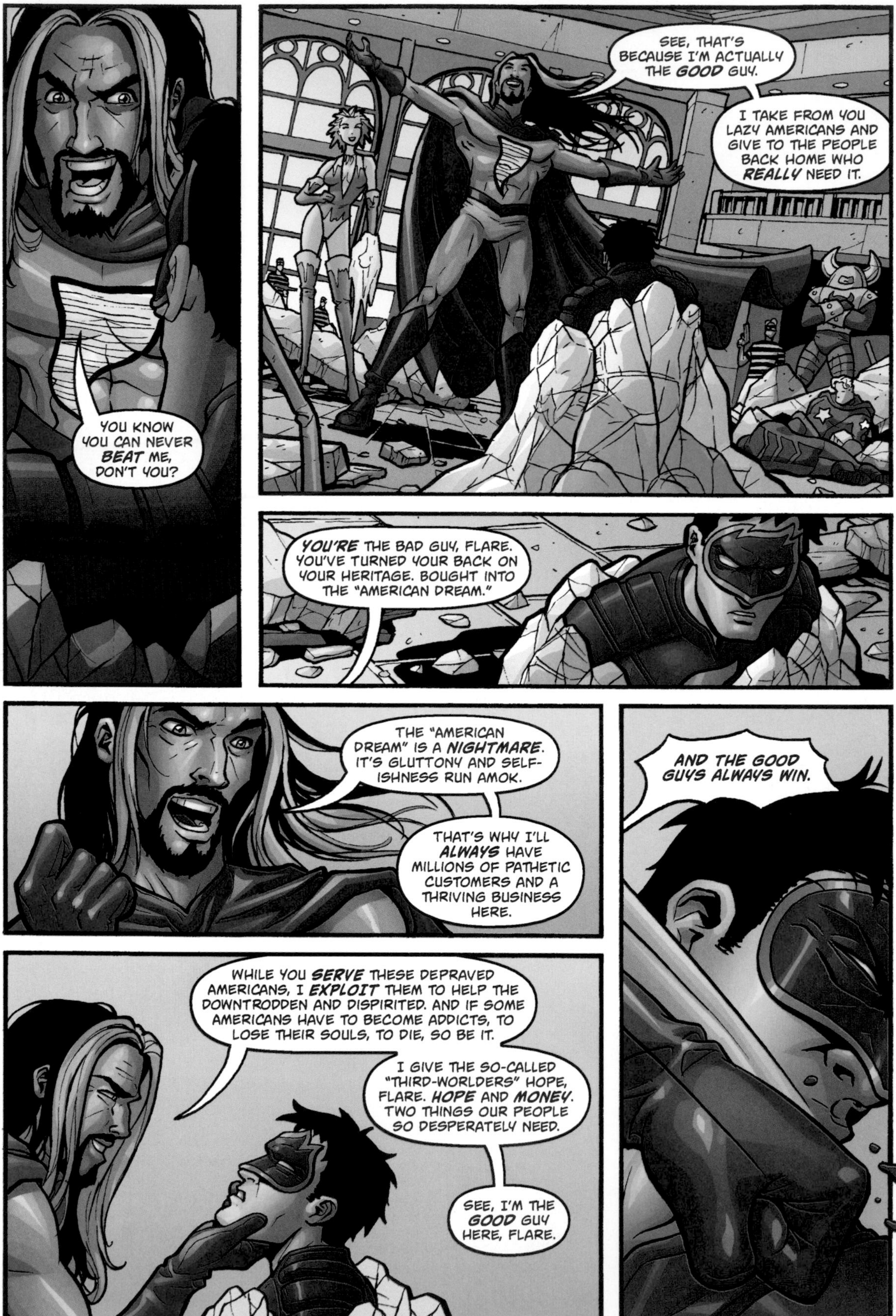
YOU KNOW YOU CAN NEVER BEAT ME, DON'T YOU?
SEE, THAT'S BECAUSE I'M ACTUALLY THE GOOD GUY.
I TAKE FROM YOU LAZY AMERICANS AND GIVE TO THE PEOPLE BACK HOME WHO REALLY NEED IT.
YOU'RE THE BAD GUY, FLARE. YOU'VE TURNED YOUR BACK ON YOUR HERITAGE. BOUGHT INTO THE "AMERICAN DREAM."
THE "AMERICAN DREAM" IS A NIGHTMARE. IT'S GLUTTONY AND SELF-ISHNESS RUN AMOK.
THAT'S WHY I'LL ALWAYS HAVE MILLIONS OF PATHETIC CUSTOMERS AND A THRIVING BUSINESS HERE.
WHILE YOU SERVE THESE DEPRAVED AMERICANS, I EXPLOIT THEM TO HELP THE DOWNTRODDEN AND DISPIRITED. AND IF SOME AMERICANS HAVE TO BECOME ADDICTS, TO LOSE THEIR SOULS, TO DIE, SO BE IT.
I GIVE THE SO-CALLED "THIRD-WORLDERS" HOPE, FLARE. HOPE AND MONEY. TWO THINGS OUR PEOPLE SO DESPERATELY NEED.
SEE, I'M THE GOOD GUY HERE, FLARE.
AND THE GOOD GUYS ALWAYS WIN.

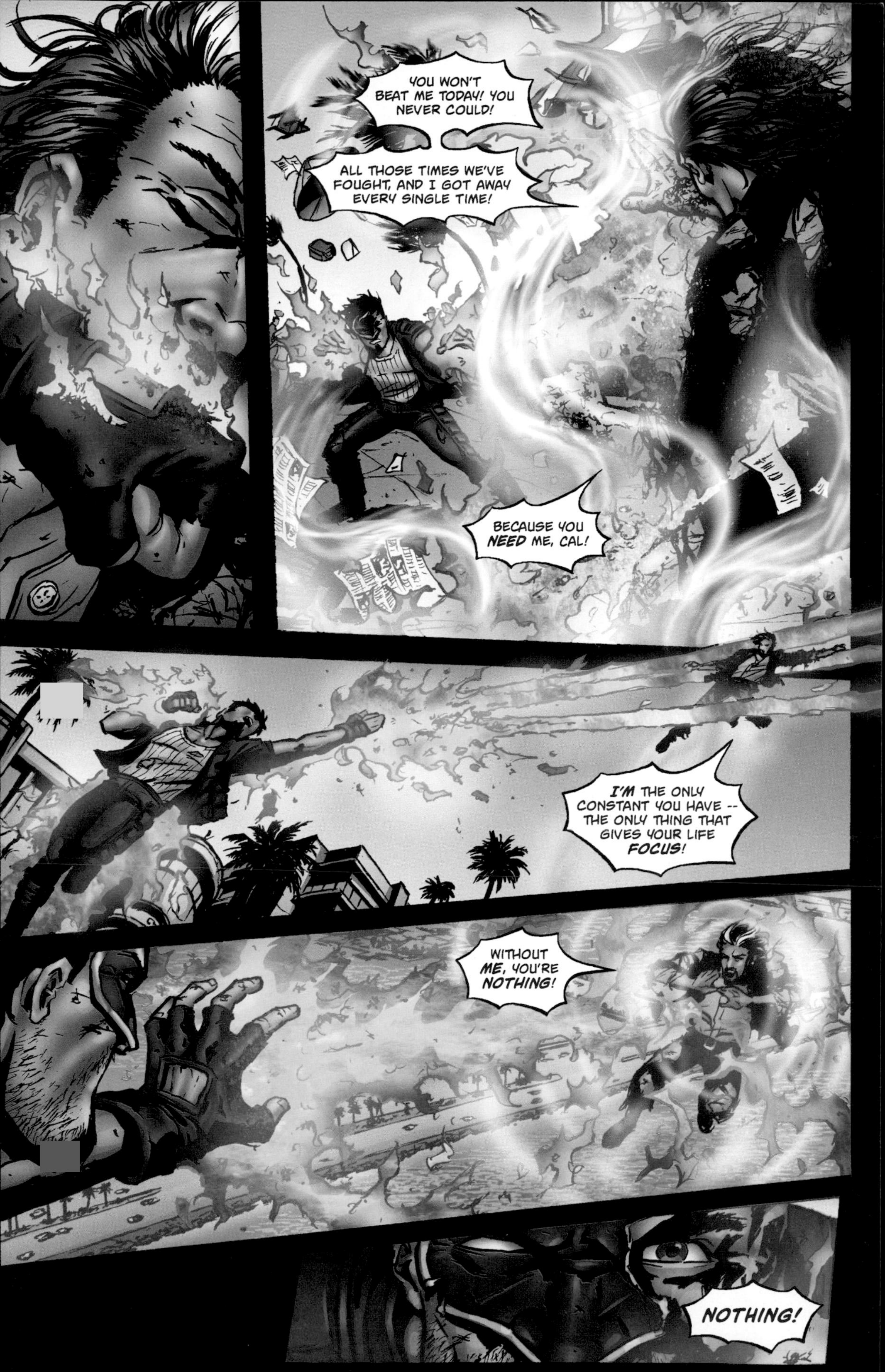

YOU WON'T BEAT ME TODAY! YOU NEVER COULD!
ALL THOSE TIMES WE'VE FOUGHT, AND I GOT AWAY EVERY SINGLE TIME!
BECAUSE YOU **NEED** ME, CAL!
I'M THE ONLY CONSTANT YOU HAVE -- THE ONLY THING THAT GIVES YOUR LIFE ***FOCUS***!
WITHOUT ***ME***, YOU'RE ***NOTHING***!
NOTHING!

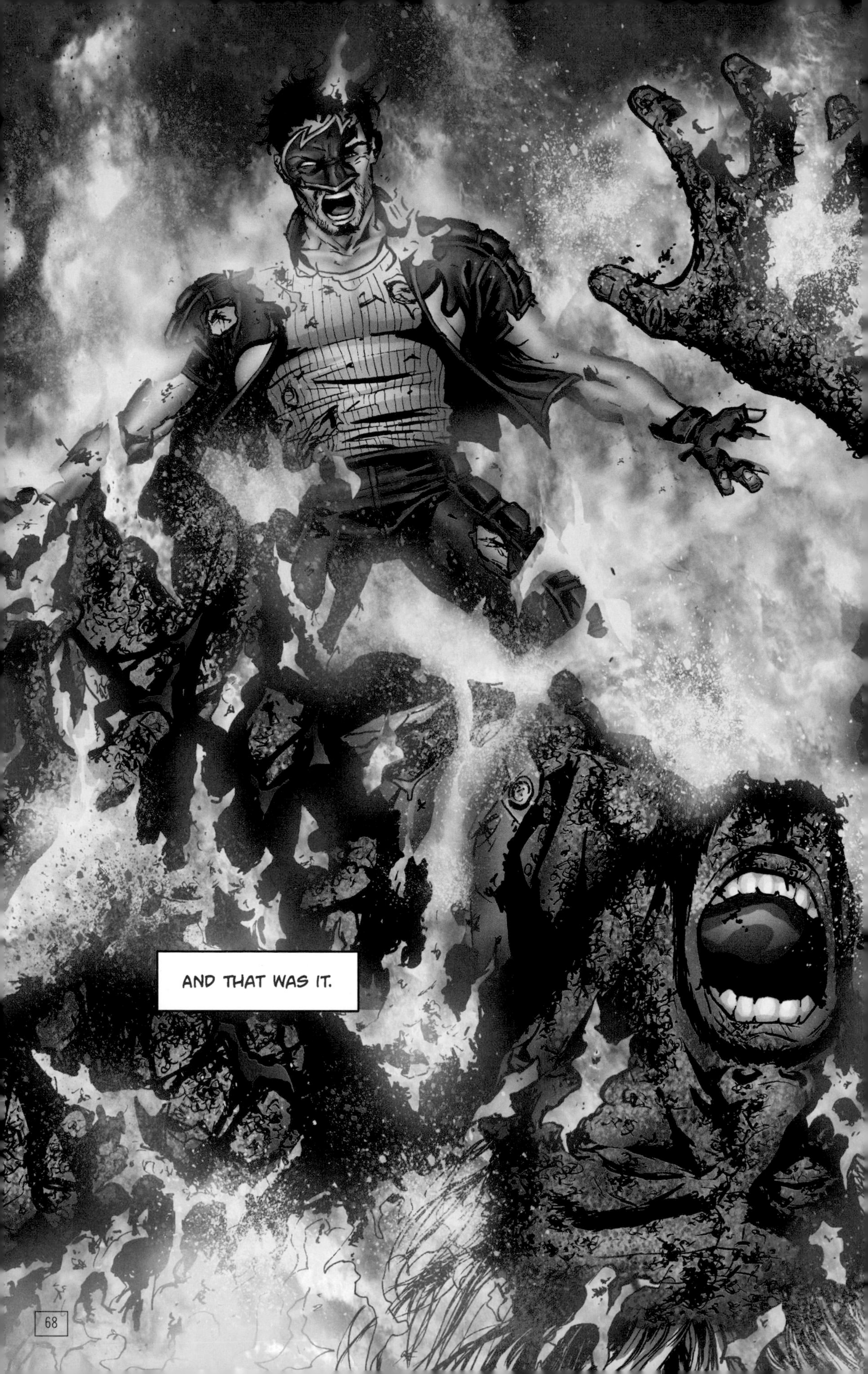
AND THAT WAS IT.

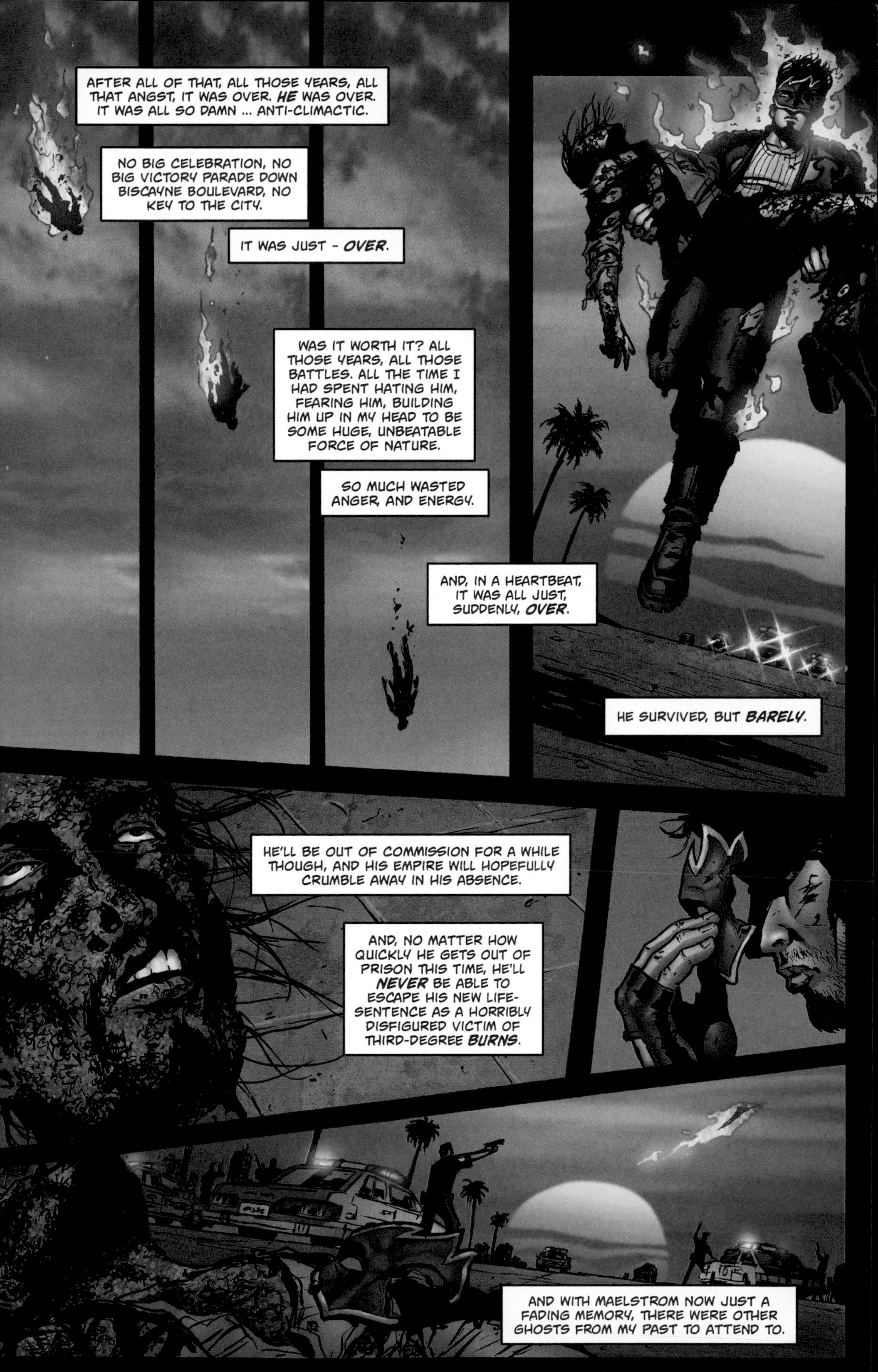

AFTER ALL OF THAT, ALL THOSE YEARS, ALL THAT ANGST, IT WAS OVER. HE WAS OVER. IT WAS ALL SO DAMN ... ANTI-CLIMACTIC.
NO BIG CELEBRATION, NO BIG VICTORY PARADE DOWN BISCAYNE BOULEVARD, NO KEY TO THE CITY.
IT WAS JUST - OVER.
WAS IT WORTH IT? ALL THOSE YEARS, ALL THOSE BATTLES. ALL THE TIME I HAD SPENT HATING HIM, FEARING HIM, BUILDING HIM UP IN MY HEAD TO BE SOME HUGE, UNBEATABLE FORCE OF NATURE.
SO MUCH WASTED ANGER, AND ENERGY.
AND, IN A HEARTBEAT, IT WAS ALL JUST, SUDDENLY, OVER.
HE SURVIVED, BUT BARELY.
HE'LL BE OUT OF COMMISSION FOR A WHILE THOUGH, AND HIS EMPIRE WILL HOPEFULLY CRUMBLE AWAY IN HIS ABSENCE.
AND, NO MATTER HOW QUICKLY HE GETS OUT OF PRISON THIS TIME, HE'LL NEVER BE ABLE TO ESCAPE HIS NEW LIFE-SENTENCE AS A HORRIBLY DISFIGURED VICTIM OF THIRD-DEGREE BURNS.
AND WITH MAELSTROM NOW JUST A FADING MEMORY, THERE WERE OTHER GHOSTS FROM MY PAST TO ATTEND TO.

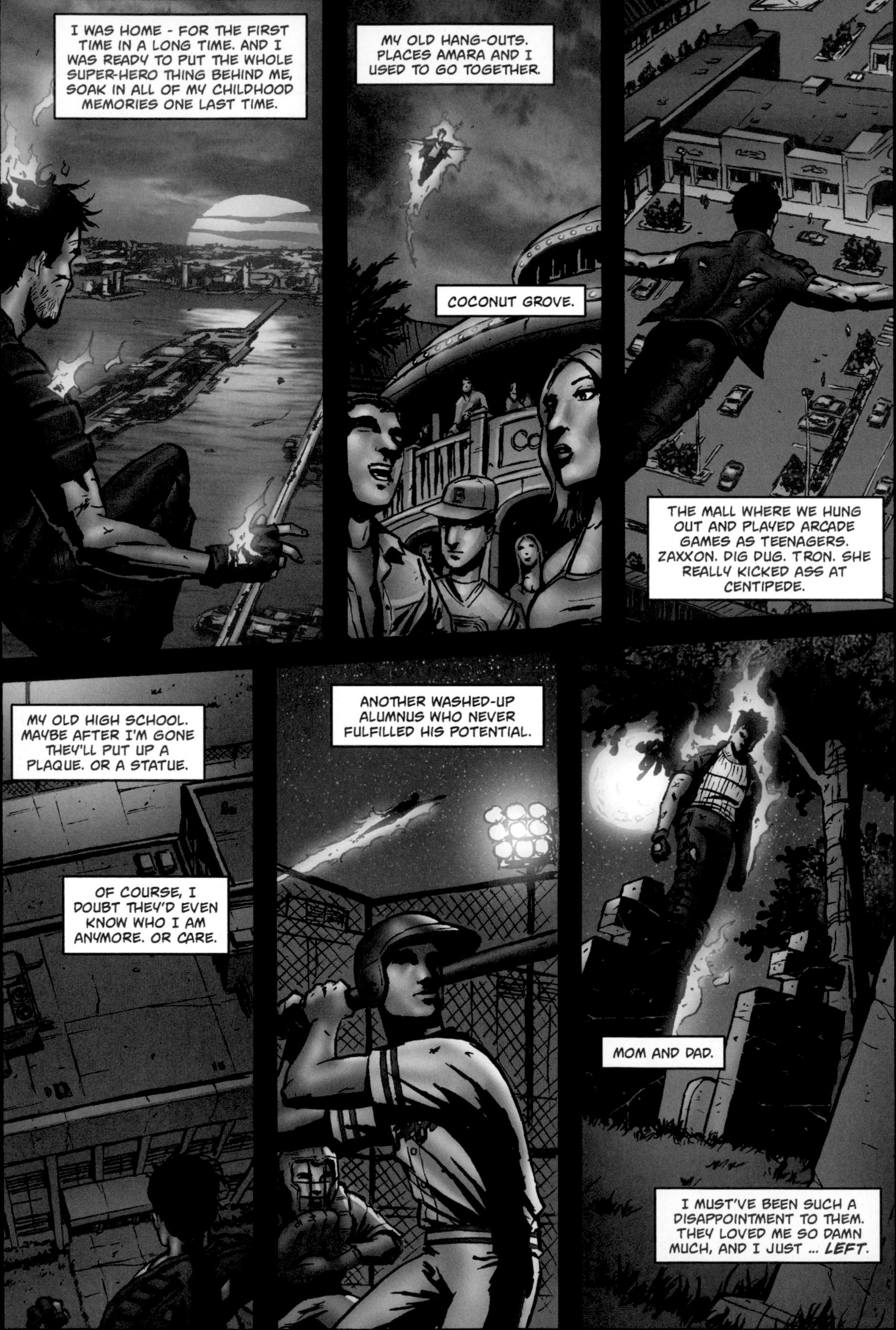
I WAS HOME - FOR THE FIRST TIME IN A LONG TIME. AND I WAS READY TO PUT THE WHOLE SUPER-HERO THING BEHIND ME, SOAK IN ALL OF MY CHILDHOOD MEMORIES ONE LAST TIME.
MY OLD HANG-OUTS. PLACES AMARA AND I USED TO GO TOGETHER.
COCONUT GROVE.
THE MALL WHERE WE HUNG OUT AND PLAYED ARCADE GAMES AS TEENAGERS. ZAXXON. DIG DUG. TRON. SHE REALLY KICKED ASS AT CENTIPEDE.
MY OLD HIGH SCHOOL. MAYBE AFTER I'M GONE THEY'LL PUT UP A PLAQUE. OR A STATUE.
OF COURSE, I DOUBT THEY'D EVEN KNOW WHO I AM ANYMORE. OR CARE.
ANOTHER WASHED-UP ALUMNUS WHO NEVER FULFILLED HIS POTENTIAL.
MOM AND DAD.
I MUST'VE BEEN SUCH A DISAPPOINTMENT TO THEM. THEY LOVED ME SO DAMN MUCH, AND I JUST ... *LEFT*.

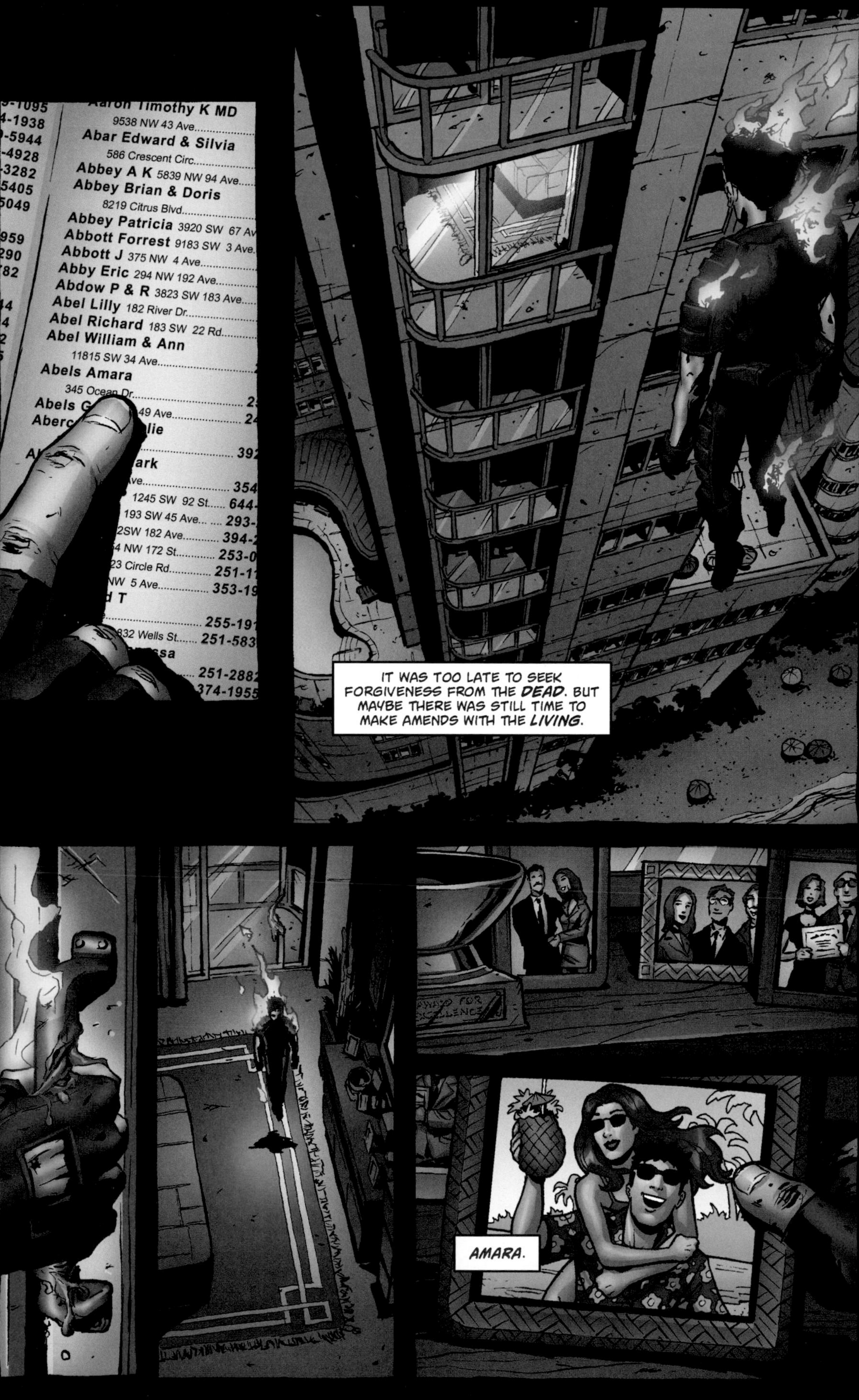
Abar Edward & Silvia
586 Crescent Circ.
Abbey A K 5839 NW 94 Ave.
Abbey Brian & Doris
8219 Citrus Blvd.
Abbey Patricia 3920 SW 67
Abbott Forrest 9183 SW 3 Ave.
Abbott J 375 NW 4 Ave.
Abby Eric 294 NW 192 Ave.
Abdow P & R 3823 SW 183 Ave.
Abel Lilly 182 River Dr.
Abel Richard 183 SW 22 Rd.
Abel William & Ann
11815 SW 34 Ave.
Abels Amara
IT WAS TOO LATE TO SEEK FORGIVENESS FROM THE DEAD. BUT MAYBE THERE WAS STILL TIME TO MAKE AMENDS WITH THE LIVING.
AWARD FOR EXCELLENCE
AMARA.

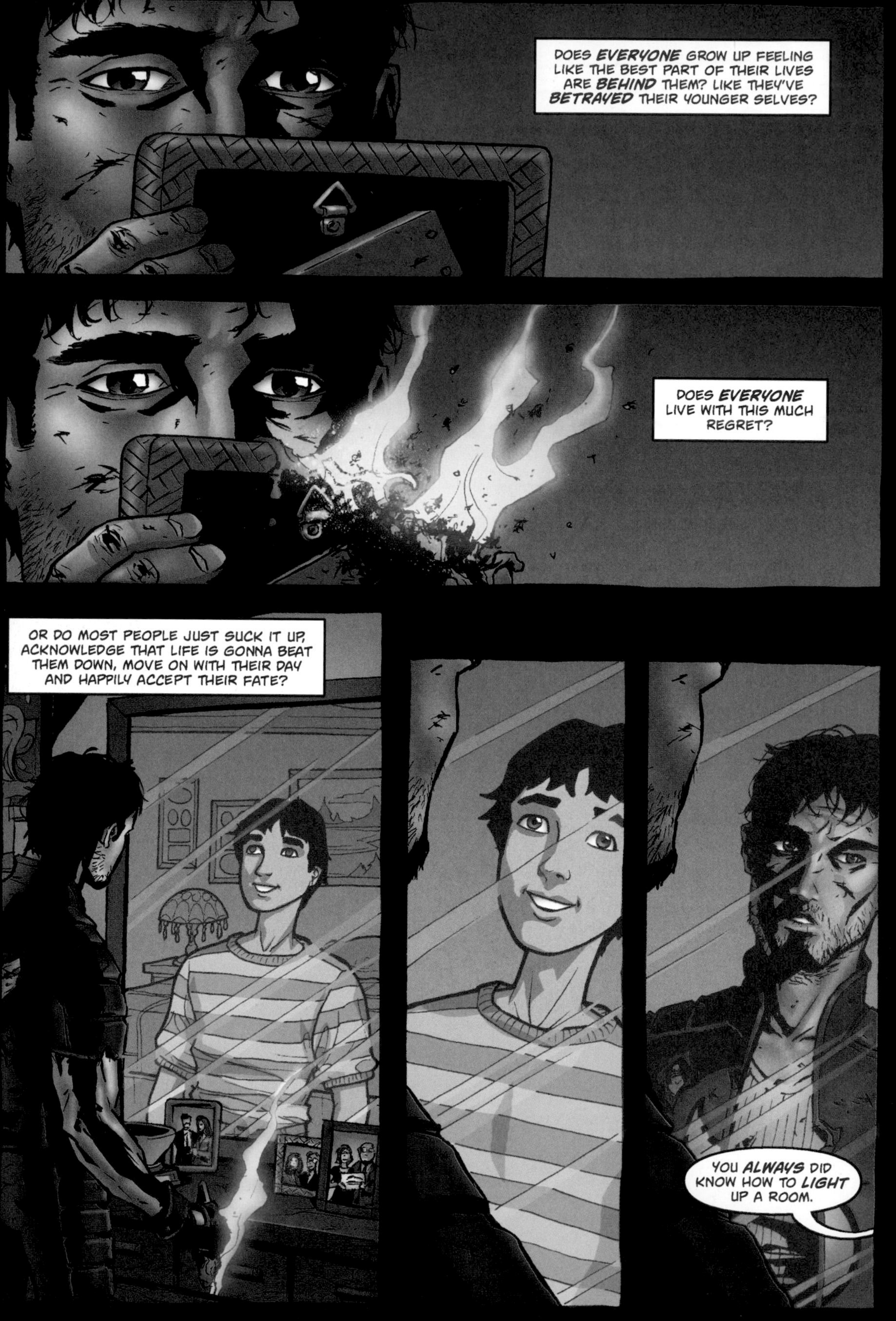
DOES EVERYONE GROW UP FEELING LIKE THE BEST PART OF THEIR LIVES ARE BEHIND THEM? LIKE THEY'VE BETRAYED THEIR YOUNGER SELVES?
DOES EVERYONE LIVE WITH THIS MUCH REGRET?
OR DO MOST PEOPLE JUST SUCK IT UP, ACKNOWLEDGE THAT LIFE IS GONNA BEAT THEM DOWN, MOVE ON WITH THEIR DAY AND HAPPILY ACCEPT THEIR FATE?
YOU ALWAYS DID KNOW HOW TO LIGHT UP A ROOM.

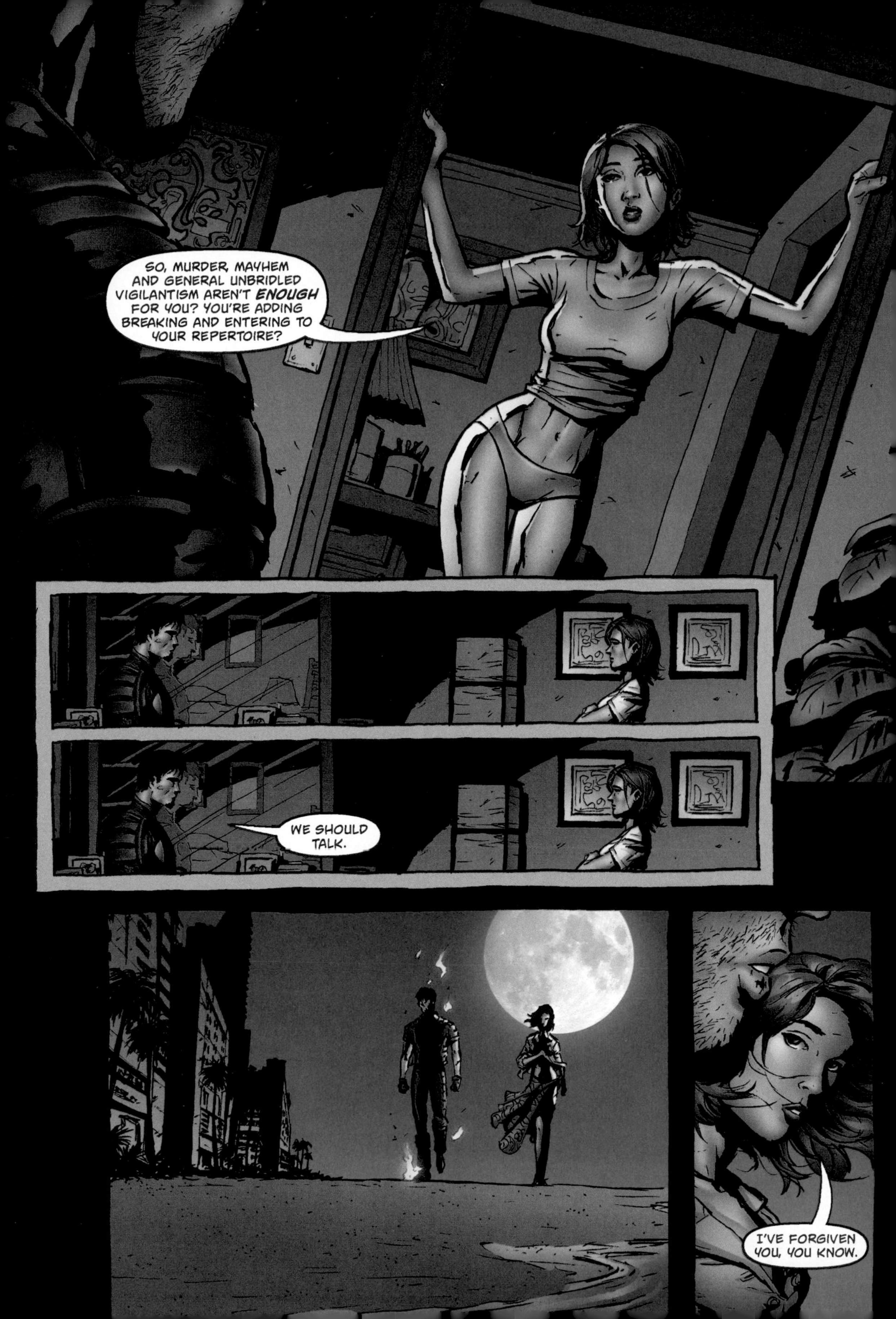
SO, MURDER, MAYHEM AND GENERAL UNBRIDLED VIGILANTISM AREN'T *ENOUGH* FOR YOU? YOU'RE ADDING BREAKING AND ENTERING TO YOUR REPERTOIRE?
WE SHOULD TALK.
I'VE FORGIVEN YOU, YOU KNOW.

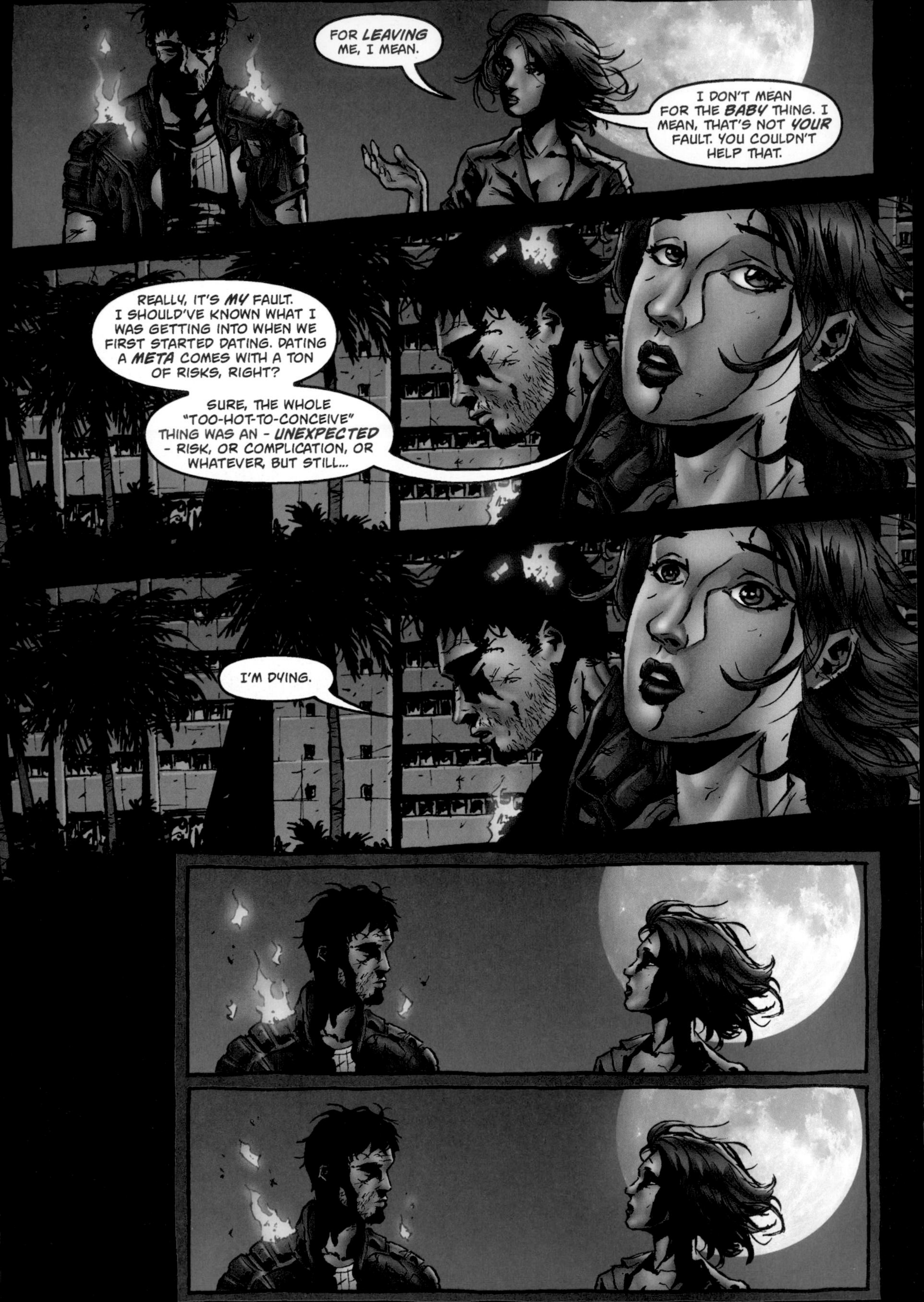
FOR LEAVING ME, I MEAN.
I DON'T MEAN FOR THE BABY THING. I MEAN, THAT'S NOT YOUR FAULT. YOU COULDN'T HELP THAT.
REALLY, IT'S MY FAULT. I SHOULD'VE KNOWN WHAT I WAS GETTING INTO WHEN WE FIRST STARTED DATING. DATING A META COMES WITH A TON OF RISKS, RIGHT?
SURE, THE WHOLE "TOO-HOT-TO-CONCEIVE" THING WAS AN - UNEXPECTED - RISK, OR COMPLICATION, OR WHATEVER, BUT STILL...
I'M DYING.

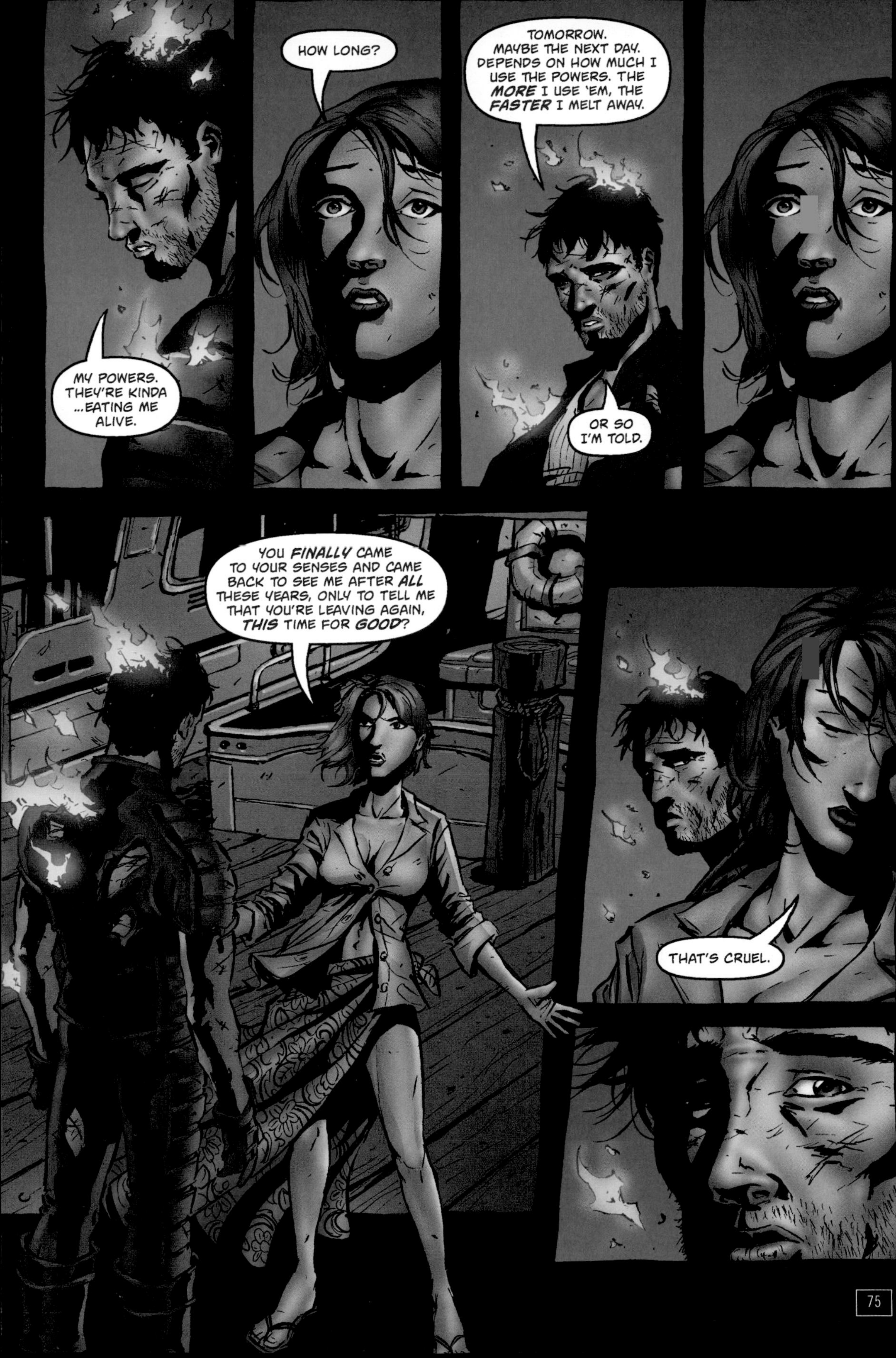
MY POWERS. THEY'RE KINDA ...EATING ME ALIVE.
HOW LONG?
TOMORROW. MAYBE THE NEXT DAY. DEPENDS ON HOW MUCH I USE THE POWERS. THE **MORE** I USE 'EM, THE **FASTER** I MELT AWAY.
OR SO I'M TOLD.
YOU **FINALLY** CAME TO YOUR SENSES AND CAME BACK TO SEE ME AFTER **ALL** THESE YEARS, ONLY TO TELL ME THAT YOU'RE LEAVING AGAIN, **THIS** TIME FOR **GOOD**?
THAT'S CRUEL.

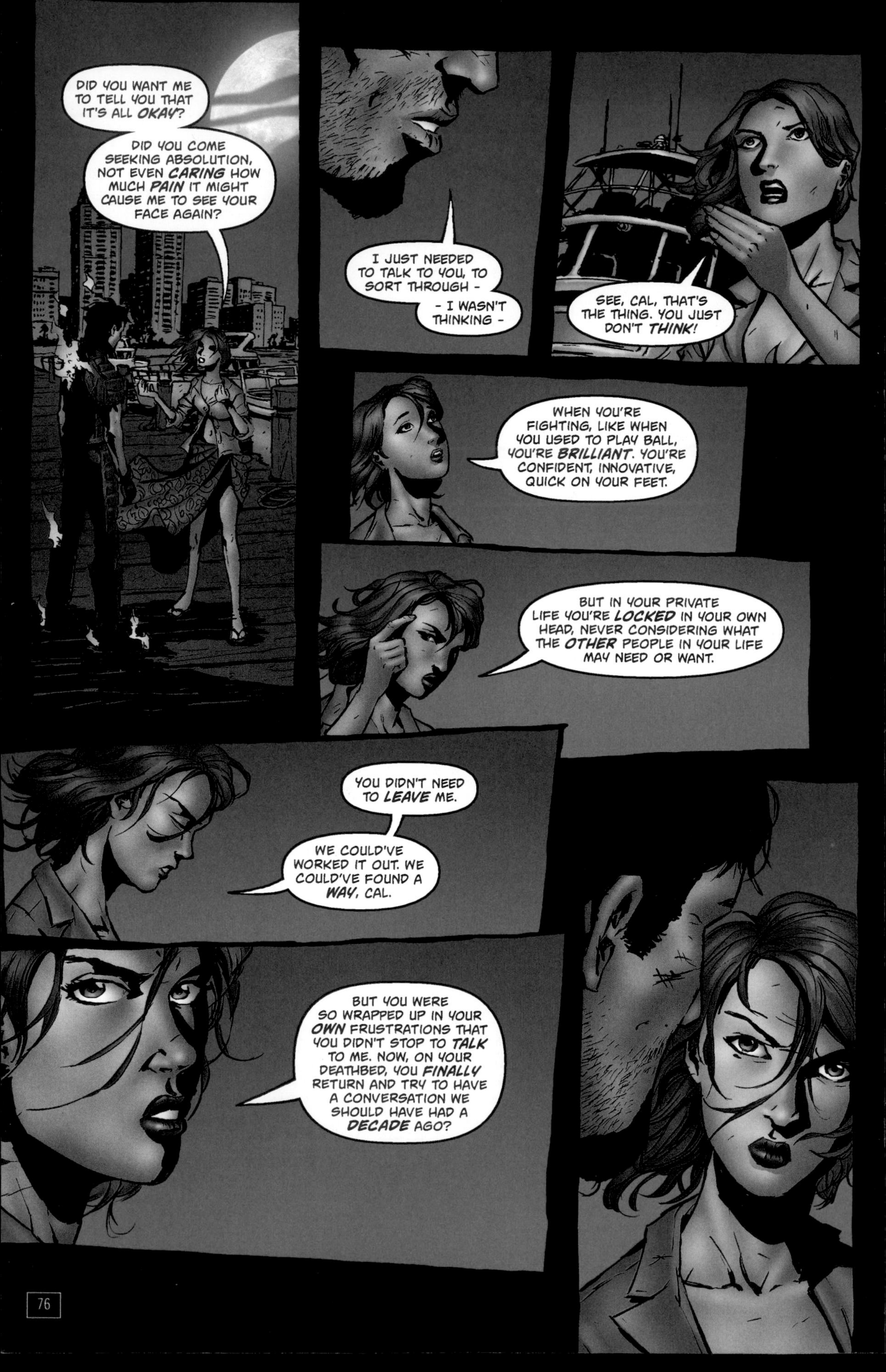
DID YOU WANT ME TO TELL YOU THAT IT'S ALL OKAY?
DID YOU COME SEEKING ABSOLUTION, NOT EVEN CARING HOW MUCH PAIN IT MIGHT CAUSE ME TO SEE YOUR FACE AGAIN?
I JUST NEEDED TO TALK TO YOU, TO SORT THROUGH -
- I WASN'T THINKING -
SEE, CAL, THAT'S THE THING. YOU JUST DON'T THINK!
WHEN YOU'RE FIGHTING, LIKE WHEN YOU USED TO PLAY BALL, YOU'RE BRILLIANT. YOU'RE CONFIDENT, INNOVATIVE, QUICK ON YOUR FEET.
BUT IN YOUR PRIVATE LIFE YOU'RE LOCKED IN YOUR OWN HEAD, NEVER CONSIDERING WHAT THE OTHER PEOPLE IN YOUR LIFE MAY NEED OR WANT.
YOU DIDN'T NEED TO LEAVE ME.
WE COULD'VE WORKED IT OUT. WE COULD'VE FOUND A WAY, CAL.
BUT YOU WERE SO WRAPPED UP IN YOUR OWN FRUSTRATIONS THAT YOU DIDN'T STOP TO TALK TO ME. NOW, ON YOUR DEATHBED, YOU FINALLY RETURN AND TRY TO HAVE A CONVERSATION WE SHOULD HAVE HAD A DECADE AGO?

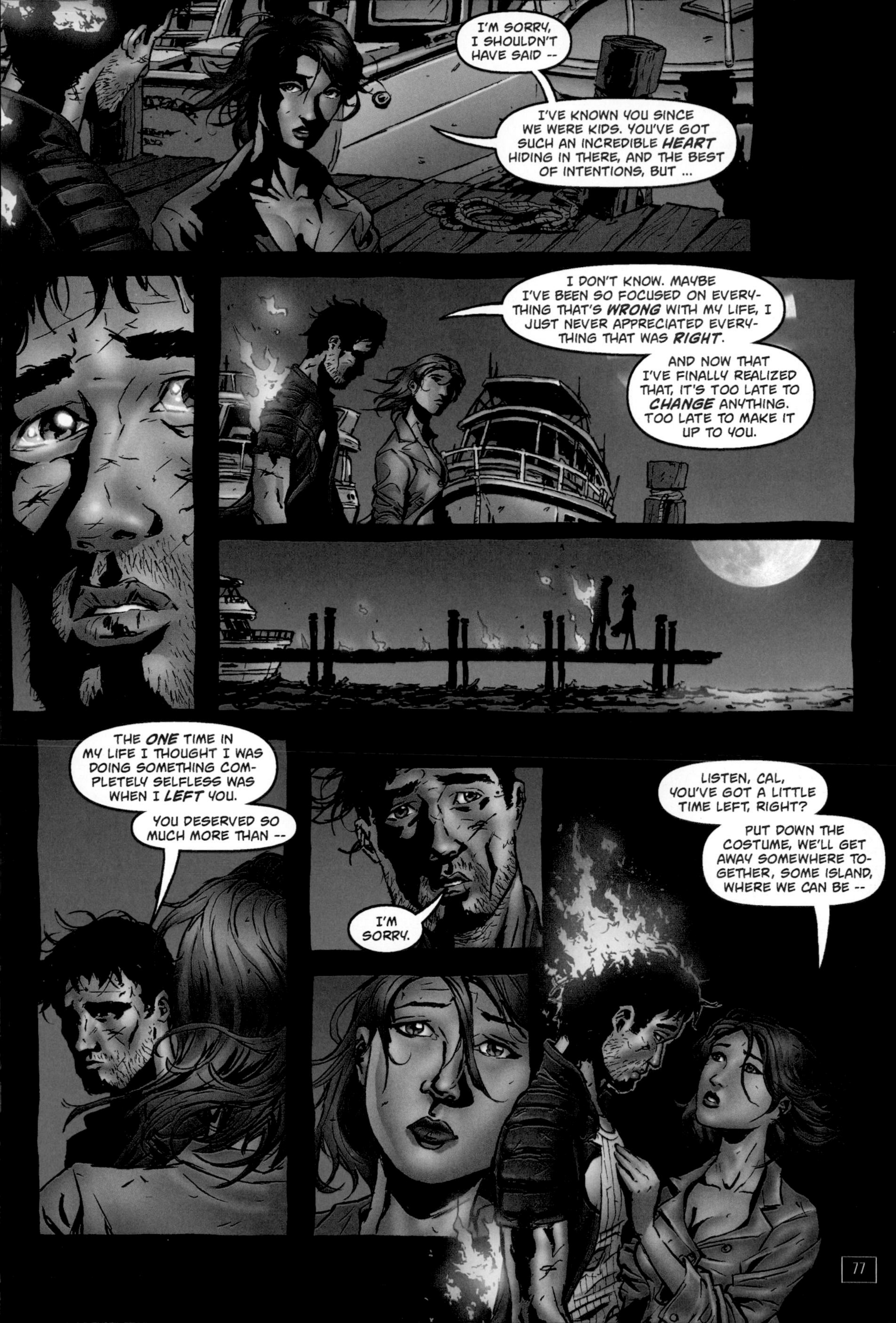
I'M SORRY, I SHOULDN'T HAVE SAID --
I'VE KNOWN YOU SINCE WE WERE KIDS. YOU'VE GOT SUCH AN INCREDIBLE *HEART* HIDING IN THERE, AND THE BEST OF INTENTIONS, BUT ...
I DON'T KNOW. MAYBE I'VE BEEN SO FOCUSED ON EVERYTHING THAT'S *WRONG* WITH MY LIFE, I JUST NEVER APPRECIATED EVERYTHING THAT WAS *RIGHT*.
AND NOW THAT I'VE FINALLY REALIZED THAT, IT'S TOO LATE TO *CHANGE* ANYTHING. TOO LATE TO MAKE IT UP TO YOU.
THE *ONE* TIME IN MY LIFE I THOUGHT I WAS DOING SOMETHING COMPLETELY SELFLESS WAS WHEN I *LEFT* YOU.
YOU DESERVED SO MUCH MORE THAN --
I'M SORRY.
LISTEN, CAL, YOU'VE GOT A LITTLE TIME LEFT, RIGHT?
PUT DOWN THE COSTUME, WE'LL GET AWAY SOMEWHERE TOGETHER, SOME ISLAND, WHERE WE CAN BE --

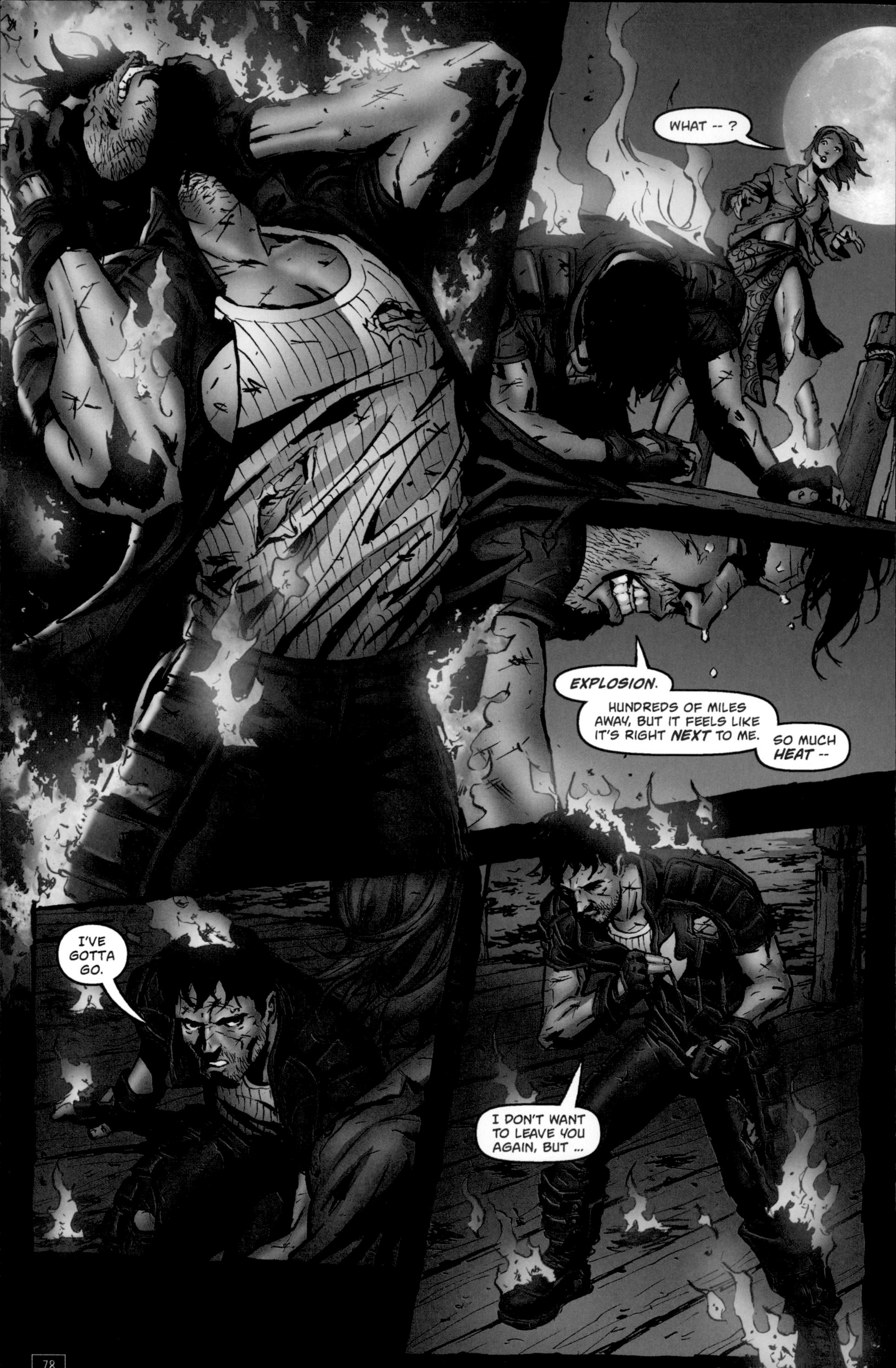

WHAT -- ?
EXPLOSION.
HUNDREDS OF MILES AWAY, BUT IT FEELS LIKE IT'S RIGHT NEXT TO ME.
SO MUCH HEAT --
I'VE GOTTA GO.
I DON'T WANT TO LEAVE YOU AGAIN, BUT ...

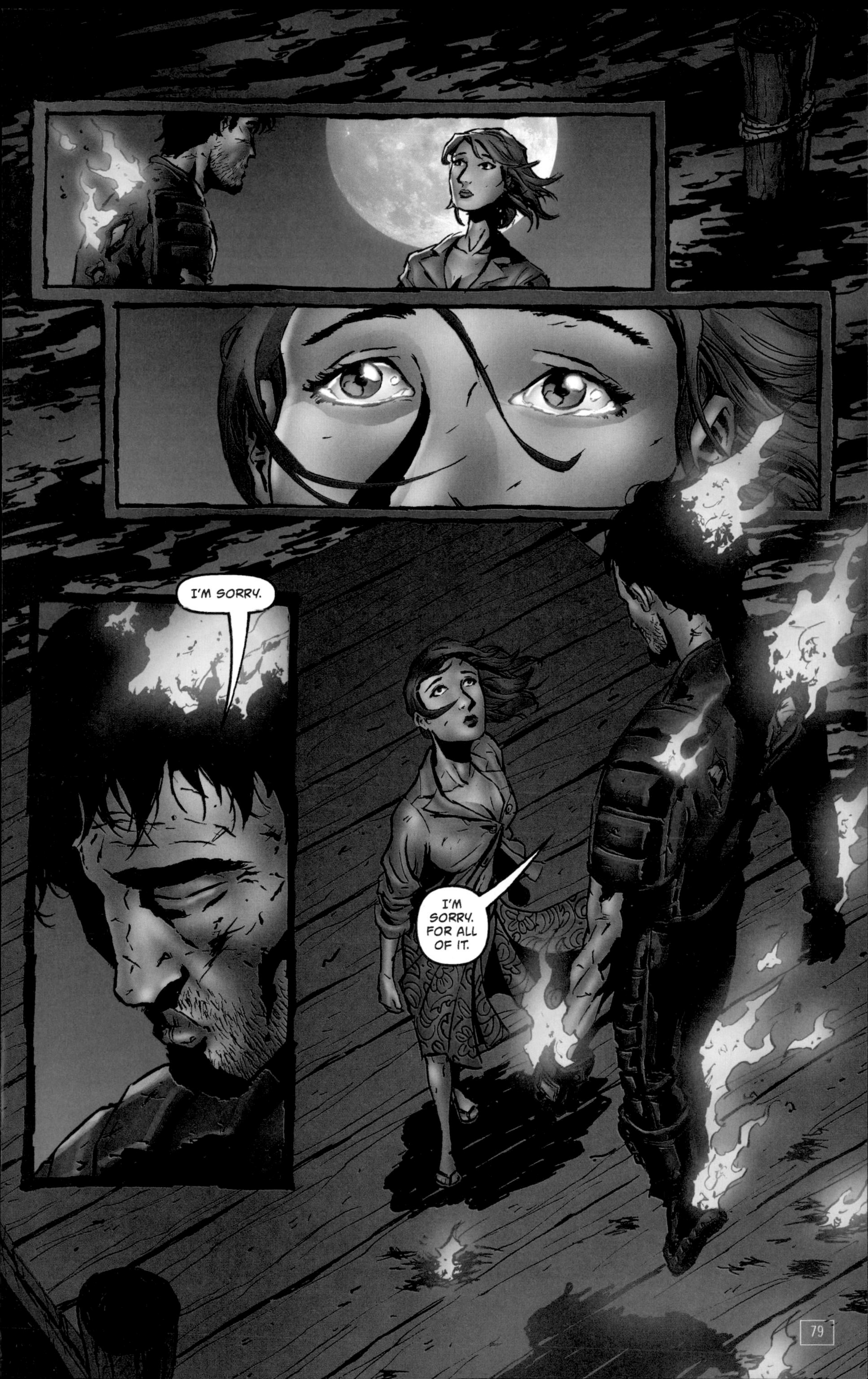
I'M SORRY.
I'M SORRY. FOR ALL OF IT.

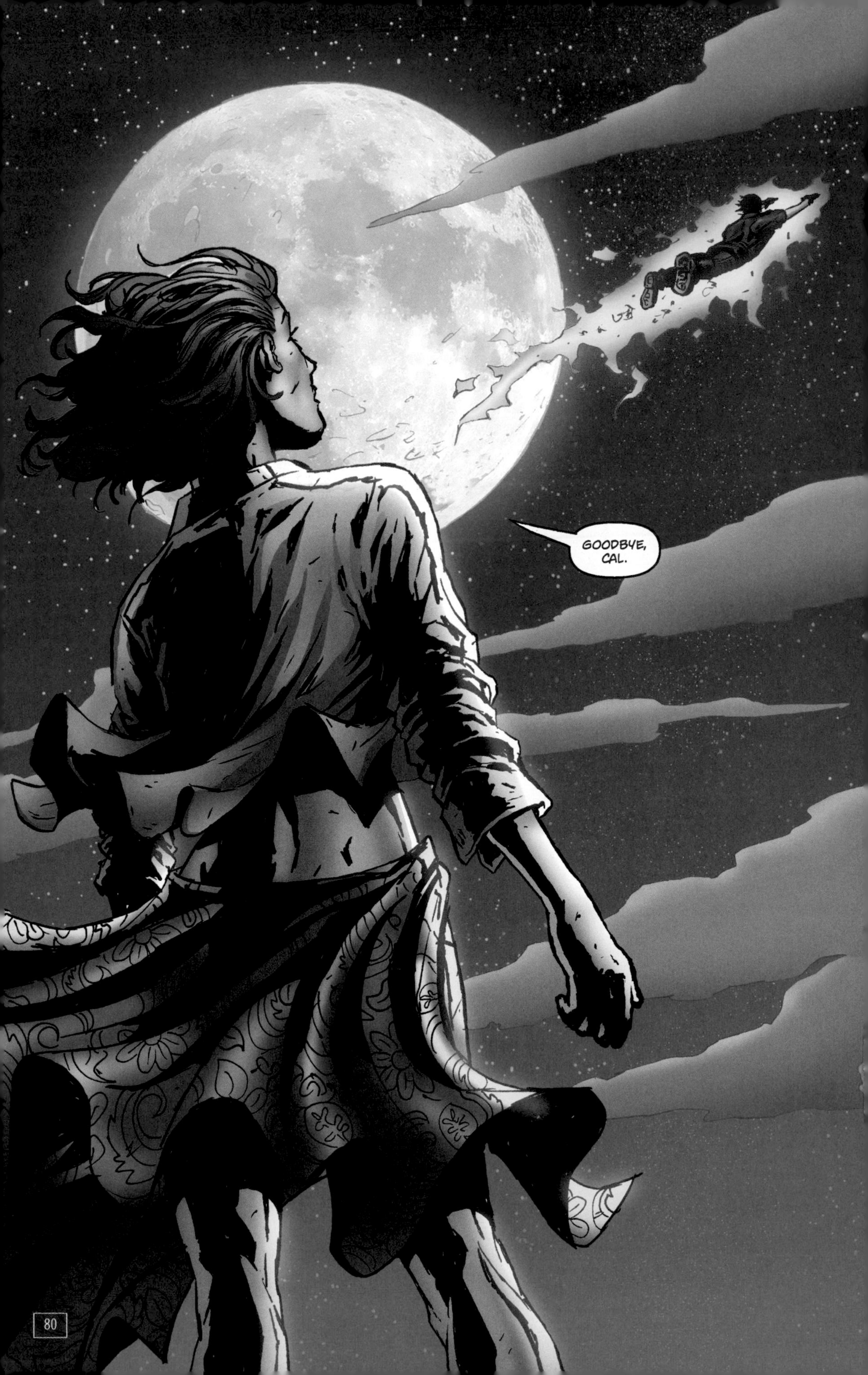
GOODBYE, CAL.

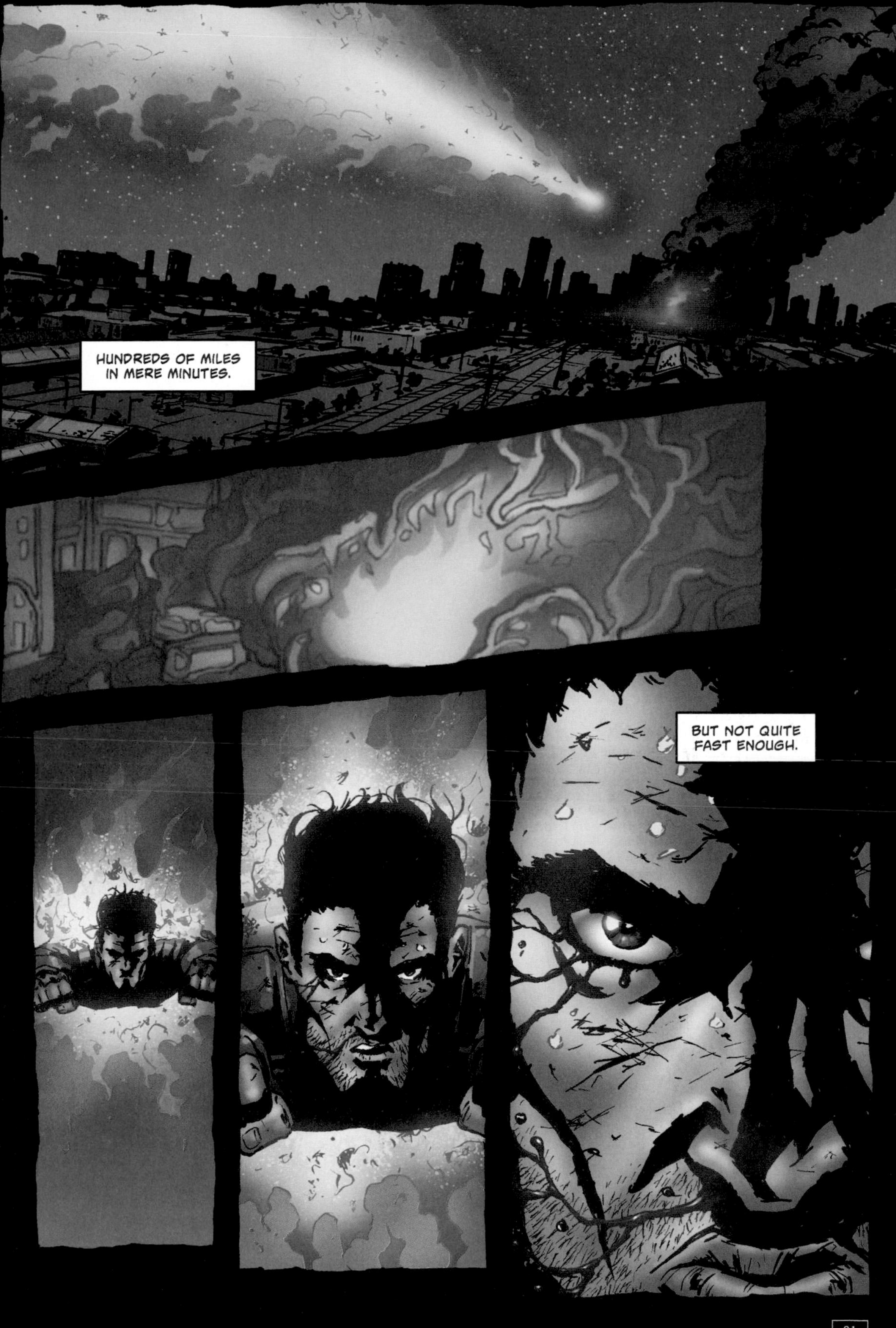
HUNDREDS OF MILES IN MERE MINUTES.
BUT NOT QUITE FAST ENOUGH.

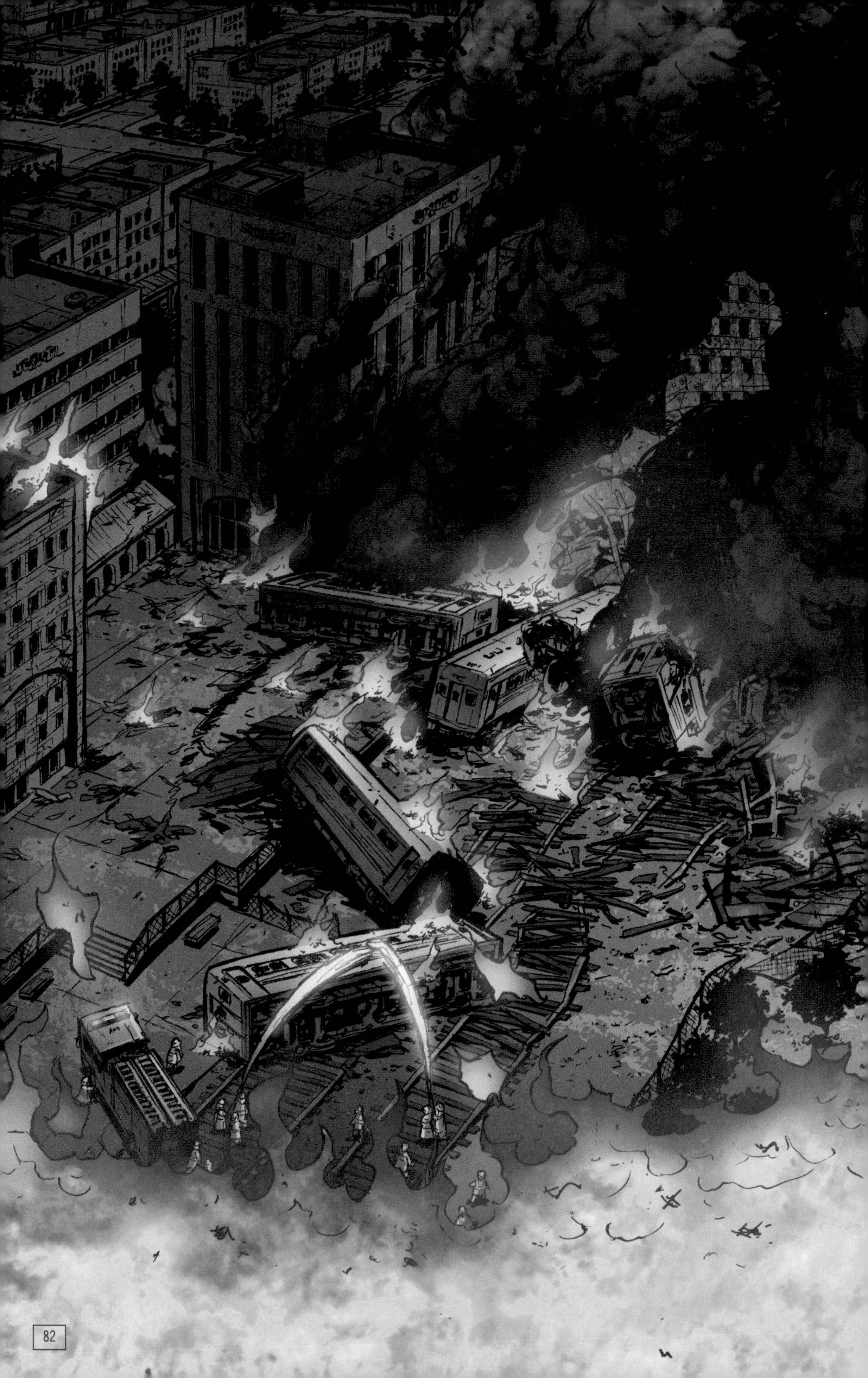

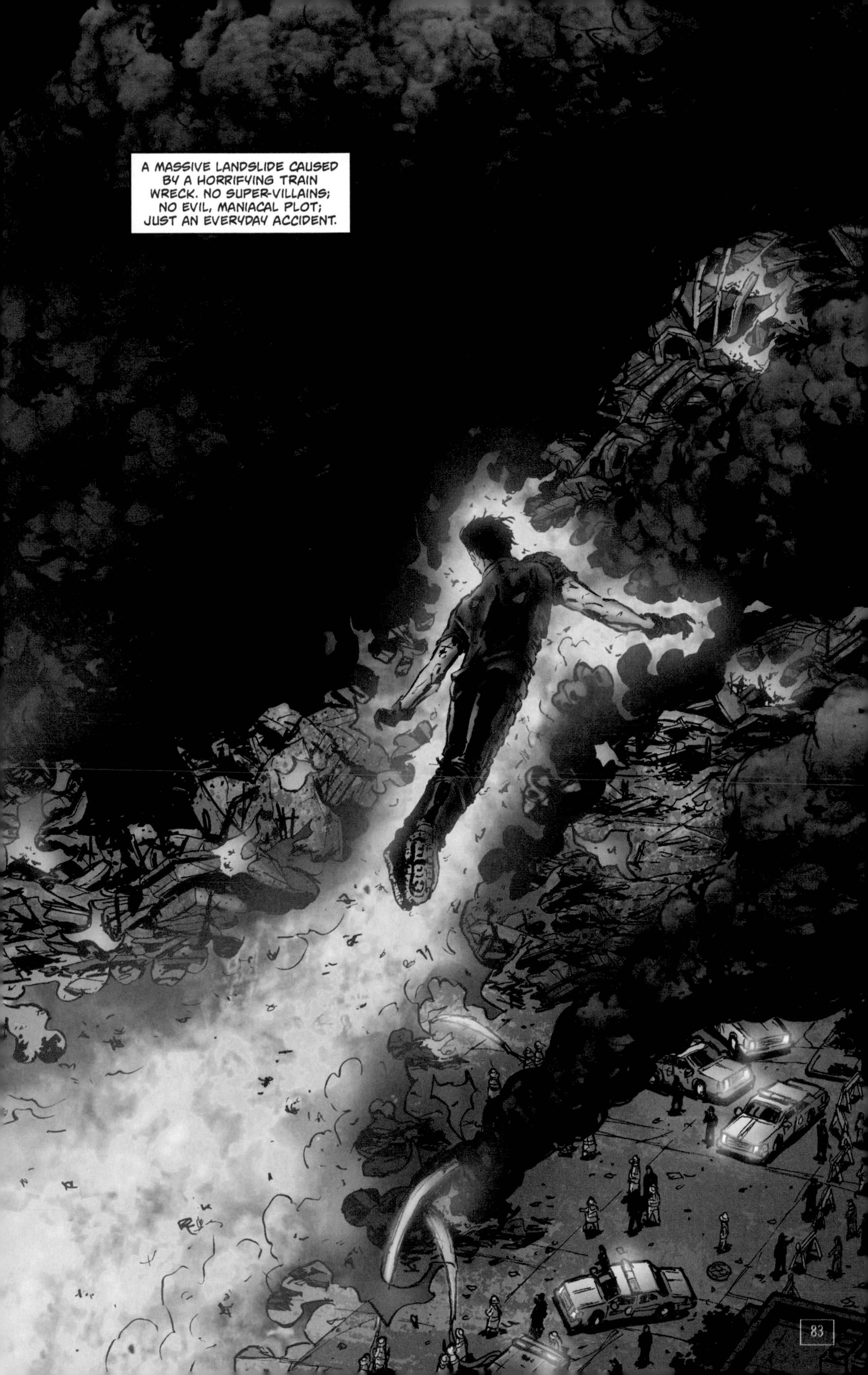
A MASSIVE LANDSLIDE CAUSED BY A HORRIFYING TRAIN WRECK. NO SUPER-VILLAINS; NO EVIL, MANIACAL PLOT; JUST AN EVERYDAY ACCIDENT.

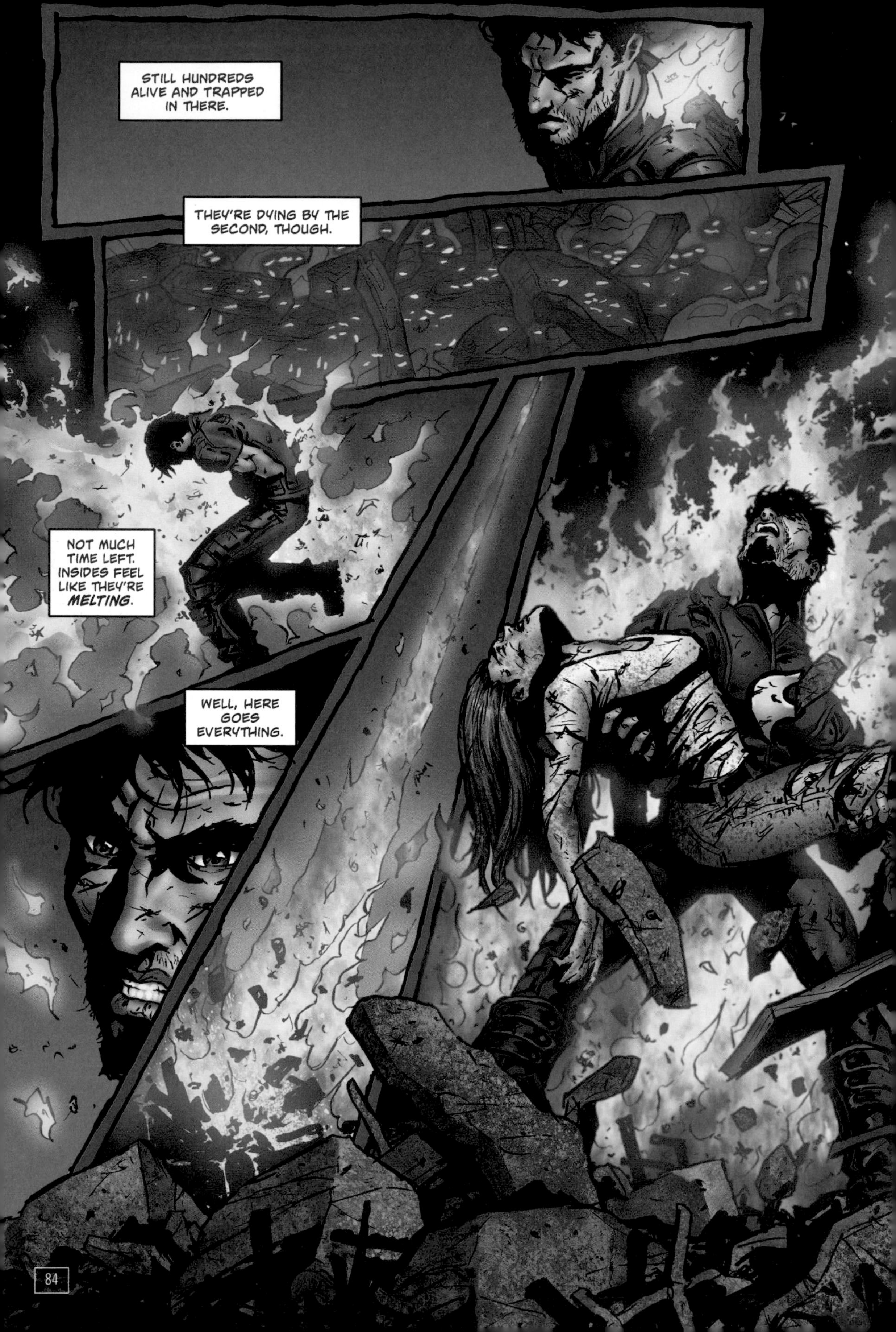
STILL HUNDREDS ALIVE AND TRAPPED IN THERE.
THEY'RE DYING BY THE SECOND, THOUGH.
NOT MUCH TIME LEFT. INSIDES FEEL LIKE THEY'RE *MELTING*.
WELL, HERE GOES EVERYTHING.

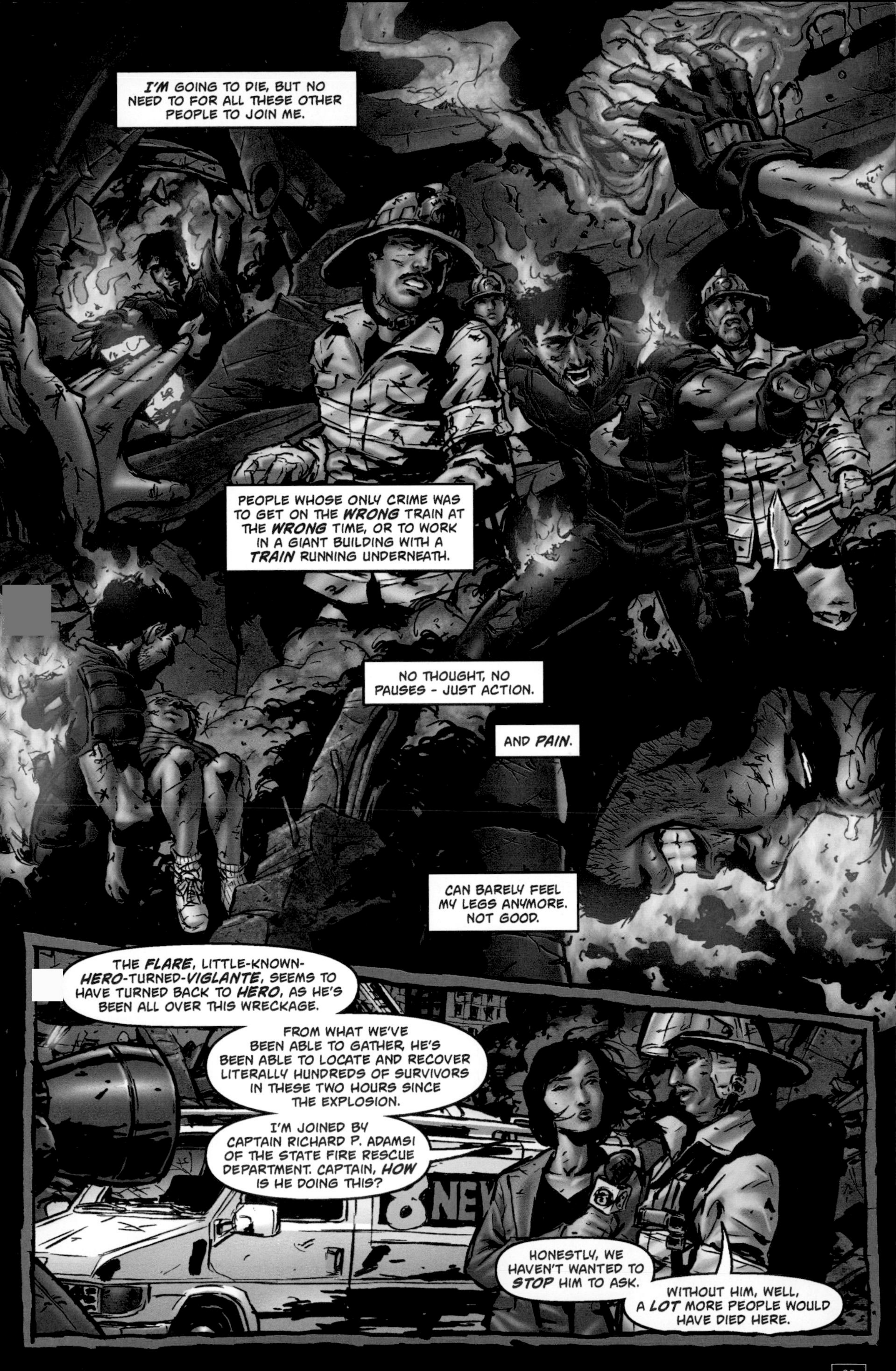
I'M GOING TO DIE, BUT NO NEED TO FOR ALL THESE OTHER PEOPLE TO JOIN ME.
PEOPLE WHOSE ONLY CRIME WAS TO GET ON THE WRONG TRAIN AT THE WRONG TIME, OR TO WORK IN A GIANT BUILDING WITH A TRAIN RUNNING UNDERNEATH.
NO THOUGHT, NO PAUSES - JUST ACTION.
AND PAIN.
CAN BARELY FEEL MY LEGS ANYMORE. NOT GOOD.
THE FLARE, LITTLE-KNOWN-HERO-TURNED-VIGLANTE, SEEMS TO HAVE TURNED BACK TO HERO, AS HE'S BEEN ALL OVER THIS WRECKAGE.
FROM WHAT WE'VE BEEN ABLE TO GATHER, HE'S BEEN ABLE TO LOCATE AND RECOVER LITERALLY HUNDREDS OF SURVIVORS IN THESE TWO HOURS SINCE THE EXPLOSION.
I'M JOINED BY CAPTAIN RICHARD P. ADAMSI OF THE STATE FIRE RESCUE DEPARTMENT. CAPTAIN, HOW IS HE DOING THIS?
HONESTLY, WE HAVEN'T WANTED TO STOP HIM TO ASK.
WITHOUT HIM, WELL, A LOT MORE PEOPLE WOULD HAVE DIED HERE.

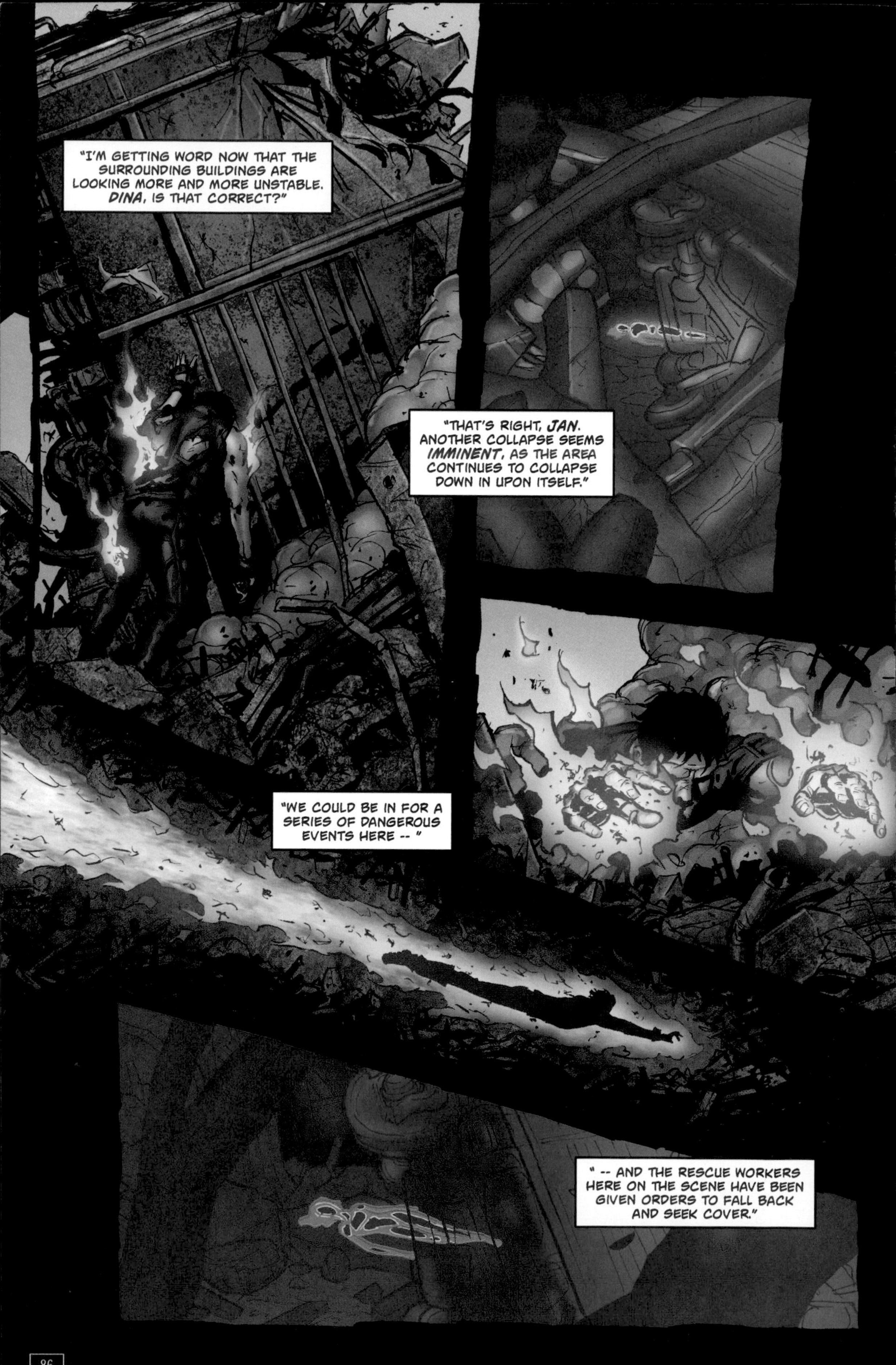
"I'M GETTING WORD NOW THAT THE SURROUNDING BUILDINGS ARE LOOKING MORE AND MORE UNSTABLE. DINA, IS THAT CORRECT?"
"THAT'S RIGHT, JAN. ANOTHER COLLAPSE SEEMS IMMINENT, AS THE AREA CONTINUES TO COLLAPSE DOWN IN UPON ITSELF."
"WE COULD BE IN FOR A SERIES OF DANGEROUS EVENTS HERE -- "
" -- AND THE RESCUE WORKERS HERE ON THE SCENE HAVE BEEN GIVEN ORDERS TO FALL BACK AND SEEK COVER."

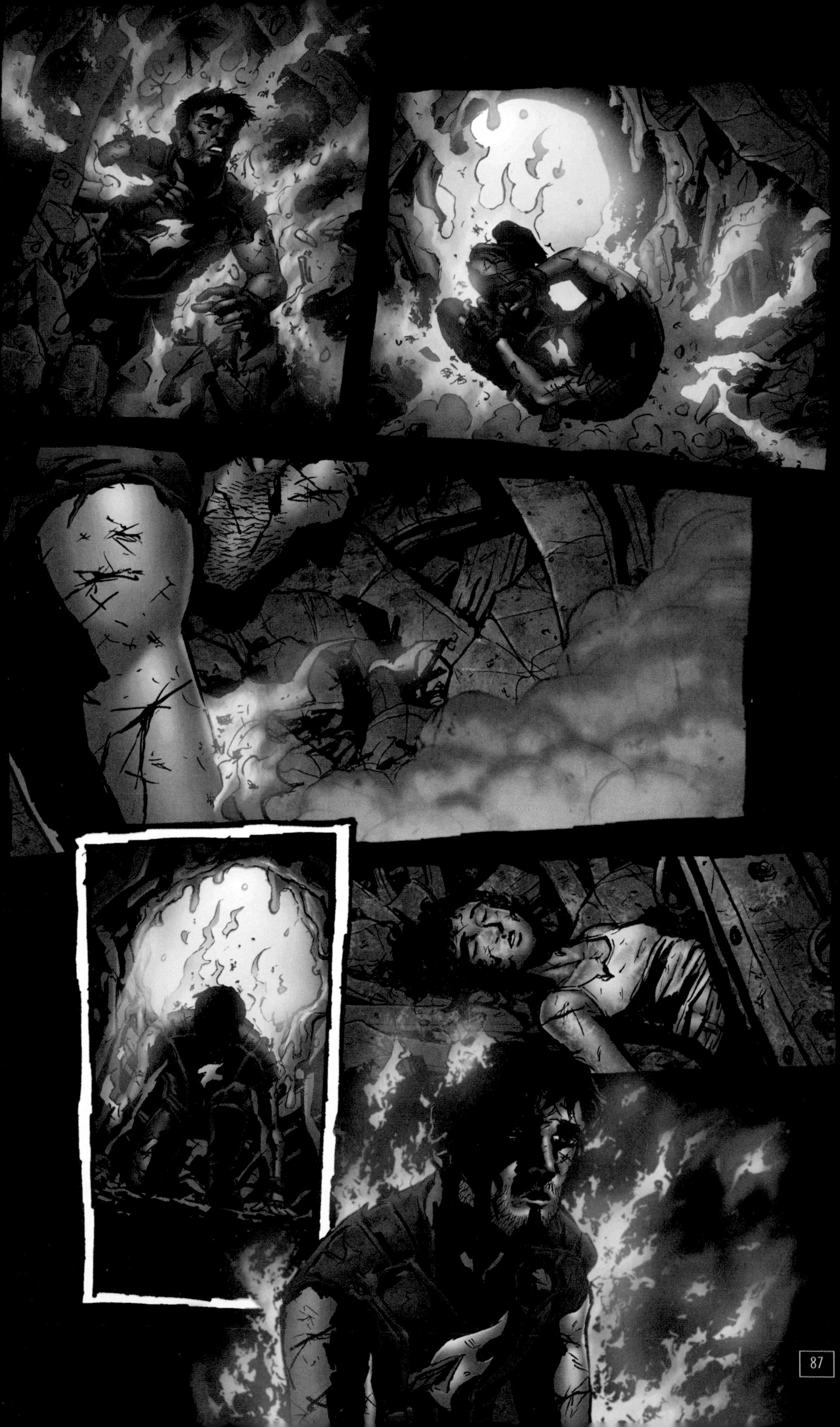

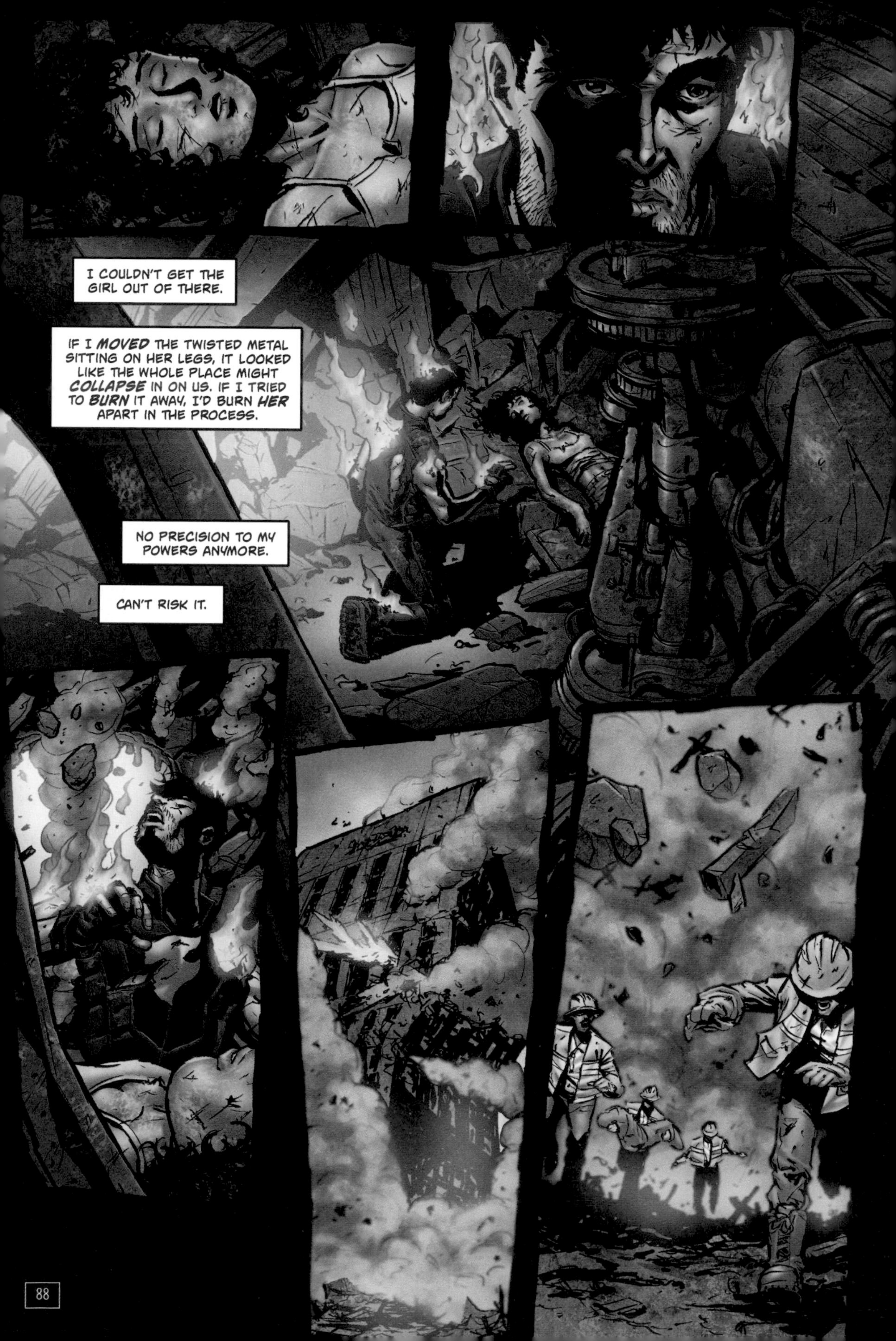
I COULDN'T GET THE GIRL OUT OF THERE.
IF I MOVED THE TWISTED METAL SITTING ON HER LEGS, IT LOOKED LIKE THE WHOLE PLACE MIGHT COLLAPSE IN ON US. IF I TRIED TO BURN IT AWAY, I'D BURN HER APART IN THE PROCESS.
NO PRECISION TO MY POWERS ANYMORE.
CAN'T RISK IT.

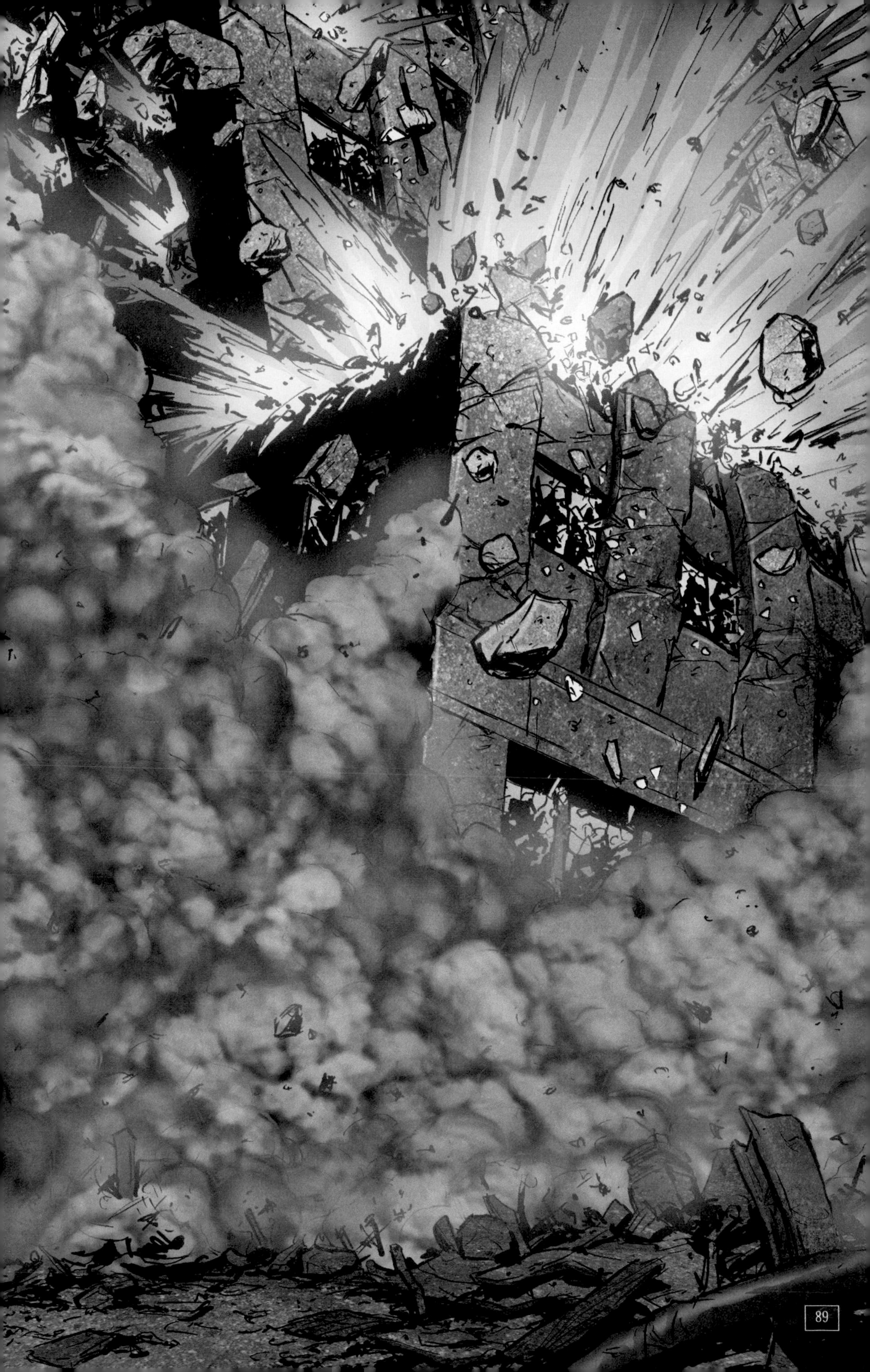

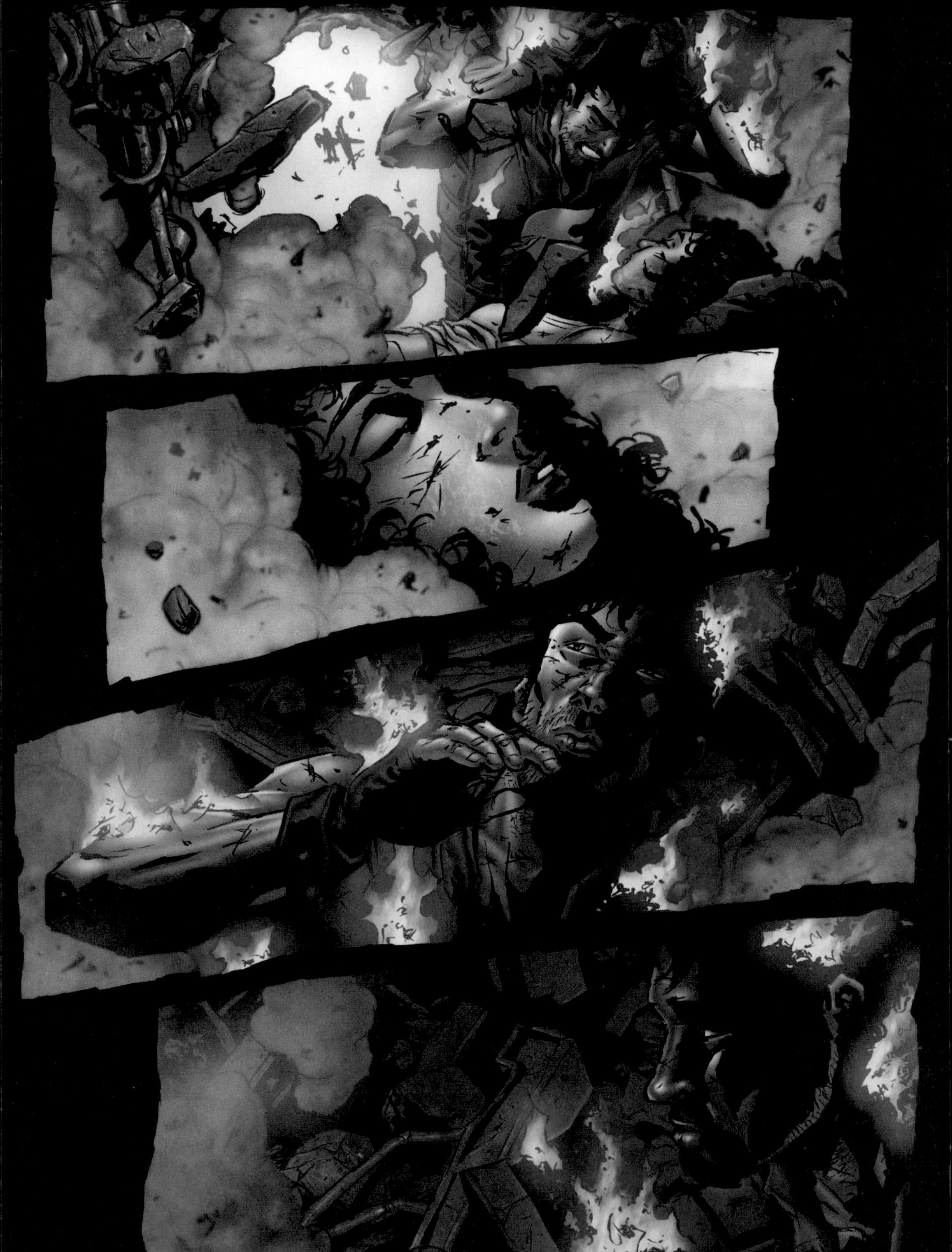

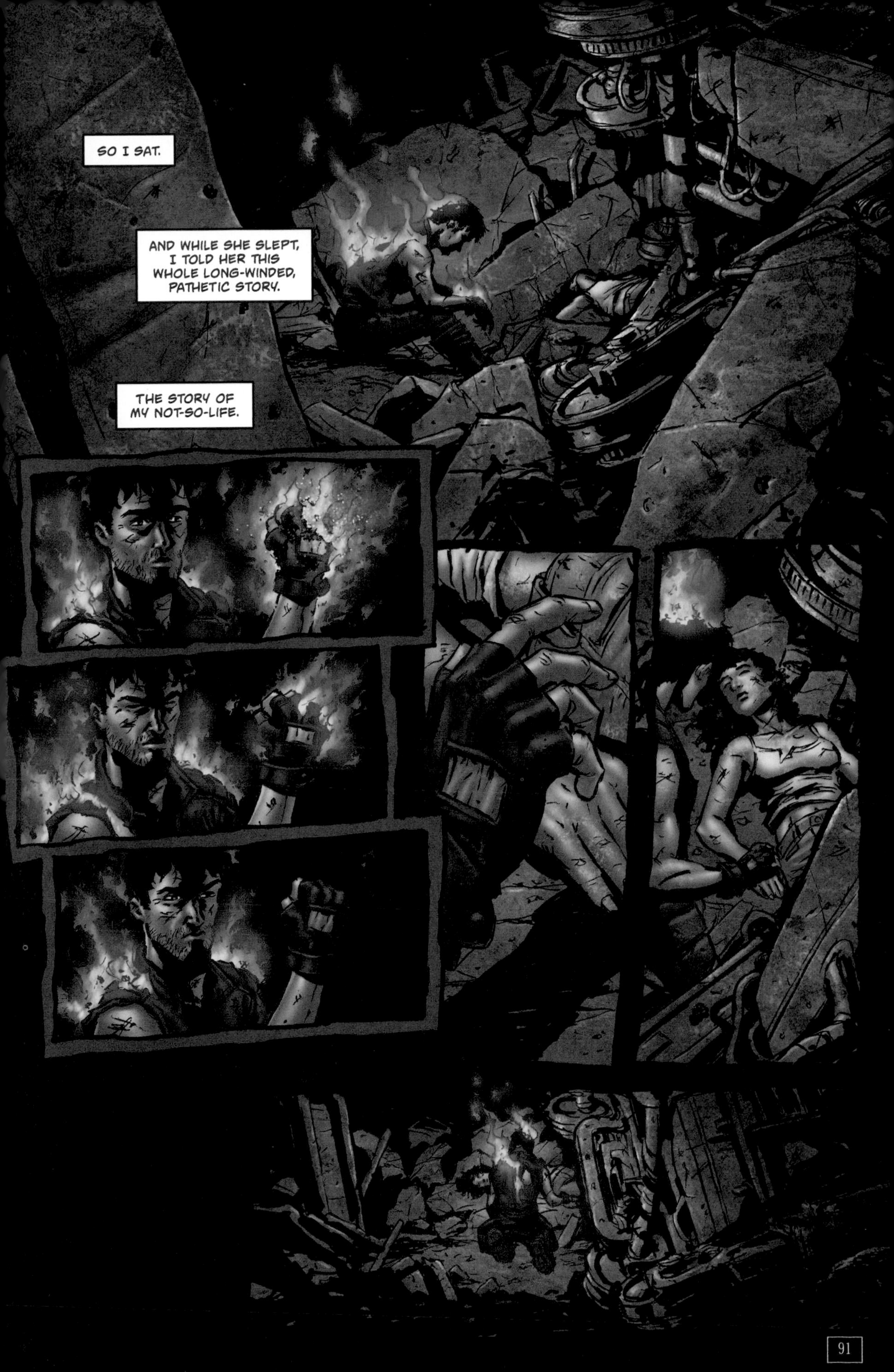
SO I SAT.
AND WHILE SHE SLEPT, I TOLD HER THIS WHOLE LONG-WINDED, PATHETIC STORY.
THE STORY OF MY NOT-SO-LIFE.

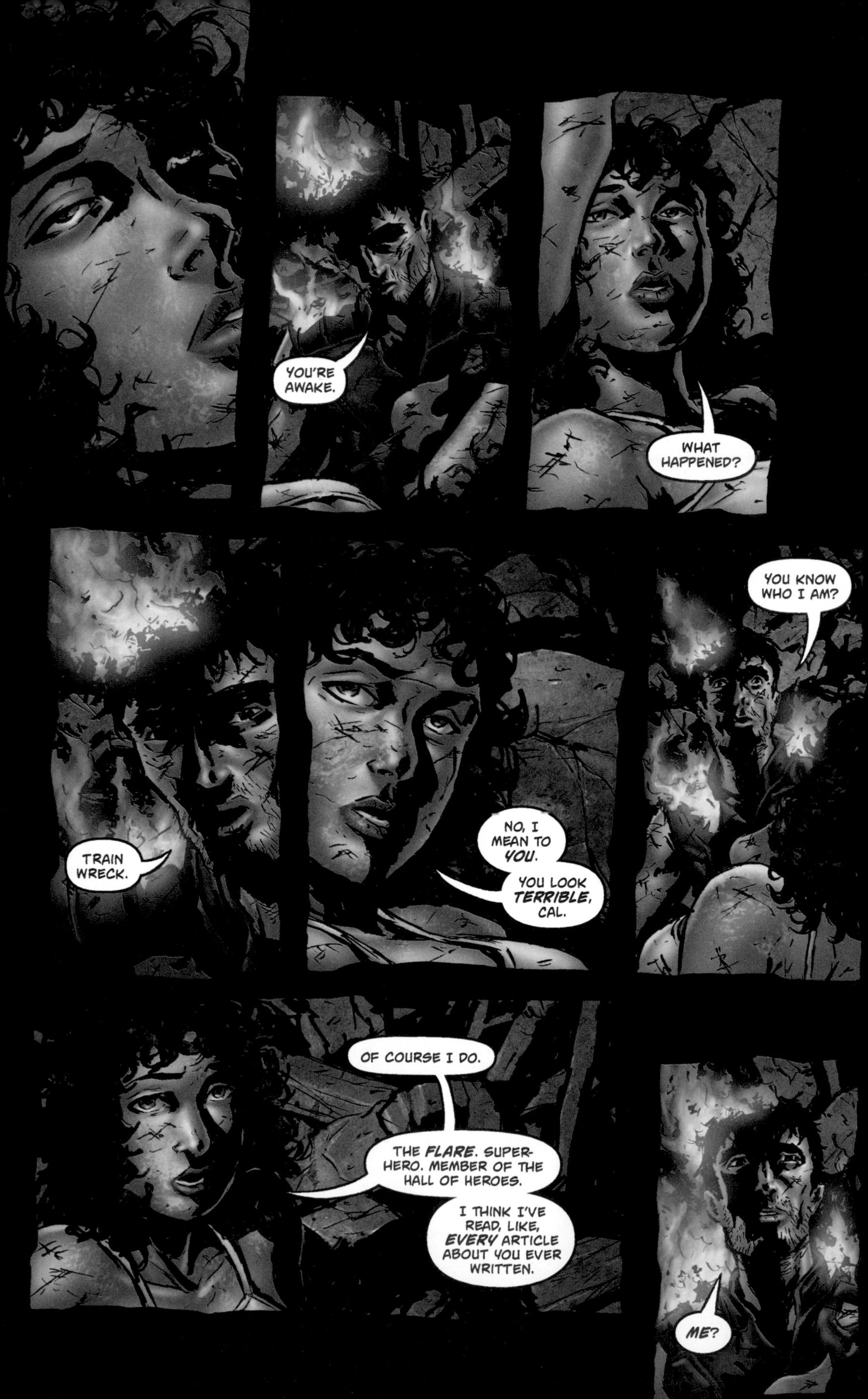
YOU'RE AWAKE.
WHAT HAPPENED?
TRAIN WRECK.
NO, I MEAN TO *YOU*.
YOU LOOK *TERRIBLE*, CAL.
YOU KNOW WHO I AM?
OF COURSE I DO.
THE *FLARE*. SUPER-HERO. MEMBER OF THE HALL OF HEROES.
I THINK I'VE READ, LIKE, *EVERY* ARTICLE ABOUT YOU EVER WRITTEN.
ME?

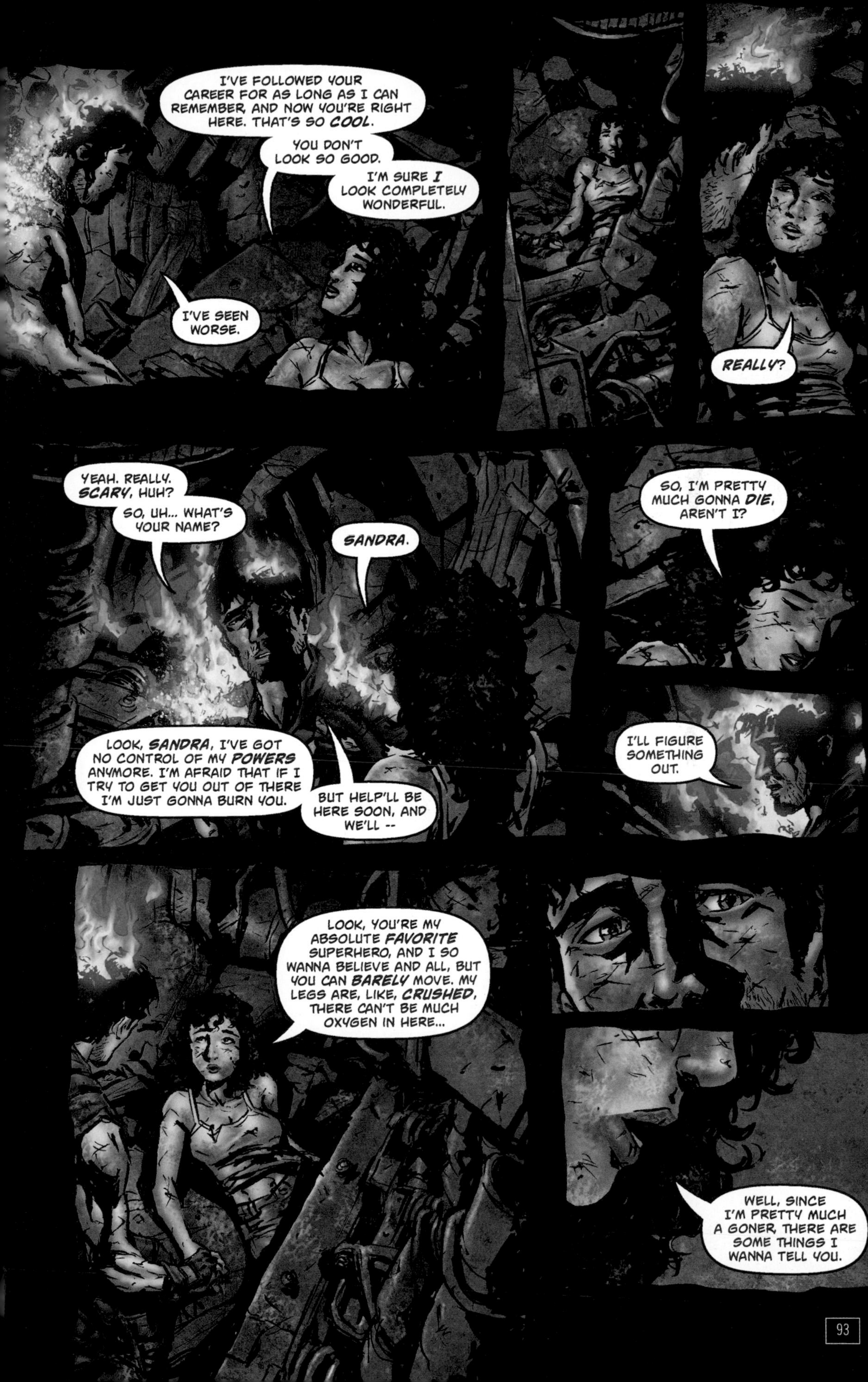
I'VE FOLLOWED YOUR CAREER FOR AS LONG AS I CAN REMEMBER, AND NOW YOU'RE RIGHT HERE. THAT'S SO COOL.
YOU DON'T LOOK SO GOOD.
I'M SURE I LOOK COMPLETELY WONDERFUL.
I'VE SEEN WORSE.
REALLY?
YEAH. REALLY. SCARY, HUH?
SO, UH... WHAT'S YOUR NAME?
SANDRA.
SO, I'M PRETTY MUCH GONNA DIE, AREN'T I?
LOOK, SANDRA, I'VE GOT NO CONTROL OF MY POWERS ANYMORE. I'M AFRAID THAT IF I TRY TO GET YOU OUT OF THERE I'M JUST GONNA BURN YOU.
BUT HELP'LL BE HERE SOON, AND WE'LL --
I'LL FIGURE SOMETHING OUT.
LOOK, YOU'RE MY ABSOLUTE FAVORITE SUPERHERO, AND I SO WANNA BELIEVE AND ALL, BUT YOU CAN BARELY MOVE. MY LEGS ARE, LIKE, CRUSHED, THERE CAN'T BE MUCH OXYGEN IN HERE...
WELL, SINCE I'M PRETTY MUCH A GONER, THERE ARE SOME THINGS I WANNA TELL YOU.

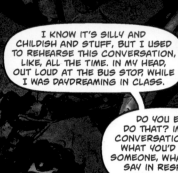

I KNOW IT'S SILLY AND CHILDISH AND STUFF, BUT I USED TO REHEARSE THIS CONVERSATION, LIKE, ALL THE TIME. IN MY HEAD, OUT LOUD AT THE BUS STOP, WHILE I WAS DAYDREAMING IN CLASS.

ALL THE TIME.

DO YOU EVER DO THAT? IMAGINE CONVERSATIONS, LIKE WHAT YOU'D SAY TO SOMEONE, WHAT THEY'D SAY IN RESPONSE, AND ALL THAT?

"BUT YOU ALWAYS LOOKED SO *SAD*, LIKE YOU WERE BROKEN INSIDE, AND I THOUGHT IT WAS IMPORTANT FOR YOU TO KNOW HOW IMPORTANT YOU'VE BEEN TO ME, HOW MUCH YOU'VE *INSPIRED* ME."

"BECAUSE MAYBE THAT WOULD MAKE A DIFFERENCE. MAYBE YOU'D *SMILE* FOR ONCE, YOU KNOW?"

SEE, AND THAT'S THE PART OF MY SPEECH WHERE YOU TOTALLY FALL IN *LOVE* WITH ME, AND YOU, LIKE, SWEEP ME OFF MY FEET AND WE FLY AWAY TOGETHER.

AT LEAST, THAT'S WHAT HAPPENS IN MY *HEAD*.

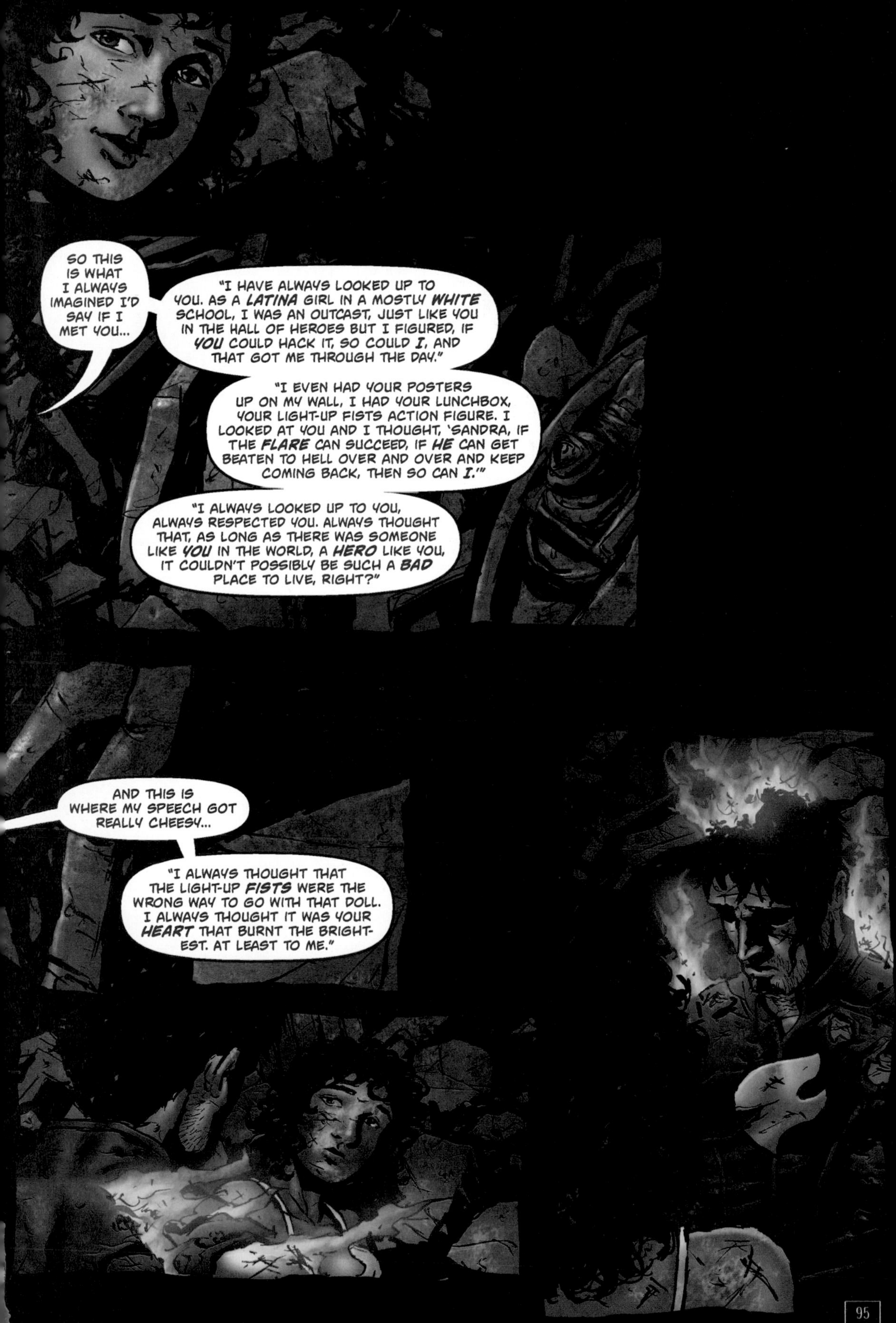
SO THIS IS WHAT I ALWAYS IMAGINED I'D SAY IF I MET YOU...
"I HAVE ALWAYS LOOKED UP TO YOU. AS A LATINA GIRL IN A MOSTLY WHITE SCHOOL, I WAS AN OUTCAST, JUST LIKE YOU IN THE HALL OF HEROES BUT I FIGURED, IF YOU COULD HACK IT, SO COULD I, AND THAT GOT ME THROUGH THE DAY."
"I EVEN HAD YOUR POSTERS UP ON MY WALL, I HAD YOUR LUNCHBOX, YOUR LIGHT-UP FISTS ACTION FIGURE. I LOOKED AT YOU AND I THOUGHT, 'SANDRA, IF THE FLARE CAN SUCCEED, IF HE CAN GET BEATEN TO HELL OVER AND OVER AND KEEP COMING BACK, THEN SO CAN I.'"
"I ALWAYS LOOKED UP TO YOU, ALWAYS RESPECTED YOU. ALWAYS THOUGHT THAT, AS LONG AS THERE WAS SOMEONE LIKE YOU IN THE WORLD, A HERO LIKE YOU, IT COULDN'T POSSIBLY BE SUCH A BAD PLACE TO LIVE, RIGHT?"
AND THIS IS WHERE MY SPEECH GOT REALLY CHEESY...
"I ALWAYS THOUGHT THAT THE LIGHT-UP FISTS WERE THE WRONG WAY TO GO WITH THAT DOLL. I ALWAYS THOUGHT IT WAS YOUR HEART THAT BURNT THE BRIGHT-EST. AT LEAST TO ME."

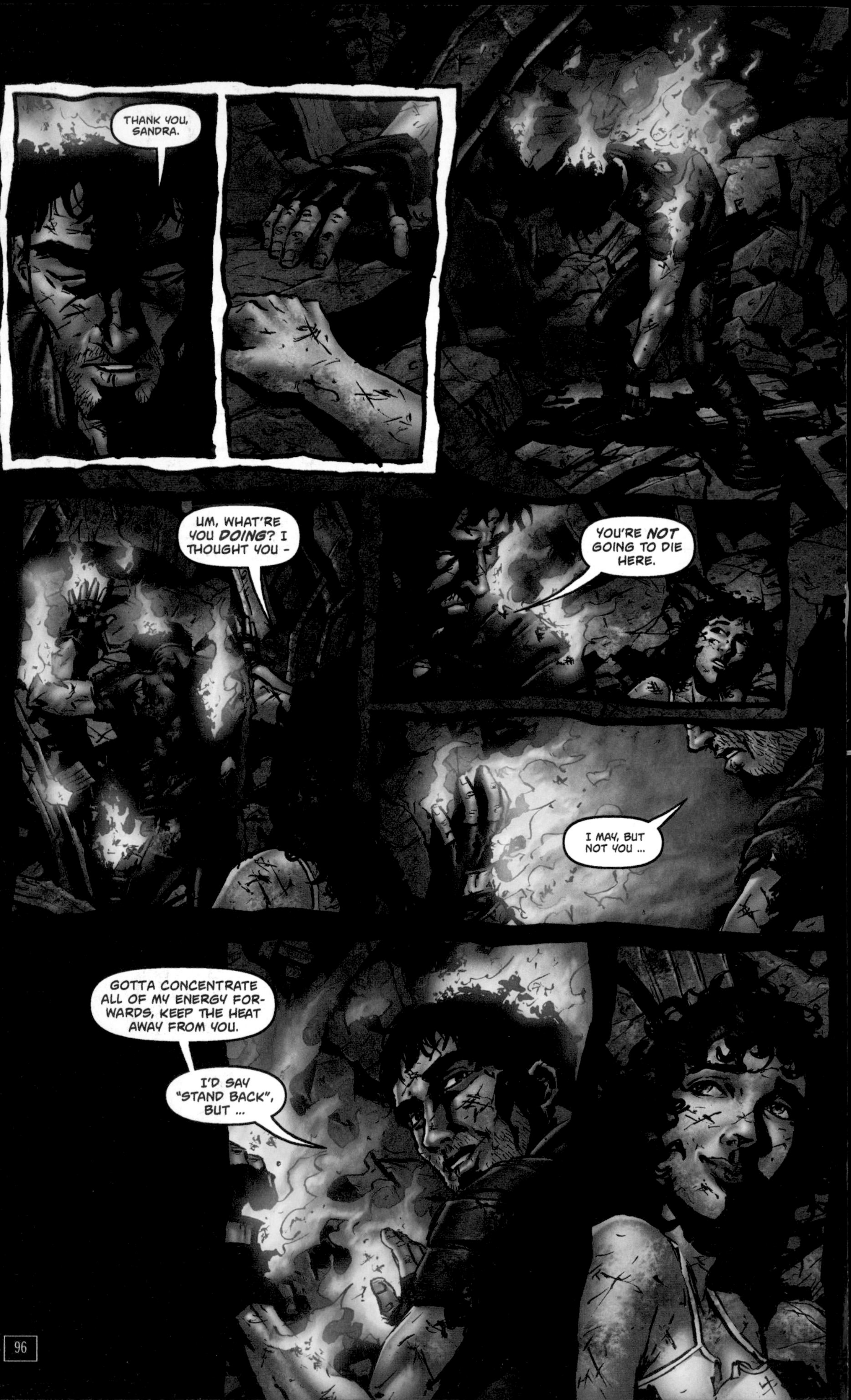
THANK YOU, SANDRA.
UM, WHAT'RE YOU DOING? I THOUGHT YOU -
YOU'RE NOT GOING TO DIE HERE.
I MAY, BUT NOT YOU ...
GOTTA CONCENTRATE ALL OF MY ENERGY FOR-WARDS, KEEP THE HEAT AWAY FROM YOU.
I'D SAY "STAND BACK", BUT ...

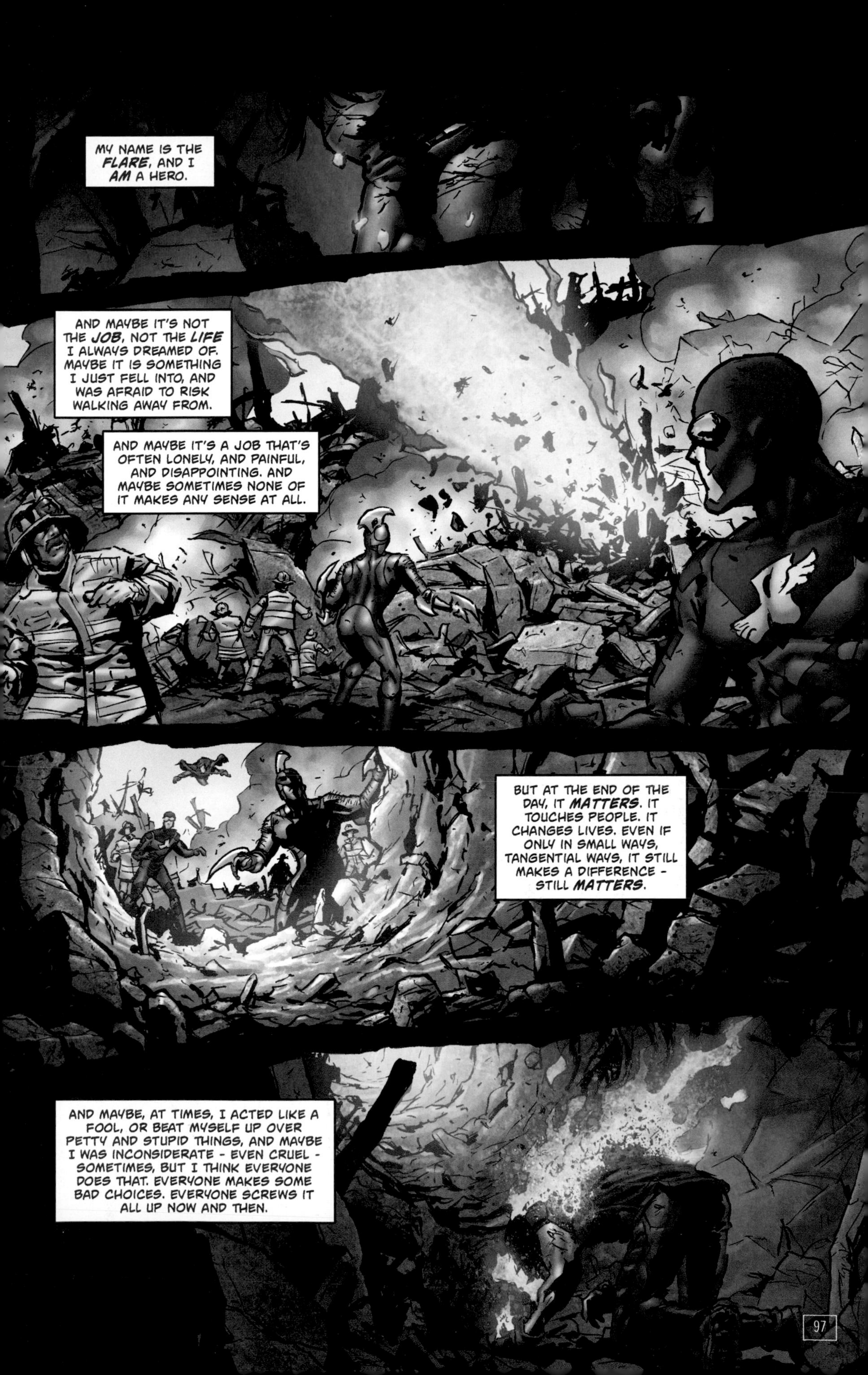
MY NAME IS THE FLARE, AND I AM A HERO.
AND MAYBE IT'S NOT THE JOB, NOT THE LIFE I ALWAYS DREAMED OF. MAYBE IT IS SOMETHING I JUST FELL INTO, AND WAS AFRAID TO RISK WALKING AWAY FROM.
AND MAYBE IT'S A JOB THAT'S OFTEN LONELY, AND PAINFUL, AND DISAPPOINTING. AND MAYBE SOMETIMES NONE OF IT MAKES ANY SENSE AT ALL.
BUT AT THE END OF THE DAY, IT MATTERS. IT TOUCHES PEOPLE. IT CHANGES LIVES. EVEN IF ONLY IN SMALL WAYS, TANGENTIAL WAYS, IT STILL MAKES A DIFFERENCE - STILL MATTERS.
AND MAYBE, AT TIMES, I ACTED LIKE A FOOL, OR BEAT MYSELF UP OVER PETTY AND STUPID THINGS, AND MAYBE I WAS INCONSIDERATE - EVEN CRUEL - SOMETIMES, BUT I THINK EVERYONE DOES THAT. EVERYONE MAKES SOME BAD CHOICES. EVERYONE SCREWS IT ALL UP NOW AND THEN.

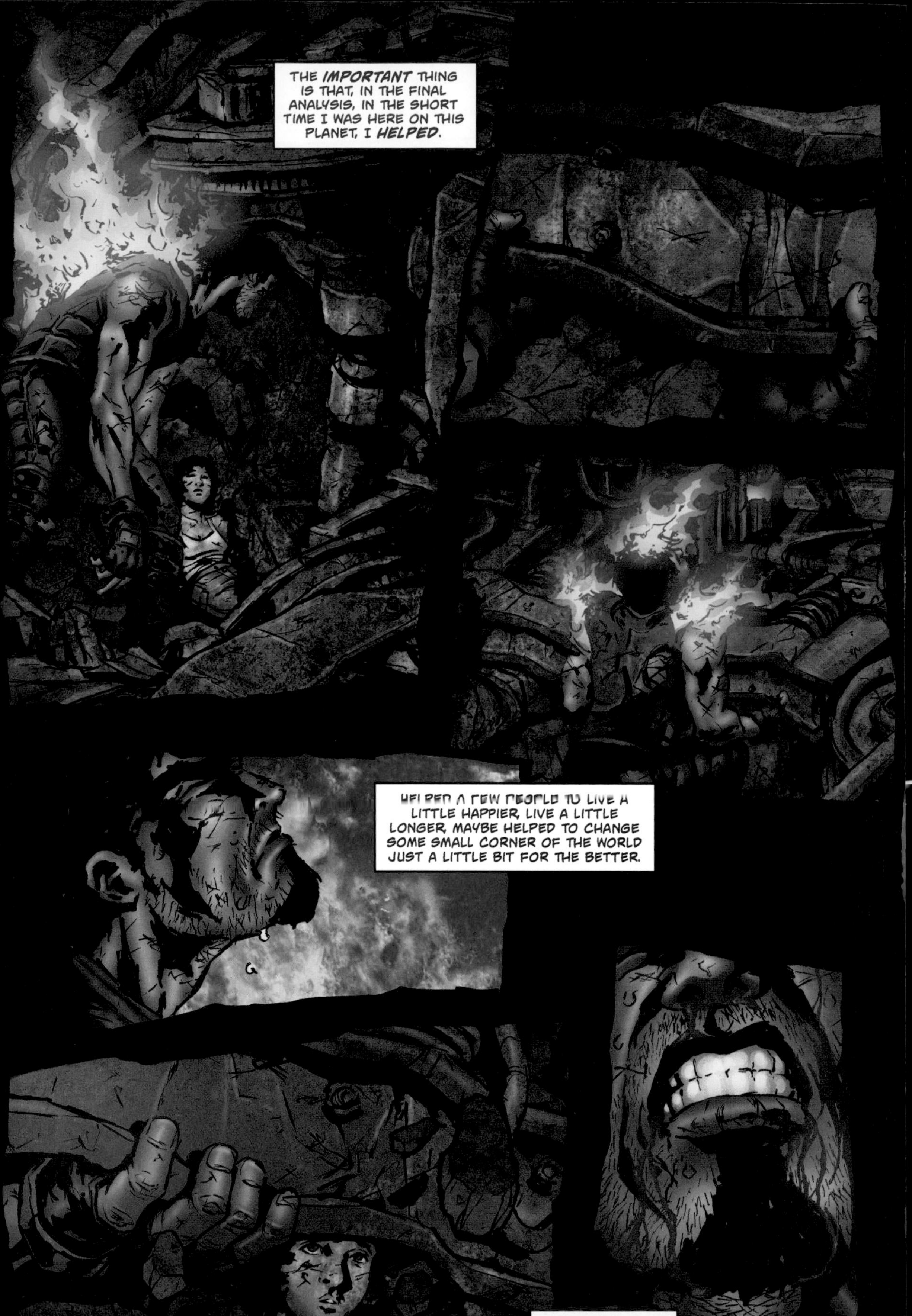
THE *IMPORTANT* THING IS THAT, IN THE FINAL ANALYSIS, IN THE SHORT TIME I WAS HERE ON THIS PLANET, I ***HELPED***.
HELPED A FEW PEOPLE TO LIVE A LITTLE HAPPIER, LIVE A LITTLE LONGER, MAYBE HELPED TO CHANGE SOME SMALL CORNER OF THE WORLD JUST A LITTLE BIT FOR THE BETTER.
THE *IMPORTANT* THING IS ...

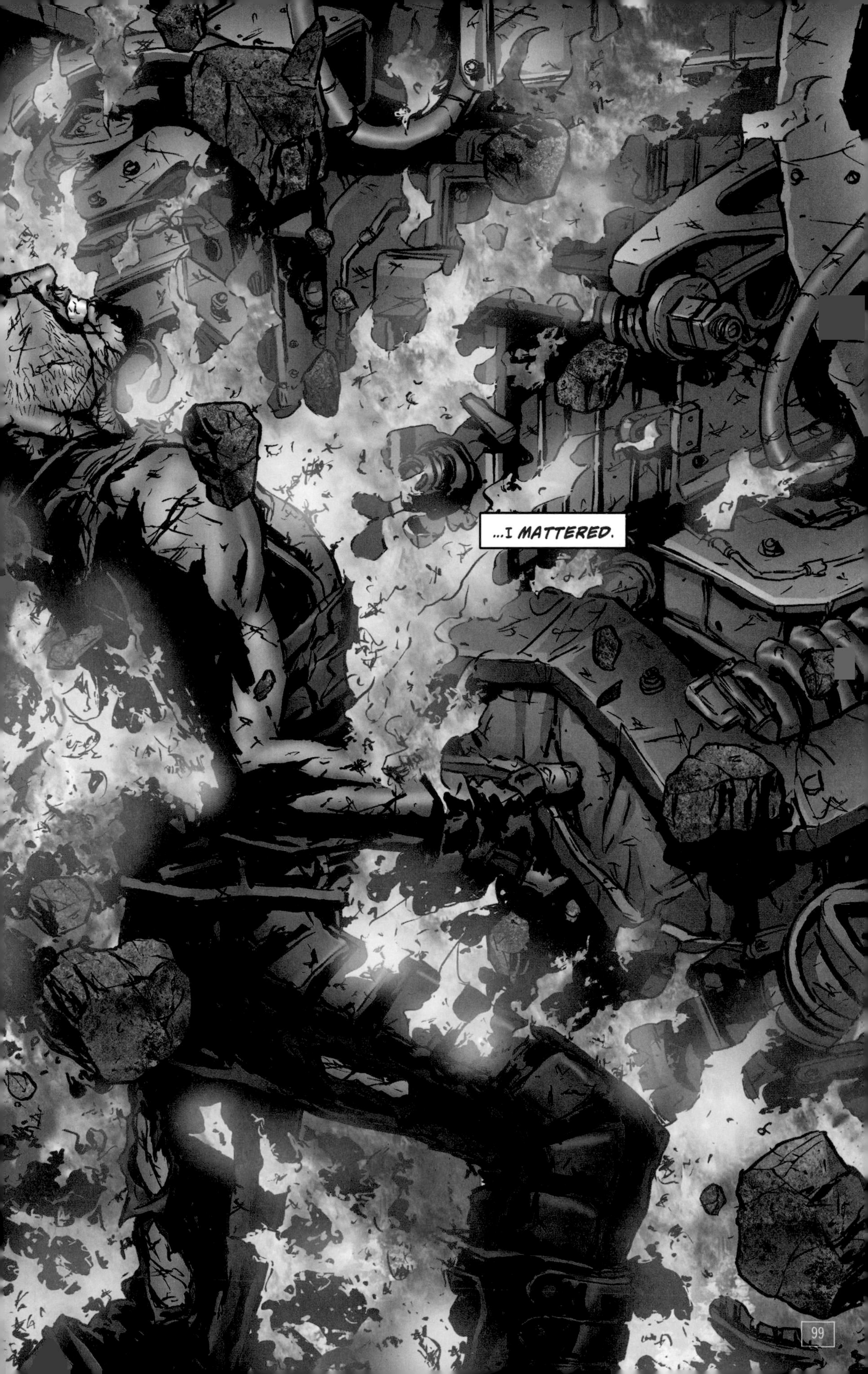
...I MATTERED.

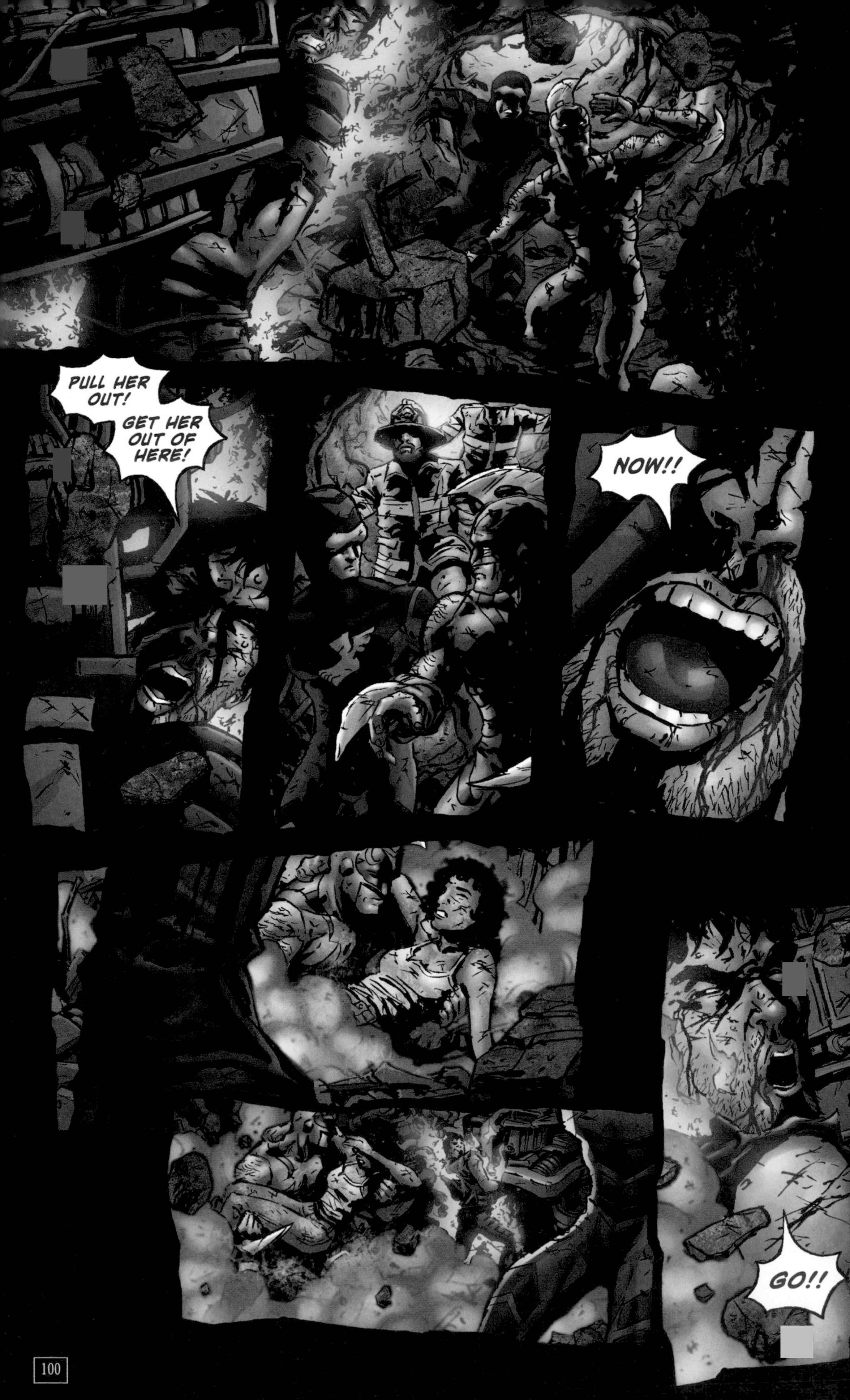
PULL HER OUT!
GET HER OUT OF HERE!
NOW!!
GO!!

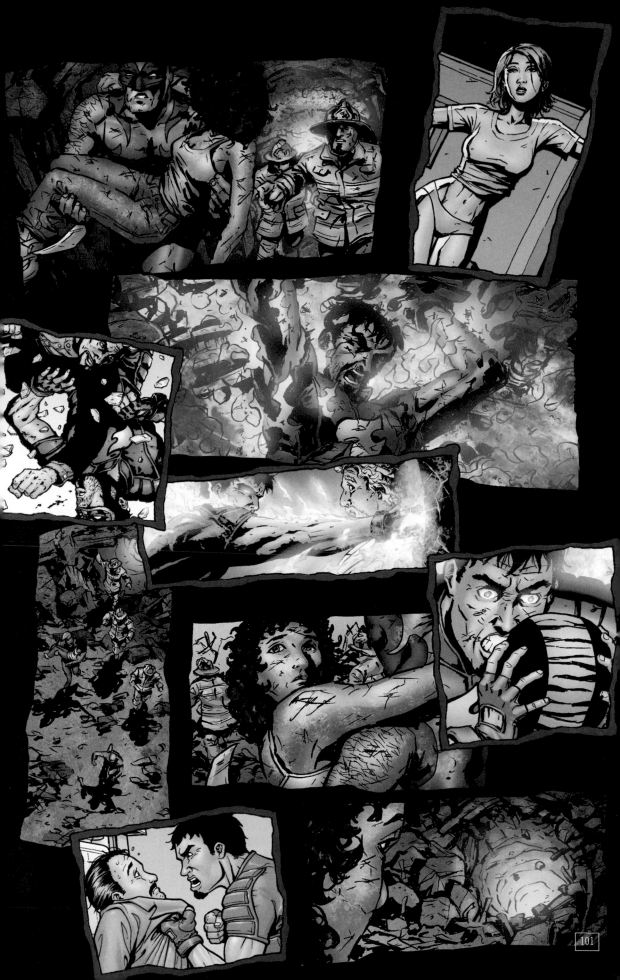

101

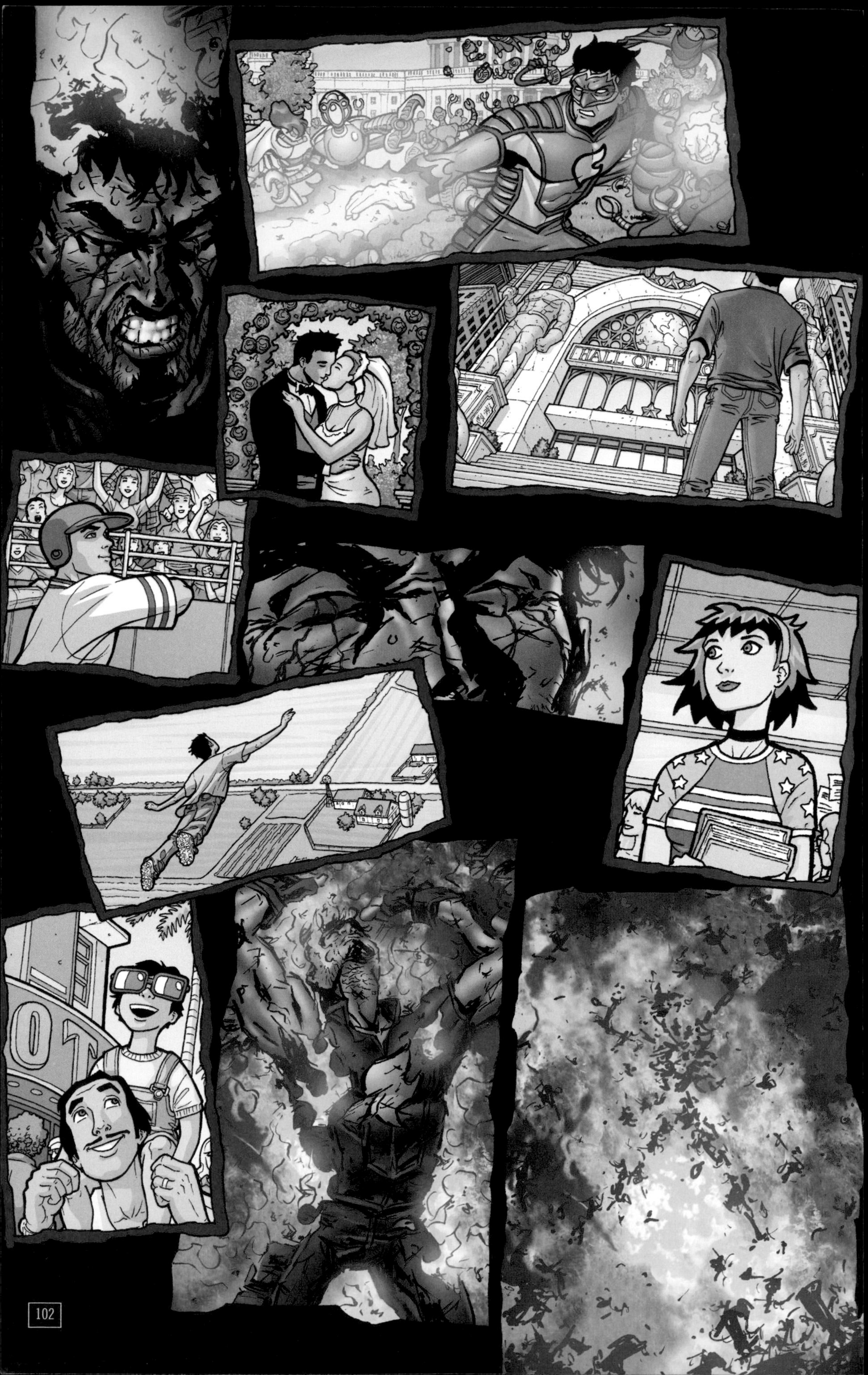

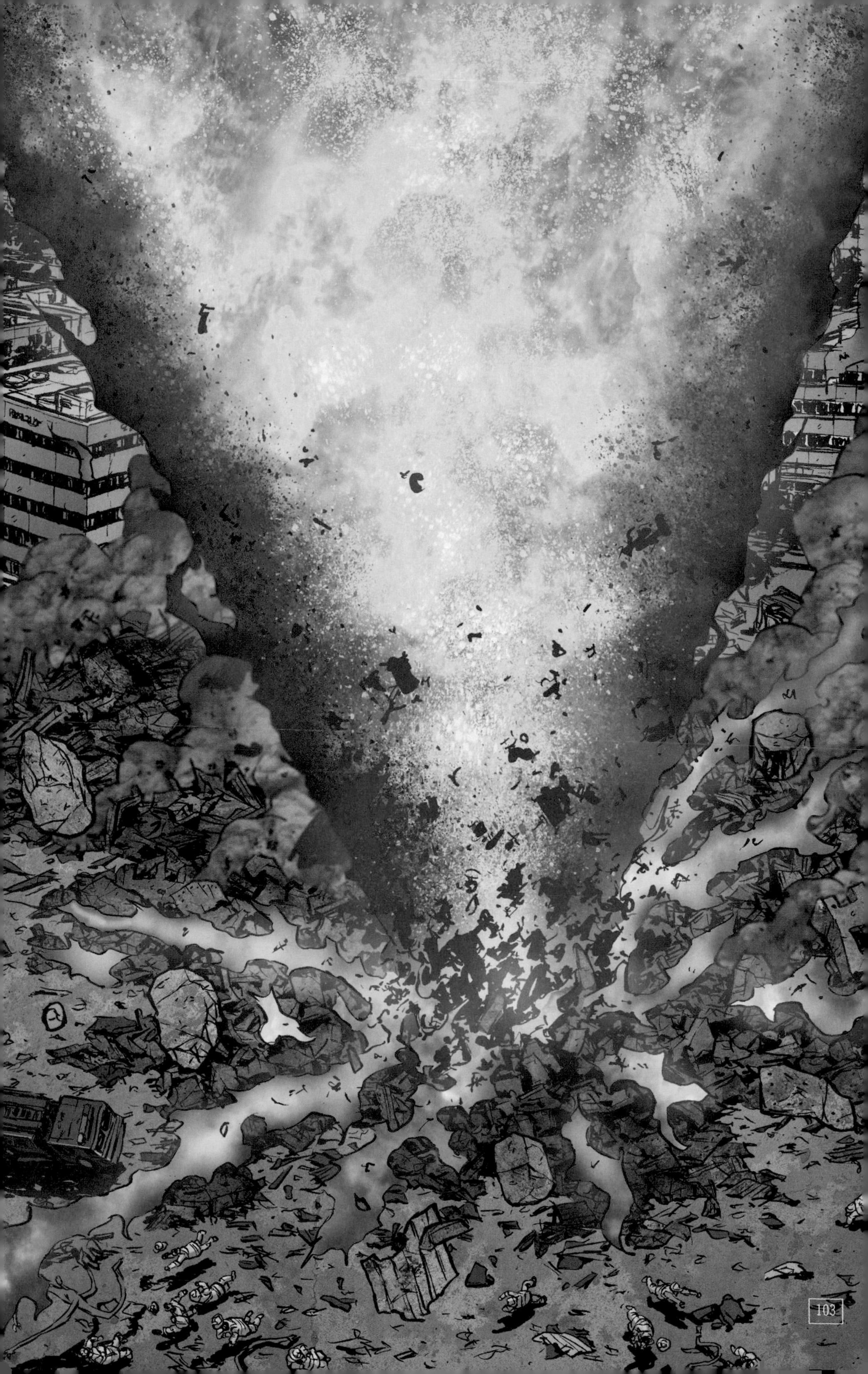

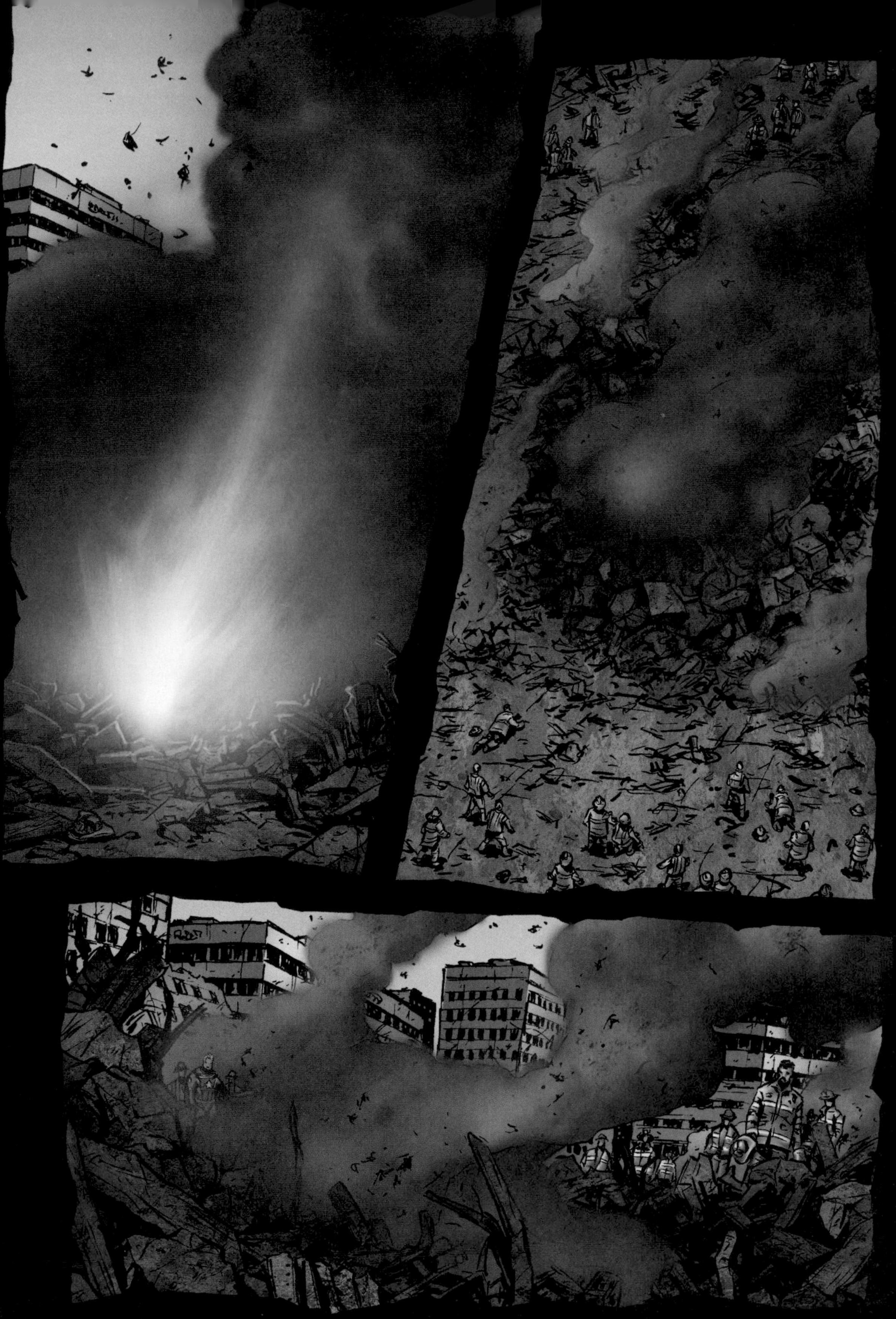

AND, FOR A SHORT WHILE, THE WORLD STOPPED.

FOLKS LAID DOWN THEIR ARMS, THEIR FEARS, THEIR HATREDS, TO PAY TRIBUTE TO A FALLEN HERO.

PEOPLE DIE EVERY DAY, BUT *SUPERHEROES*?

THAT'S FAR MORE RARE.

AND, FOR THAT SAME SHORT WHILE, THE WORLD WAS A BETTER PLACE, EVEN IF ONLY SLIGHTLY ...

THE FLARE
1974 - 2006
A HERO REMEMBERED

THE FLARE
1974 - 2006
A HERO REMEMBERED

THE FLARE
1974 -
REMEMBERED

... BECAUSE PEOPLE THE WORLD OVER HAD A GLOWING EXAMPLE OF SELFLESSNESS, OF BRAVERY, AND OF COURAGE.

BUT NEWS CYCLES COME AND GO.

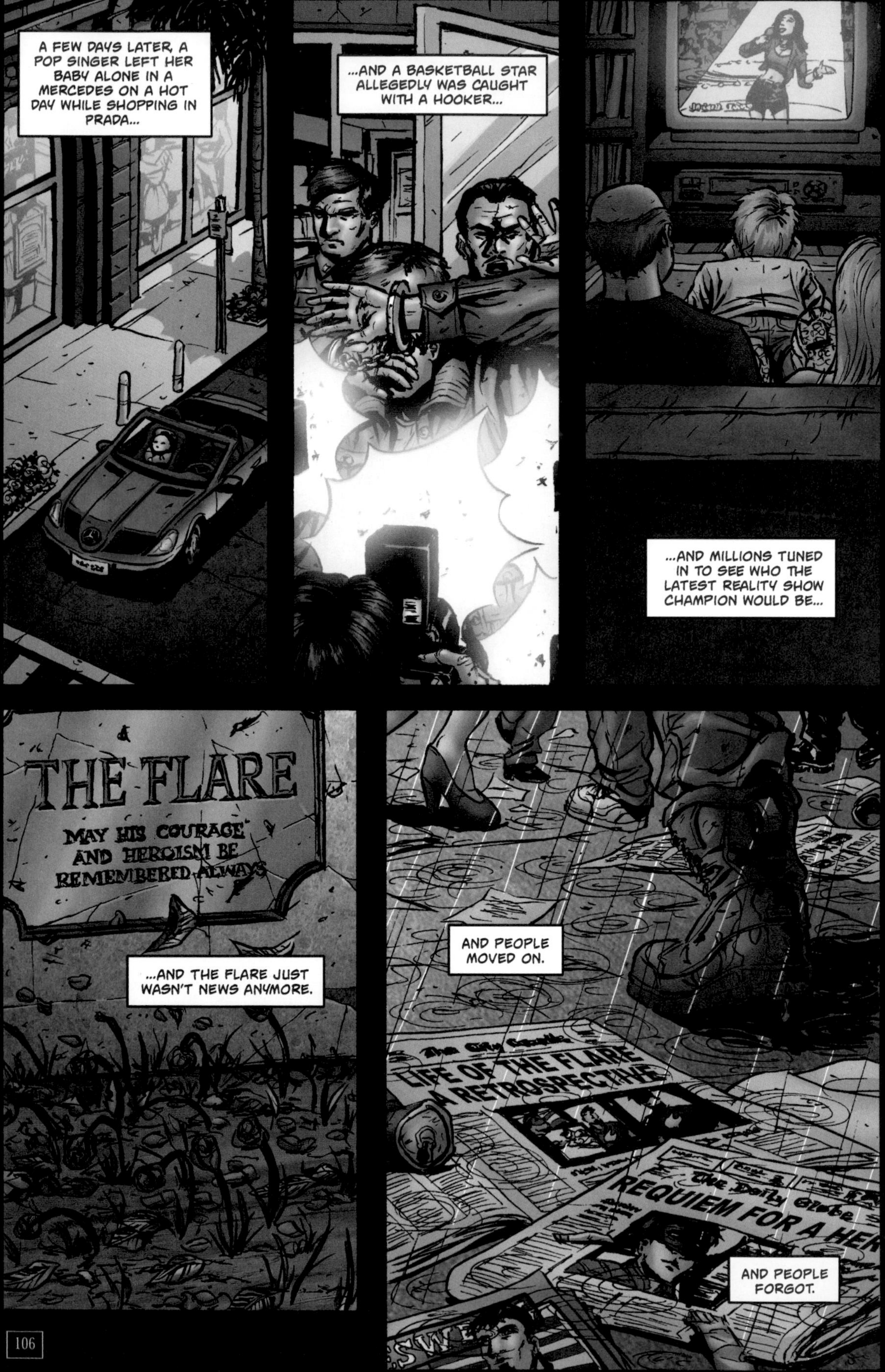
A FEW DAYS LATER, A POP SINGER LEFT HER BABY ALONE IN A MERCEDES ON A HOT DAY WHILE SHOPPING IN PRADA...
...AND A BASKETBALL STAR ALLEGEDLY WAS CAUGHT WITH A HOOKER...
...AND MILLIONS TUNED IN TO SEE WHO THE LATEST REALITY SHOW CHAMPION WOULD BE...
THE FLARE
MAY HIS COURAGE AND HEROISM BE REMEMBERED ALWAYS
...AND THE FLARE JUST WASN'T NEWS ANYMORE.
AND PEOPLE MOVED ON.
LIFE OF THE FLARE A RETROSPECTIVE
The Daily Globe
REQUIEM FOR A HER
AND PEOPLE FORGOT.

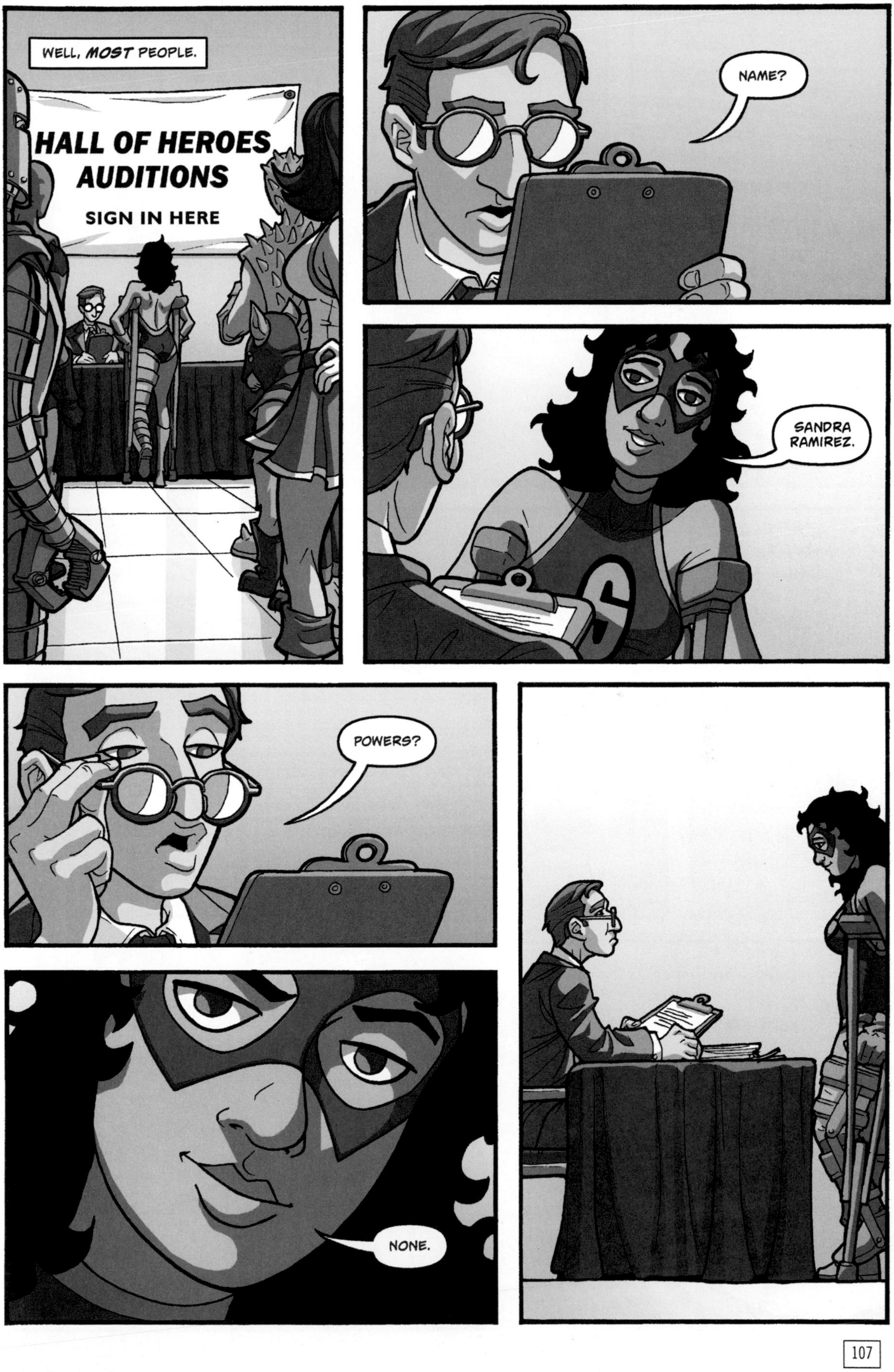
WELL, MOST PEOPLE.
HALL OF HEROES AUDITIONS
SIGN IN HERE
NAME?
SANDRA RAMIREZ.
POWERS?
NONE.

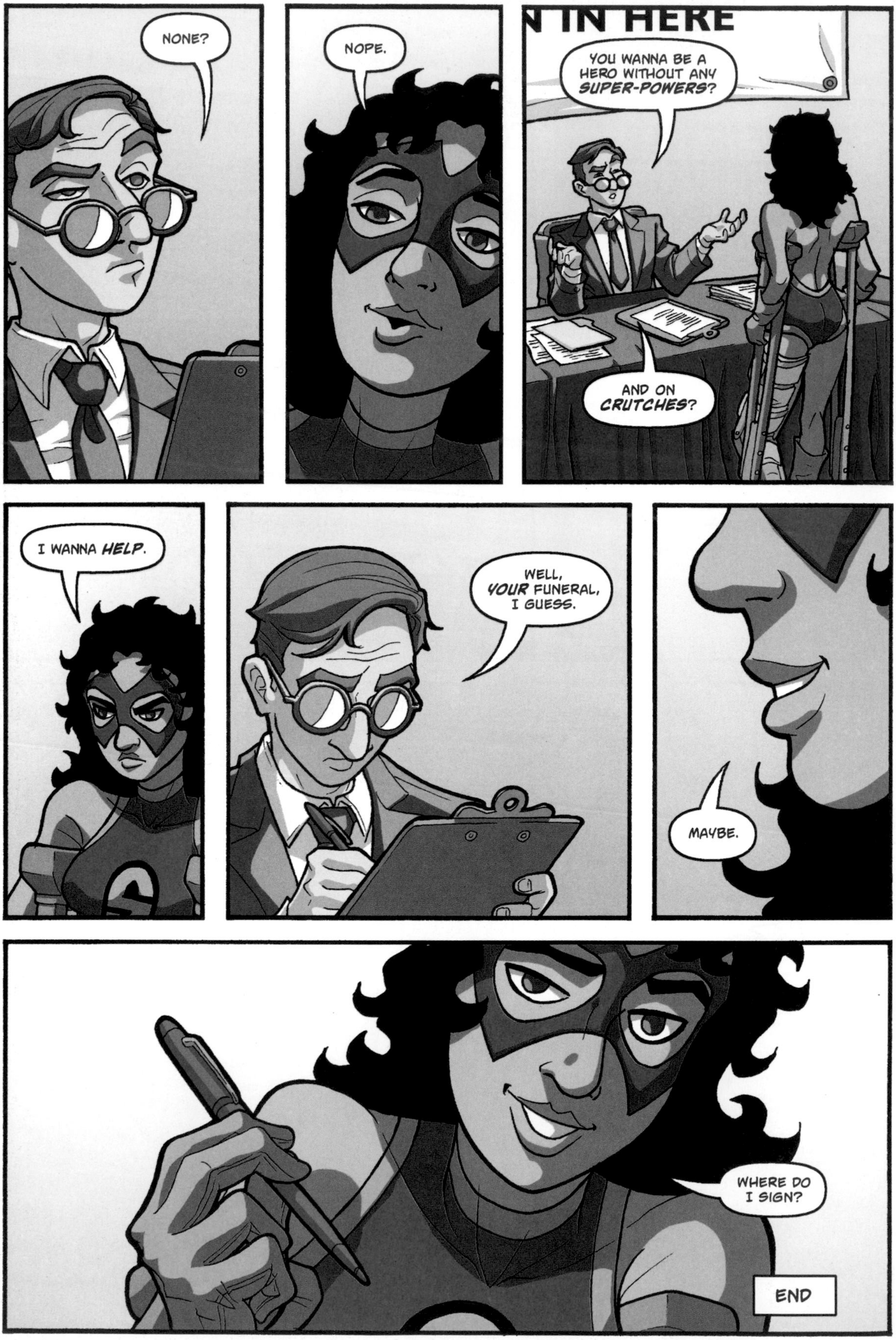
NONE?
NOPE.
N IN HERE
YOU WANNA BE A HERO WITHOUT ANY SUPER-POWERS?
AND ON CRUTCHES?
I WANNA HELP.
WELL, YOUR FUNERAL, I GUESS.
MAYBE.
WHERE DO I SIGN?
END

BEHIND THE SCENES

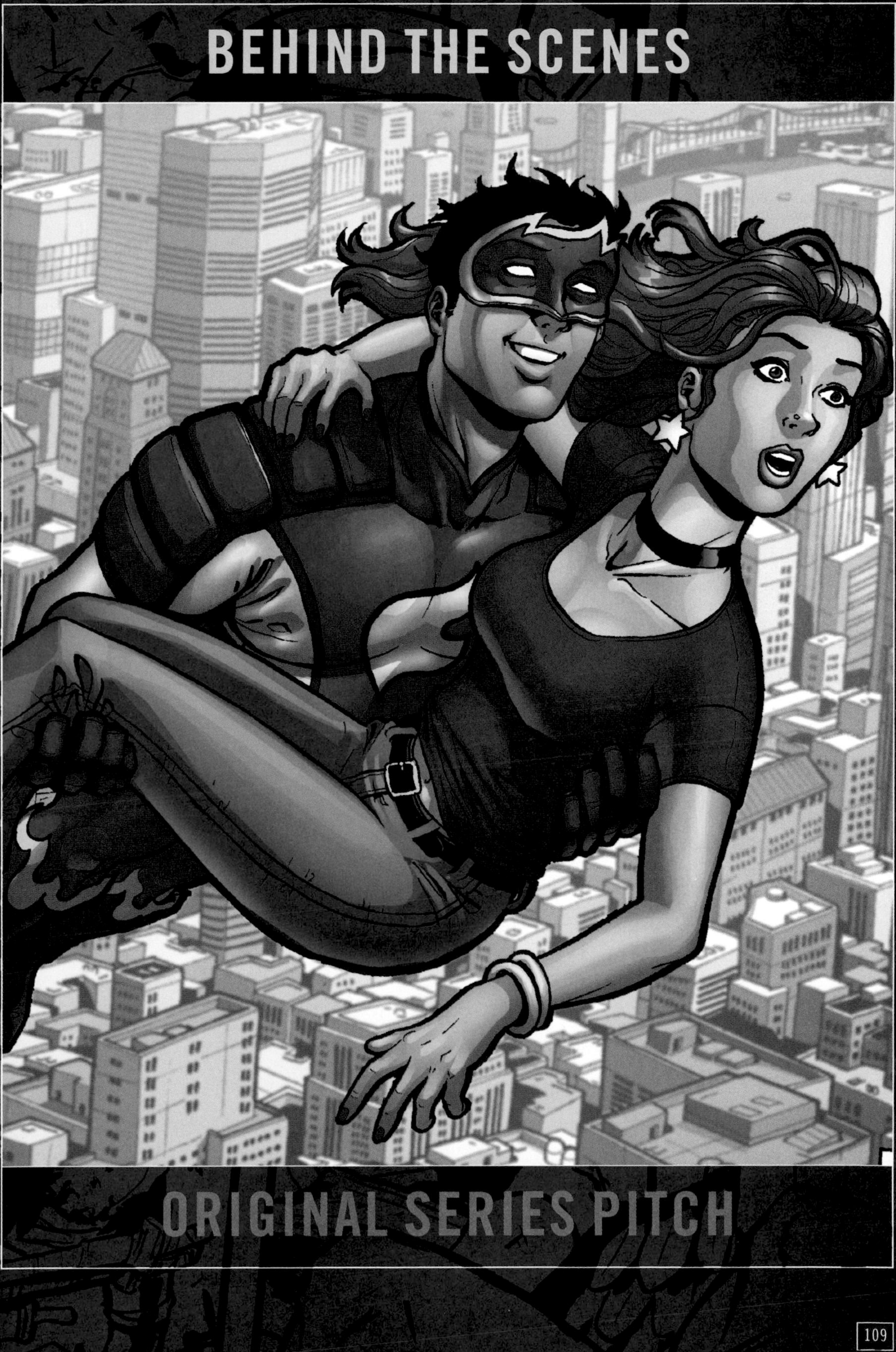

ORIGINAL SERIES PITCH

WAY BACK IN 2003, WRITER DAVID B. SCHWARTZ PITCHED A COMIC BOOK SERIES ENTITLED "LAST DAYS OF THE FLARE" TO IMAGE COMICS. "LAST DAYS OF THE FLARE" WOULD EVENTUALLY EVOLVE INTO "MELTDOWN." THE FOLLOWING IS THE TEXT OF THAT ORIGINAL SERIES PITCH.

A dying super-hero with a chip on his shoulder attempts to set his life in order. In doing so, he comes to understand the number of lives that he touched, the number of people that look up to him, and that he was, in fact, much more of a hero than he ever dreamed himself to be.

It's all about HEAT. The Flare, a little-known super-hero, has always been able to control fire, but now he can sense heat, feel it, to a degree a hundred times more acute than any human ever could. He's becoming a living infra-red radar, sensing immediately the presence of every living thing around him. He can feel the heat of a body, the pinprick of warmth generated by a newly-conceived child, the glow of a small house plant a mile away.

And it's becoming too much for him.

Just as he can sense minor heat fluctuations in others, he can feel his own patterns as well, and he knows that something's not right within. His blood is slowly boiling, bursts of anger shooting out at inappropriate moments.

As the ozone layer disappears and the sun's rays become more and more powerful, he's overloading. He's always been able to discharge whatever energy he's taken in, but, now, no discharge is enough to stop the build-up. He's dying slowly, the end approaching more and more rapidly with each passing day.

In the midst of battle he snaps, taking the life of a group of villains, burning them to cinders. He seeks help from the best and brightest minds among his fellow heroes, but to no avail - they only confirm his worst fears. He's willing to try anything in order to survive.

"Lock me away in a room with no light."

"You'll die just as quickly. Sunlight is as essential to you as air or water."

"I'll blow it all off in one giant blast."

"You'll destroy a continent, perhaps more. And you'll just fill up once again, in time."

His fellow heroes ask The Flare to spend his remaining days heroically, helping them to combat evil, but The Flare can't elude his own self-absorption. He sinks into a pit of despair, trying anything and everything he can think of in order to evade this fate. Slowly, realization sinks in, and he returns home to Miami to set his life in order.

He's rapidly losing control of his emotions. Old angers well up, joined by new ones as he says his goodbyes to old friends and family. He came seeking peace, resolution and absolution, but he's finding the opposite - he can't control the flood of sensations that are burrowing into his head.

The Flare is pulled out of his emotional chaos as he senses an explosion and intense heat - thousands of miles away in Seattle.

His true nature as a hero kicks in.

He immediately rockets off to Seattle, arriving to a melee surrounding a collapsed sports arena. He can feel the rapidly-ebbing heat of 20,000 bodies trapped under the rubble, a last few people surviving for precious moments in small pockets of air beneath the devastation.

The Flare blasts his way down and finds a young woman trapped - Hispanic, like himself. He can't melt away the steel that's pinning her down, as to do so would burn her to death. He can't move it, for fear of collapsing the entire structure and trapping the rescue workers above.

He holds her hand. They talk. She's not afraid to die. He can feel her calm, and her bravery touches him. As a fellow Latino, she's always looked up to him as a shining example of the best the world has to offer. He finally comes to terms with himself and his life, as she helps him to understand the number of people he's touched and been an inspiration for.

As he holds her, he feels her heat slipping away, and her body turns slowly cold.

Epilogue: On a TV news report, we see that The Flare was able to find and save a few survivors of the crash, thanks to his ability to home in on their heat. Although only one of numerous heroes who came and helped, he was lauded as the first to arrive, and the only one to actually bring anyone out alive. Pull back from the TV to reveal The Flare speaking with several of the heroes he had met with earlier, while trying on a new costume. These heroes, touched by The Flare's actions, have redoubled their efforts on his behalf and designed a new suit for him that will filter the light sufficiently for him to survive, although he can never take it off.

Hard-hitting and topical, LAST DAYS OF THE FLARE is a dark and introspective story, with a blast of light and hope at the end. The series explores themes of heroism, racism, nationalism, war, hatred, the media and more, ultimately focusing on the idea that, if you can touch even one person in need, your life has been worthwhile, all while counting down the last few days The Flare believes are remaining in his life.

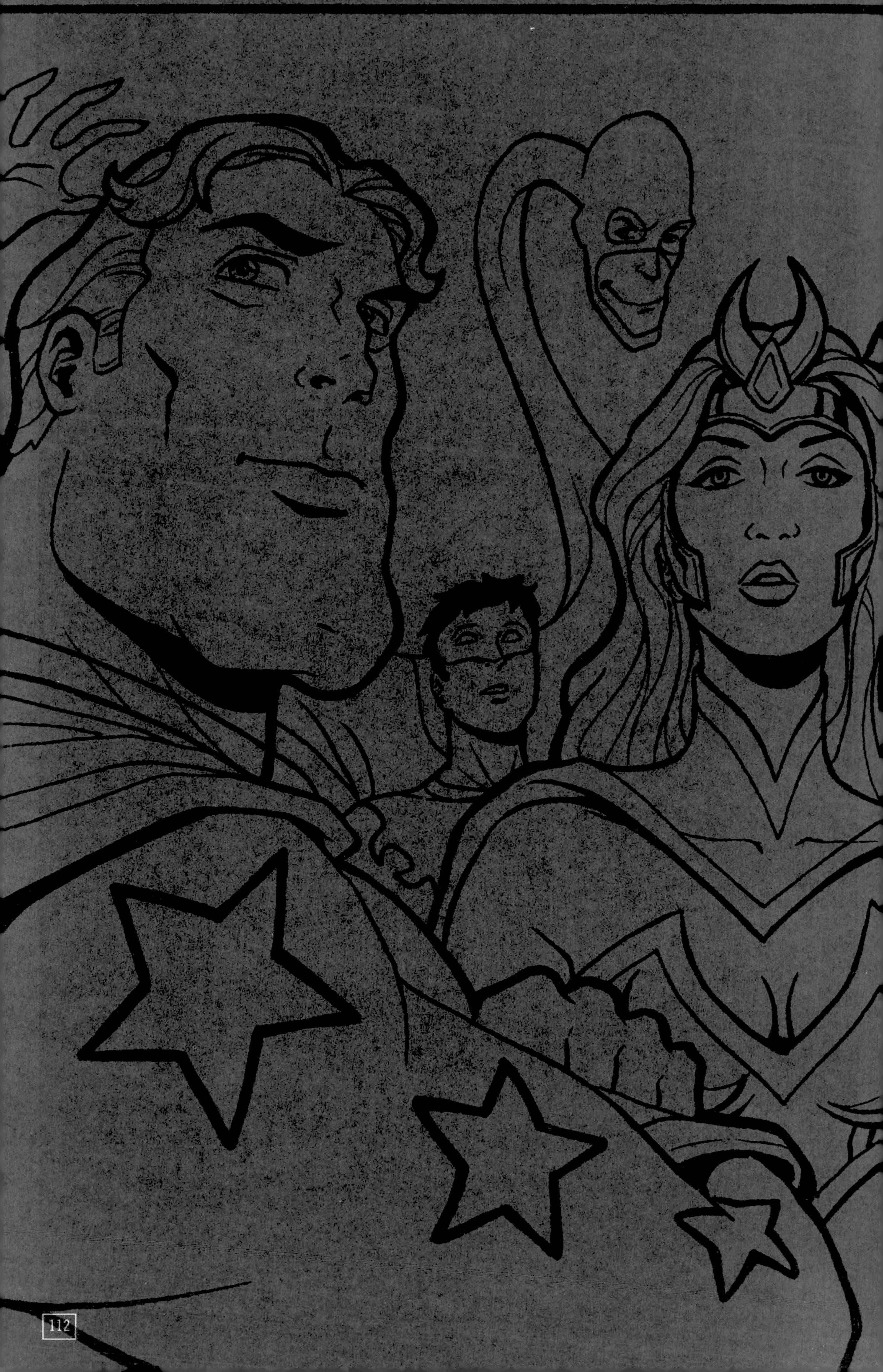

BEHIND THE SCENES

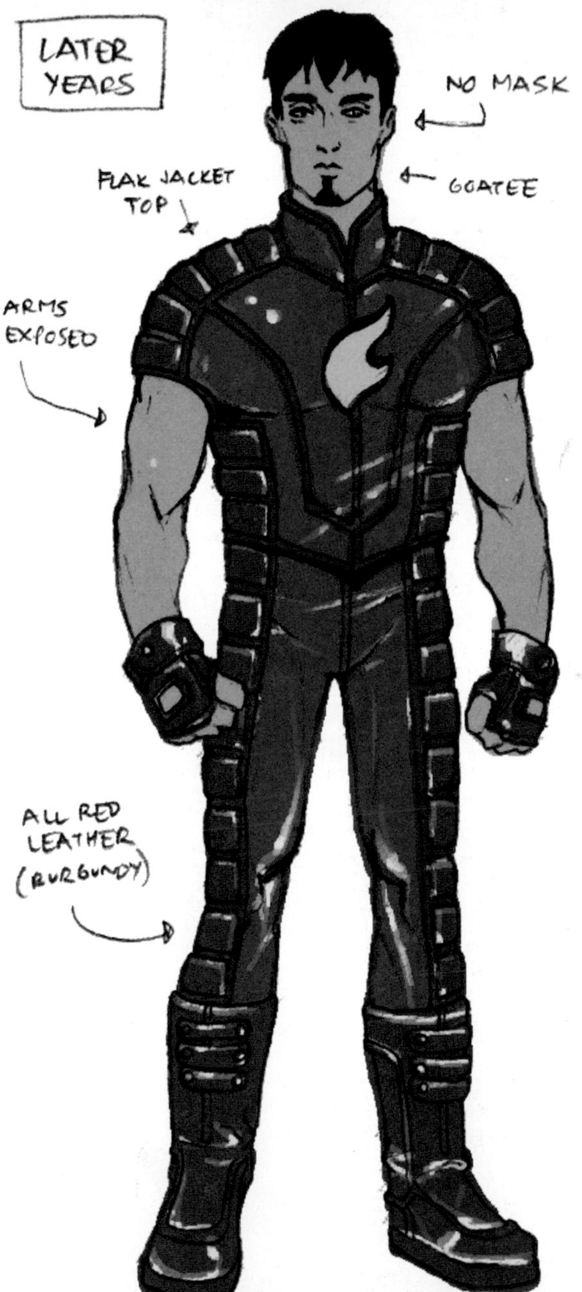
LATER YEARS
NO MASK
GOATEE
FLAK JACKET TOP
ARMS EXPOSED
ALL RED LEATHER (BURGUNDY)

DESIGNING MELTDOWN

BY SEAN WANG

STYLE TESTS

These images show some of the tests I did to hammer out the different art styles I wanted to use for the various time periods of the book. Given the number of styles I wanted to go through, I had to make myself a cheat sheet to keep track of the elements that would define one style vs another. Ultimately, the final looks varied quite a bit from these early tests, but they were a good start.

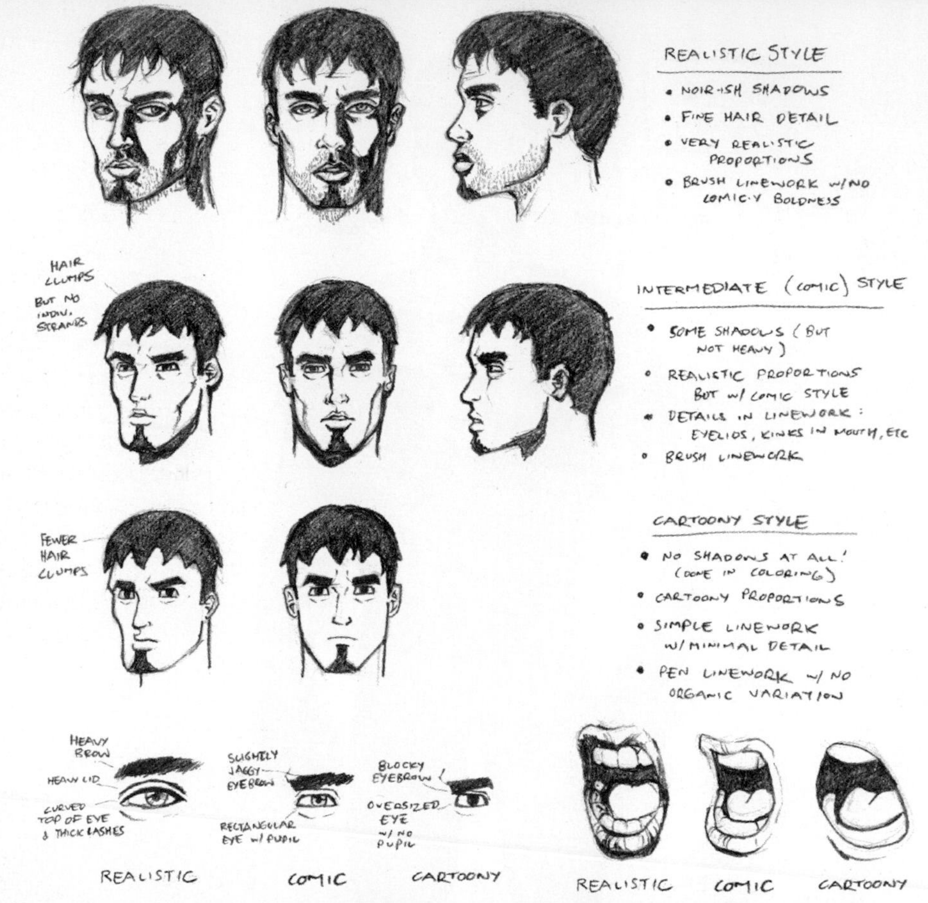

REALISTIC STYLE
• NOIR-ISH SHADOWS
• FINE HAIR DETAIL
• VERY REALISTIC PROPORTIONS
• BRUSH LINEWORK W/NO COMIC-Y BOLDNESS
HAIR CLUMPS BUT NO INDIV. STRANDS
INTERMEDIATE (COMIC) STYLE
• SOME SHADOWS (BUT NOT HEAVY)
• REALISTIC PROPORTIONS BUT W/ COMIC STYLE
• DETAILS IN LINEWORK: EYELIDS, KINKS IN MOUTH, ETC
• BRUSH LINEWORK
FEWER HAIR CLUMPS
CARTOONY STYLE
• NO SHADOWS AT ALL! (DONE IN COLORING)
• CARTOONY PROPORTIONS
• SIMPLE LINEWORK W/MINIMAL DETAIL
• PEN LINEWORK W/ NO ORGANIC VARIATION
HEAVY BROW
HEAVY LID
CURVED TOP OF EYE & THICK LASHES
SLIGHTLY JAGGY EYEBROW
RECTANGULAR EYE W/ PUPIL
BLOCKY EYEBROW
OVERSIZED EYE W/ NO PUPIL
REALISTIC
COMIC
CARTOONY
REALISTIC
COMIC
CARTOONY

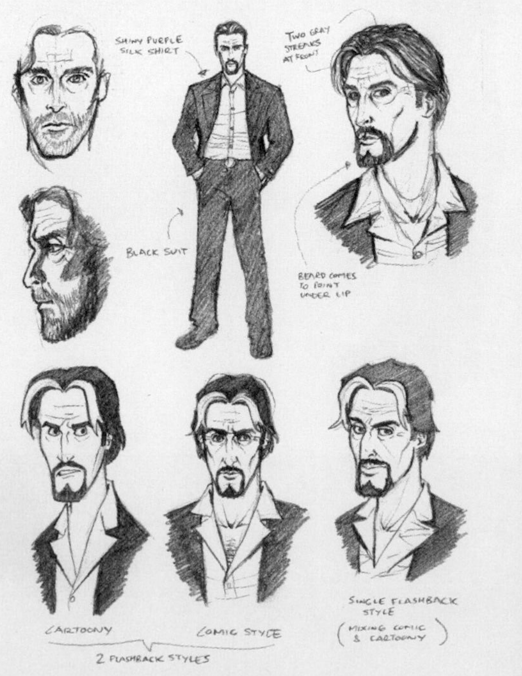

SHINY PURPLE SILK SHIRT
TWO GRAY STREAKS AT FRONT
BLACK SUIT
BEARD COMES TO POINT UNDER LIP
CARTOONY
COMIC STYLE
2 FLASHBACK STYLES
SINGLE FLASHBACK STYLE (MIXING COMIC & CARTOONY)

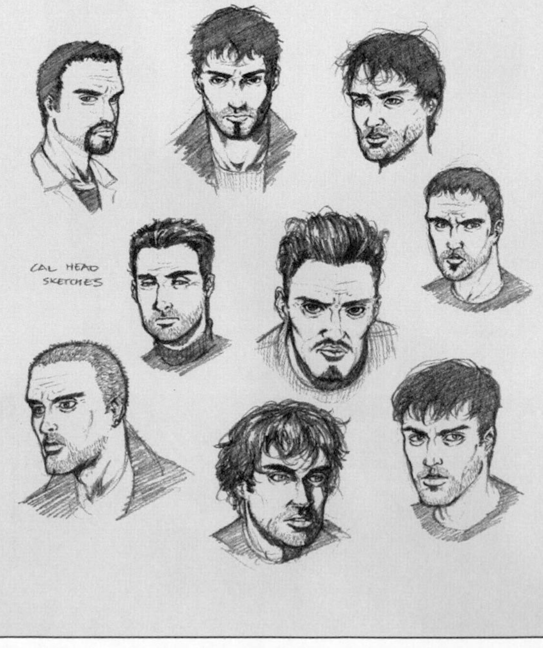

CAL HEAD SKETCHES

DESIGNING A SUPER-HERO COSTUME

The following pages detail the creative process behind one of the most important aspects of doing a superhero comic...designing the all-important superhero costume itself!

INSULATING PADS?
OR ENERGY STORAGE BACKUPS
BARE ARMS?
DARK & GRITTY?
OR BRIGHTER & SUPER-HERO-Y?
LEAN & VERY TONED (HIGH METABOLISM BURNS OFF FAT?)
UNITARD
RADIATION QUILTING ON SIDES
ZIP FRONT JACKET (SEAM NOT VISIBLE)
OPTION TO HAVE OPEN: CASUAL OR WEARY

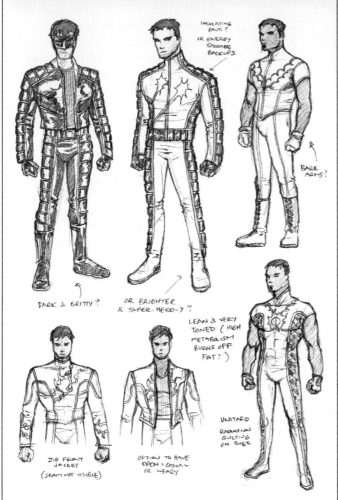

Since MELTDOWN spans the entire life and career of the main character, we wanted Cal to sport several different versions of his hero costume that he would go through and update over the years. I started with the design of the classic costume, knowing that the others would be derivations of that one.

For the classic hero costume, I initially envisioned a full-body outfit, like a racecar driver. I quickly moved away from the dark leather, which felt too contemporary, and went with brightly-colored tights for a more classic look. I also started leaning towards bare arms because I figured a fire-based hero might want more skin exposed if he tends to overheat. We also decided early on that Cal should be an everyman and have a realistic build: toned but not ridiculously muscular, since a higher metabolism would keep him from bulking up. The blocky pad shapes were intended to be technology built into the costume for backup energy storage or, more likely, to help him regulate and control his powers. Or they're just pockets to hold snacks.

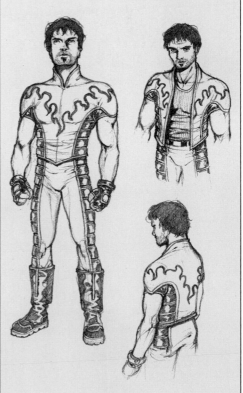

Early costume designs had a zipper jacket to give me more room to play with the visuals. During his down time, he could partially unzip it for a more casual look, and during a fight, it could get ripped open to look "battle-damaged". Ultimately, the zipper jacket and two-piece look got relegated to the leather outfit he wears later since they still looked too contemporary for the classic tights costume. The flame motif on the chest and shoulders didn't look iconic enough in the truly classic sense either, so I opted to design a more iconic superhero chest insignia. I also decided that Cal's early costume should have some sort of mask, in part to look more superhero-y and also to differentiate it from his later costume, which would be maskless (since at that point he'd no longer care about protecting his secret identity).

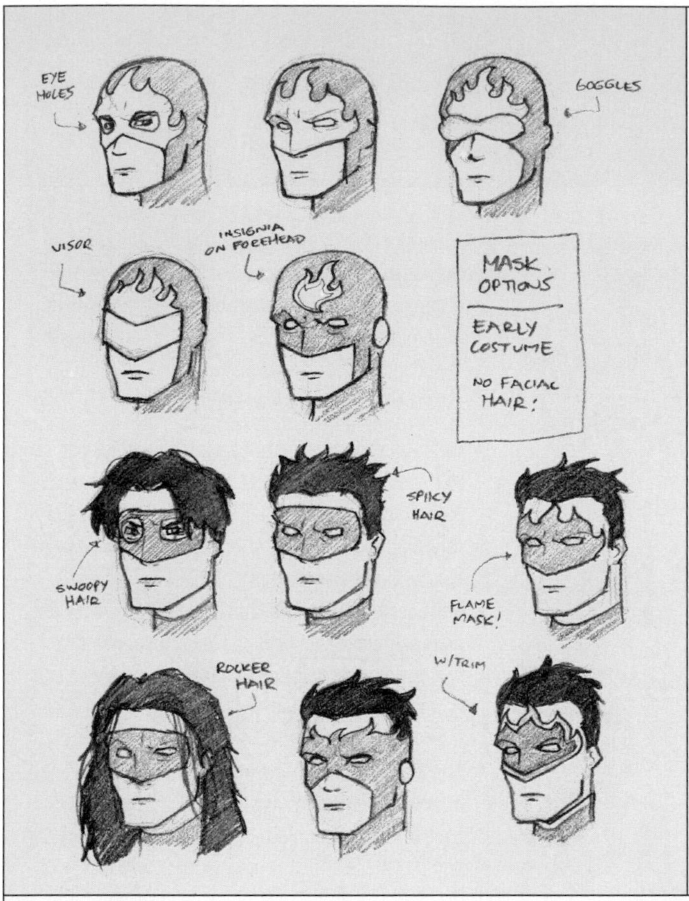
EYE HOLES
GOGGLES
VISOR
INSIGNIA ON FOREHEAD
MASK OPTIONS
EARLY COSTUME
NO FACIAL HAIR!
SPIKY HAIR
SWOOPY HAIR
FLAME MASK!
ROCKER HAIR
W/TRIM

Going through various mask concepts, including full cowls and goggle and visor looks, I finally settled on a mask that left more of his head exposed, which I liked for the same reason I wanted his arms exposed. To add a bit more flair, I added a flame outline to the top edge, which helped make it character-specific to The Flare. Basically, I wanted him to be instantly recognizable from just a head shot, and a generic hero mask wouldn't really accomplish that.

With the mask settled and the classic tights feel in mind, I went through many different costume concepts. I still played with the chest-and-shoulder flame design just to exhaust its possibilities, but I knew I was gravitating toward the chest insignia. The early fireball design eventually became the flame insignia, which I really liked since it's also a subtle "F" shape, to go with his superhero name The Flare. Finally, the flame-edges appeared on the gloves and boots, which I liked a lot since that design element, like the mask, immediately made the accessories character-specific.

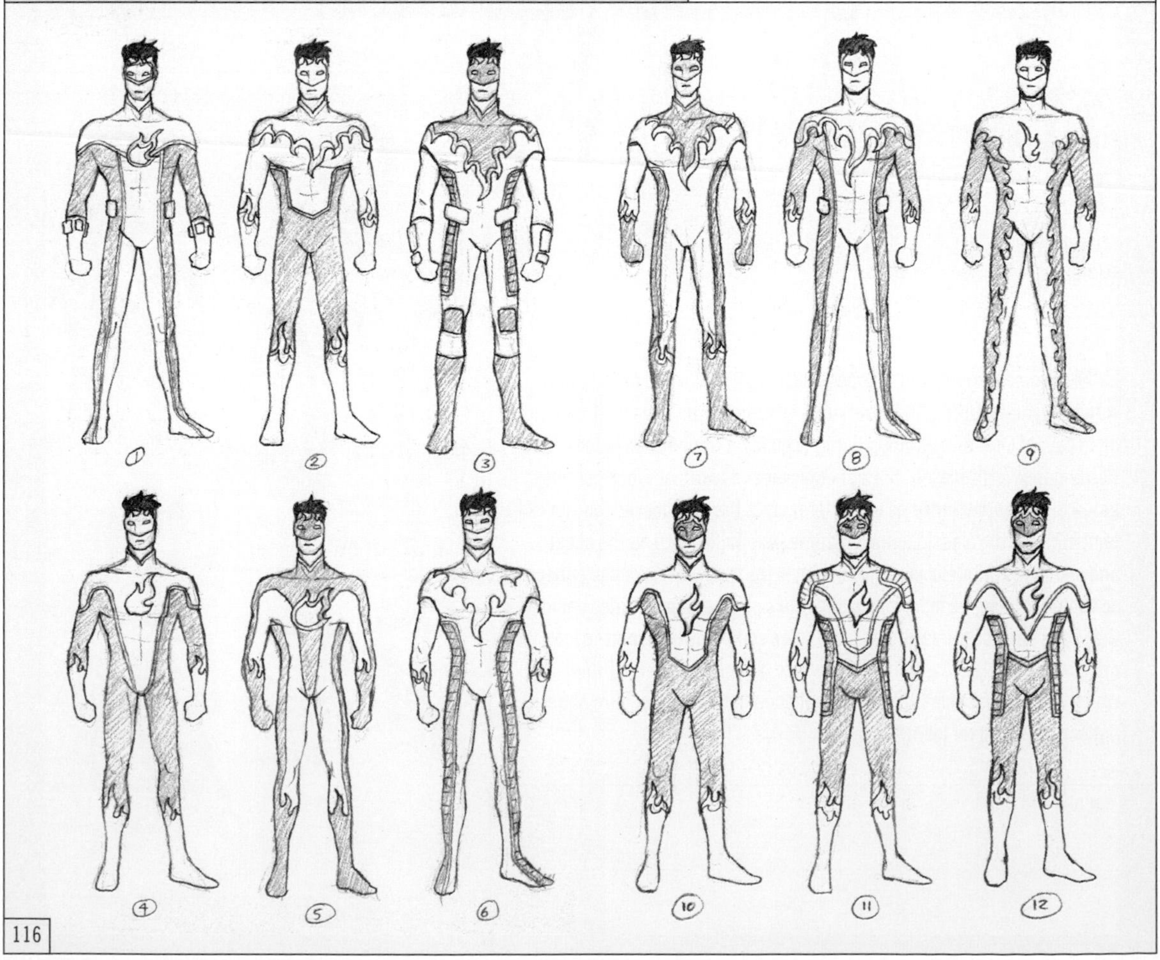
1
2
3
7
8
9
4
5
6
10
11
12

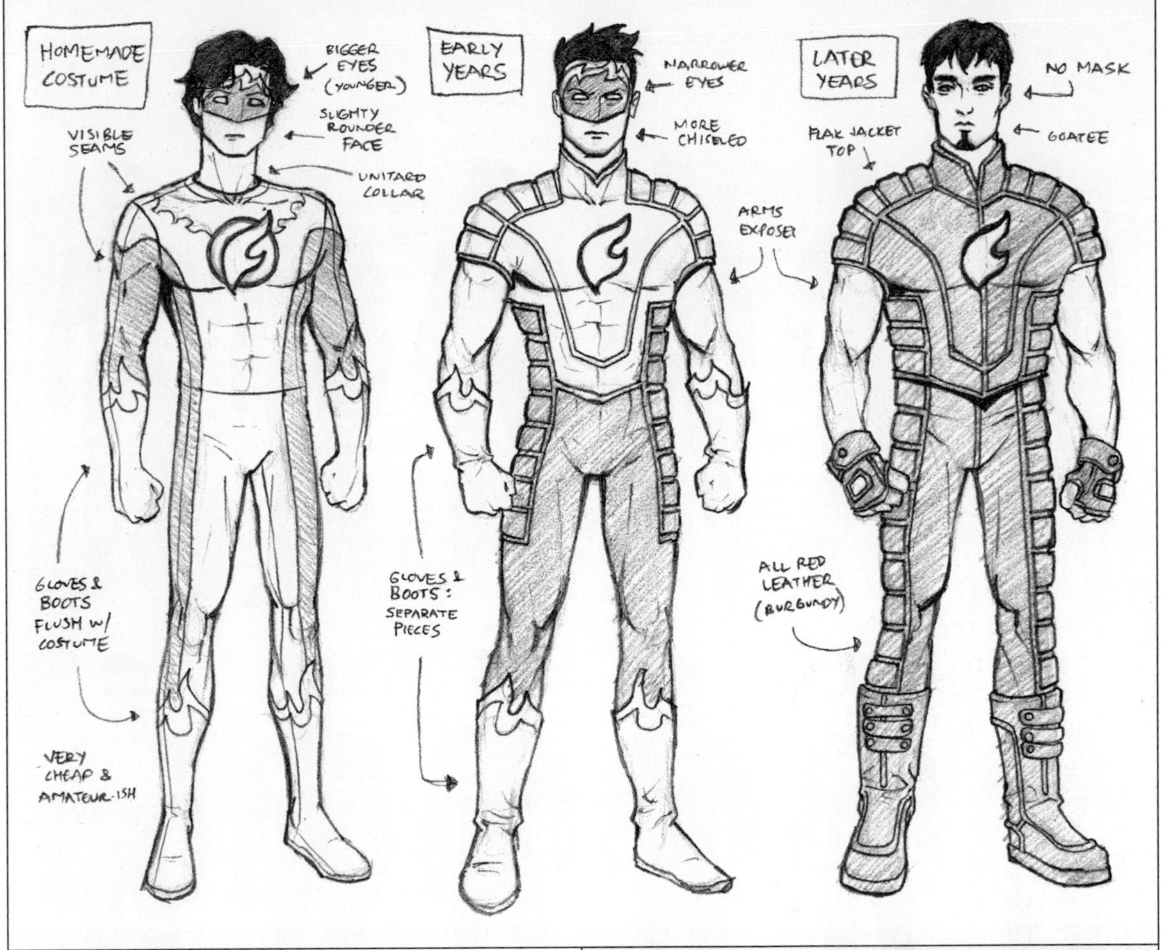
HOMEMADE COSTUME
BIGGER EYES (YOUNGER)
SLIGHTY ROUNDER FACE
VISIBLE SEAMS
UNITARD COLLAR
GLOVES & BOOTS FLUSH W/ COSTUME
VERY CHEAP & AMATEUR-ISH
EARLY YEARS
NARROWER EYES
MORE CHISELED
GLOVES & BOOTS: SEPARATE PIECES
ARMS EXPOSED
LATER YEARS
NO MASK
GOATEE
FLAK JACKET TOP
ALL RED LEATHER (BURGUNDY)

Once the classic costume was designed, the other two versions came pretty quickly. The homemade audition costume was just a cheesy unitard, with the cheesiness exemplified by the visible seams and lack of collar. The homemade costume was intentionally supposed to have a very short life, getting burned off in the heat of battle during one of Cal's very first fights as a member of the HOH.

While the classic costume is bright and colorful, I wanted the later costume to be a darker all-leather number to reflect his darker attitude later in life. I also thought a leather, maskless costume would fit the more contemporary and "realistic" look of superhero costumes in comics and movies today. Retaining the chest insignia (the only design element to span all the costumes), the rest of the costume was made more contemporary by ditching the flame-shaped gloves and boots for more standard leather accessories. The top was made into a jacket with a zipper down the middle, and more energy-modulating pads were added to the costume since at this point, Cal would need more help in controlling his powers.

There was originally going to be a fourth costume, a full head-to-toe body glove designed by Neuron to save Cal by modulating his entire body's absorption of energy. But we ultimately opted not to go that route for an ending, which was nice since it meant one less costume to design!

Finally, here are a number of color tests for the classic costume. I knew I wanted to stick with red, yellow, and orange as the primary colors, but that still left a lot of different options to play with before settling on the final color scheme.

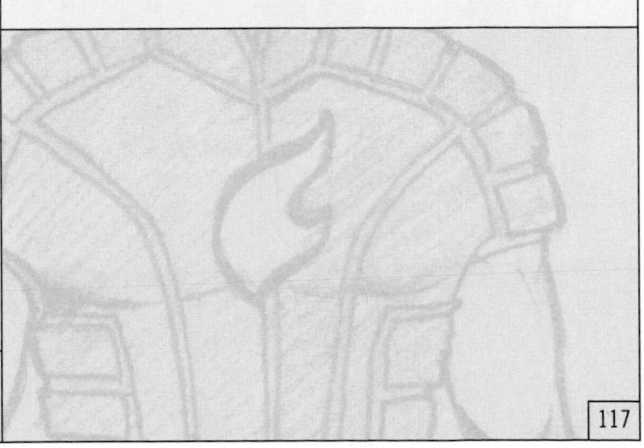

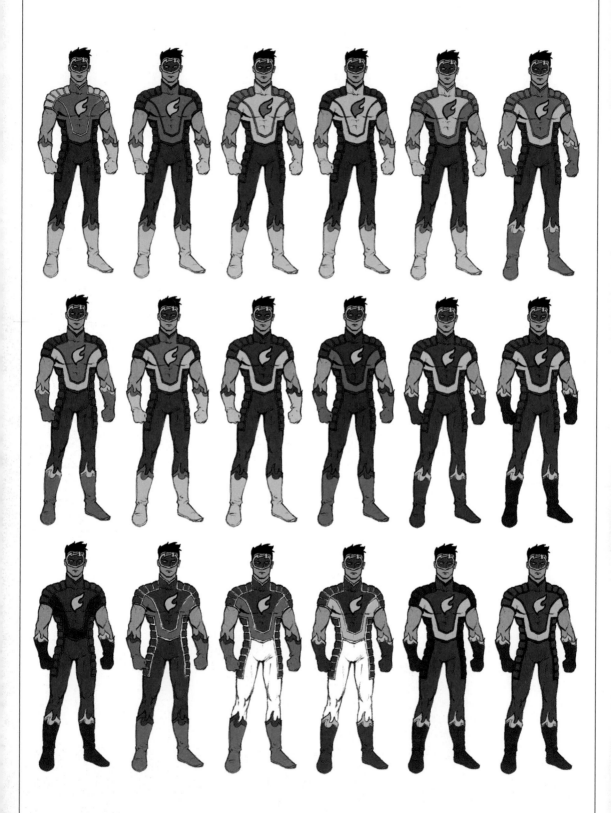

BEHIND THE SCENES

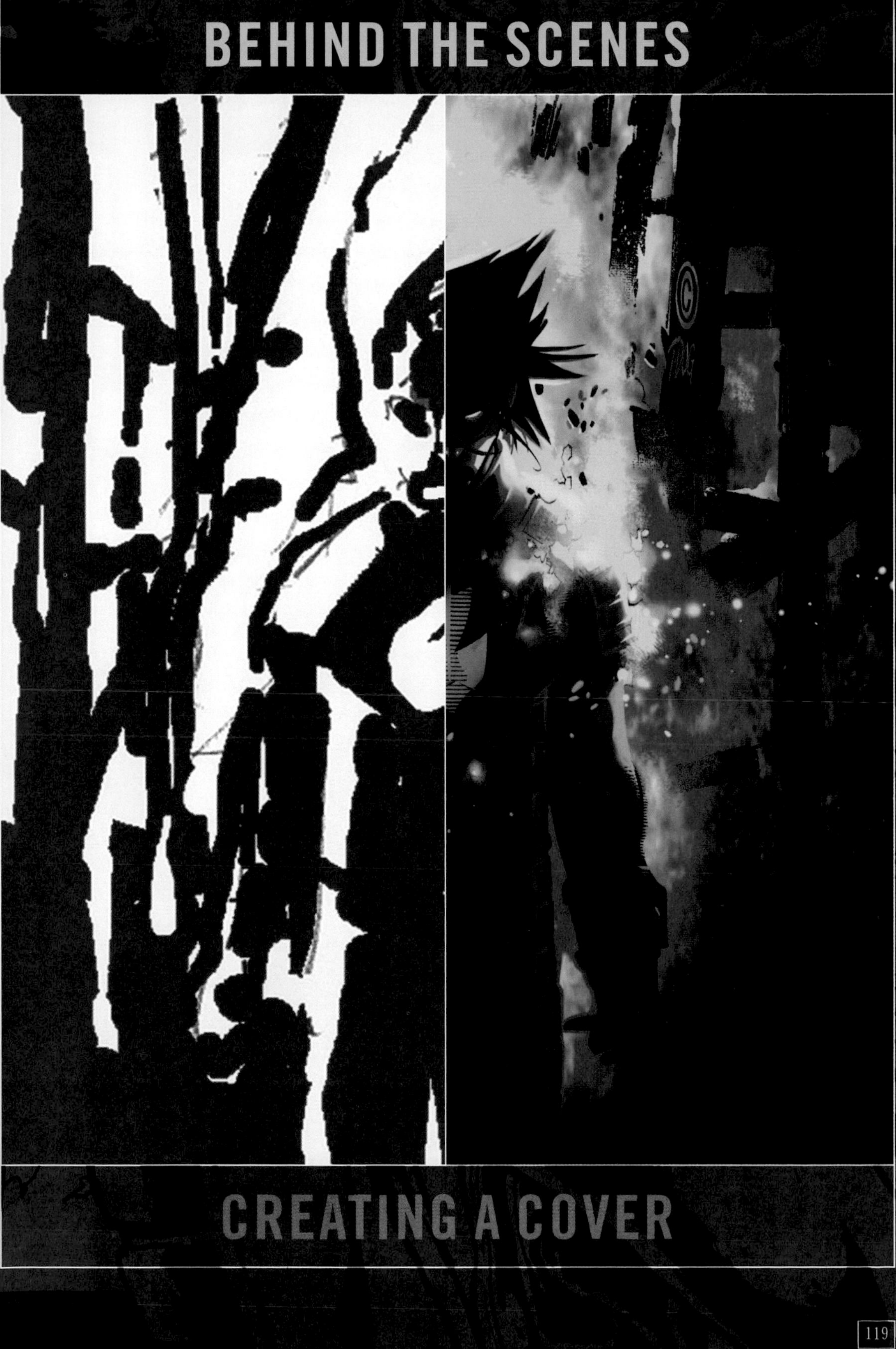

CREATING A COVER

Chris Bachalo's spectacular cover became the symbol of MELTDOWN. We used it in all of our promotion and marketing for the series, for two reasons. First, because we just thought it was really, really freakin' cool. Second, we wanted to build up some "brand awareness", so that people would recognize and be drawn to that image once they finally saw the book on the stands.

Chris started by providing us with thumbnails for five entirely different cover concepts for us to choose from. He made the decision gruelingly difficult for us, because all five were just incredible, and all five would've made great covers. Ultimately, we chose to go with the thumbnail below, presented here, for the first time, in all of its original glory. We loved that It was simple, direct, dark and haunting.

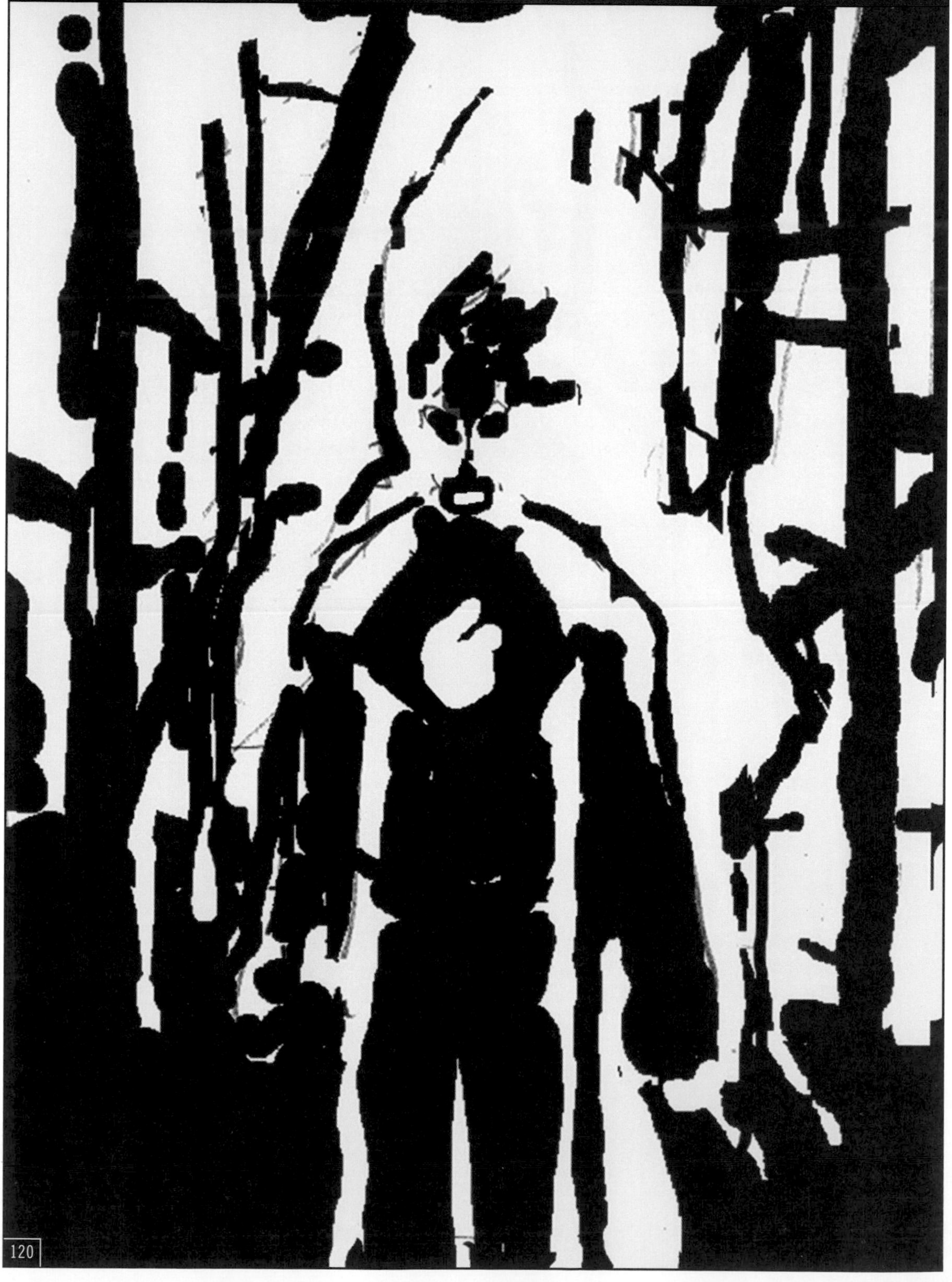

Next, of course, came the pencils, where Chris fleshed out the original concept....

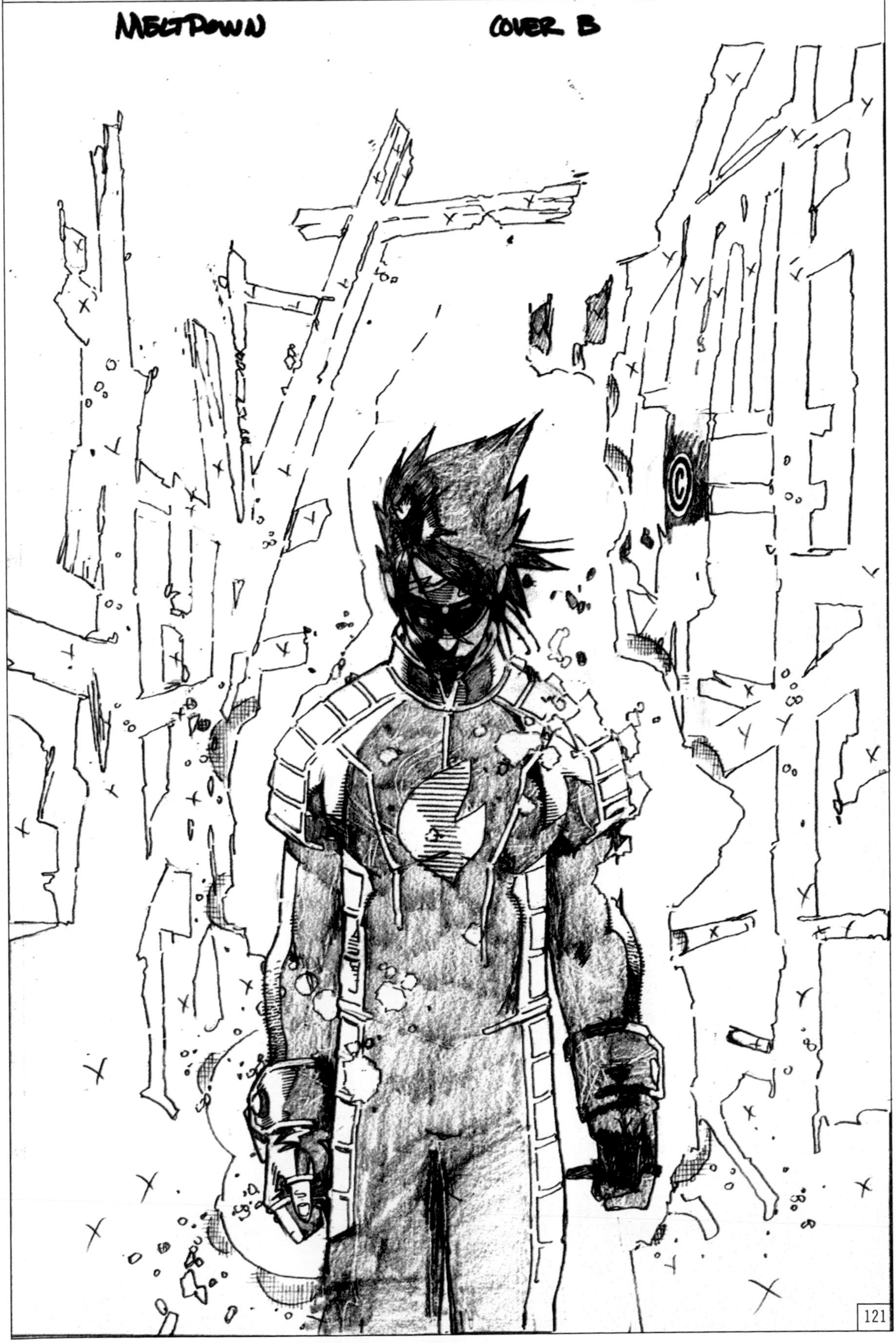
MELTDOWN
COVER B

...and then, the inks. Inks were provided by Tim Townsend, and he did a great job of it. Check out his great splatter work on the background!

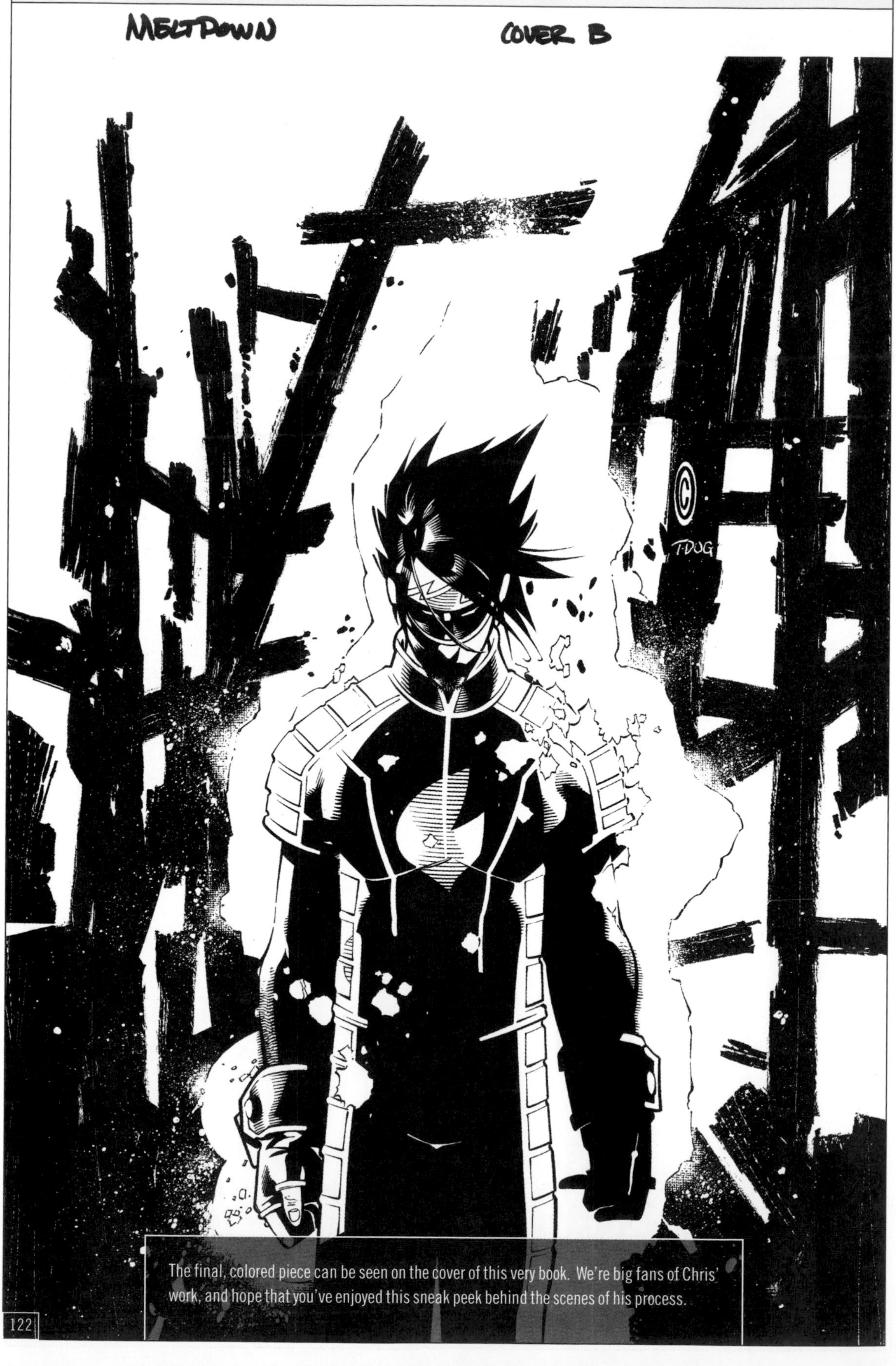
MELTDOWN
COVER B
T-DOG

The final, colored piece can be seen on the cover of this very book. We're big fans of Chris' work, and hope that you've enjoyed this sneak peek behind the scenes of his process.

Once the cover art was completed, we needed a great logo to match up with it. We turned to our friend Rory Myers, a spectacular graphic designer, to create it. Here's a few of his designs, both for our original title ("Last Days of the Flare") and for the title we finally settled on (uh, "Meltdown", of course). We'll turn this over to Rory now to walk you through his work...

LAST DAYS OF
THE FLARE

LAST DAYS OF THE
FLARE

For this set I wanted use an inline treatment to imply heat radiating from the core of each letterform. Both the typeface and the configuration of the lockup were meant to have somewhat of an Art Deco feel to reinforce the setting of much of the story. This was the first round of creative; it never made it past this stage to explore how they would work on the cover due to the title change.

LAST DAYS OF
THE FLARE

LAST DAYS OF
THE FLARE

I explored a more illustrative "flame" motif on these. On the top option the two circling fire balls frame the letter "f" to create an emblem. The Yin and Yang similarity is unavoidable but my thinking was more along the lines of the Ouroboros symbol portraying the snake consuming itself. The bottom option was a looser interpretation and was intended to grow out of the cover art.

MELTDOWN

MELTDOWN

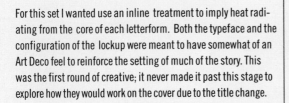

These logo options are shown on the background cover art to illustrate the composite effect. In previous rounds we settled on a banner configuration as shown. The two above solutions focused on interperating the concept of overheating. The top by actually melting or dissolving and the bottom by having the letterforms become integrated into a temperature gauge which is red lining.

MELTDOWN

MELTDOWN

I used the vernacular of warning symbols here to covey the book's storyline. The top option takes the nuclear hazard symbol and integrates it into the logotype while the bottom option took it's cue from the universal police tape. The strong san-serif font against a clean yellow bar was also a good contrast to the cover art. The bottom version, of course, developed into the current logo.

We've focused a lot on Chris' cover for issue #1, but MELTDOWN also was lucky enough to have a GREG HORN cover gracing issue #2. You've seen the final cover he came up with, but here's a look at a rough sketch of one of his early concepts. Although we didn't end up going with this one, it's a gripping, atmospheric piece that we really loved, and wanted to give you a chance to check it out.

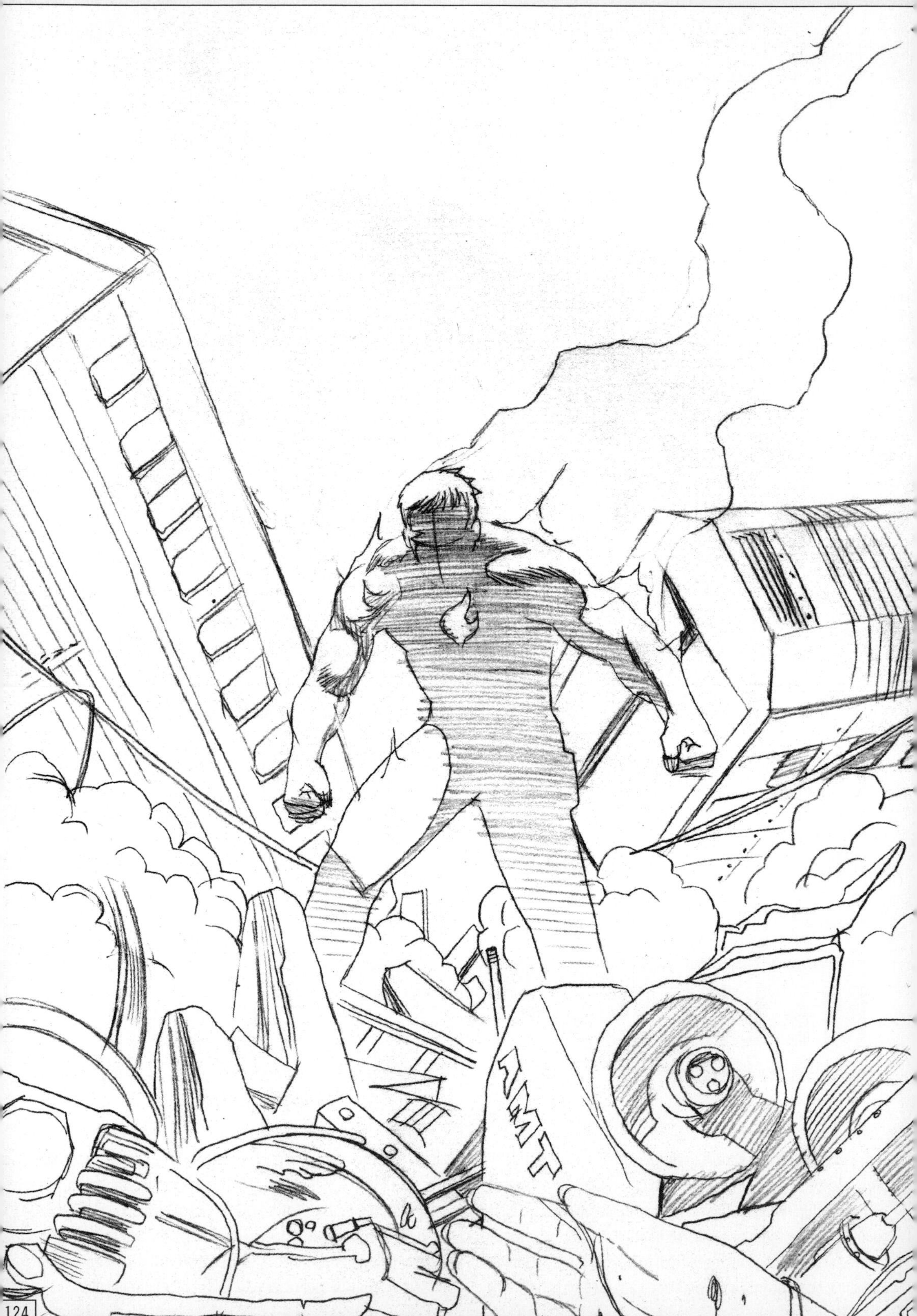

BEHIND THE SCENES

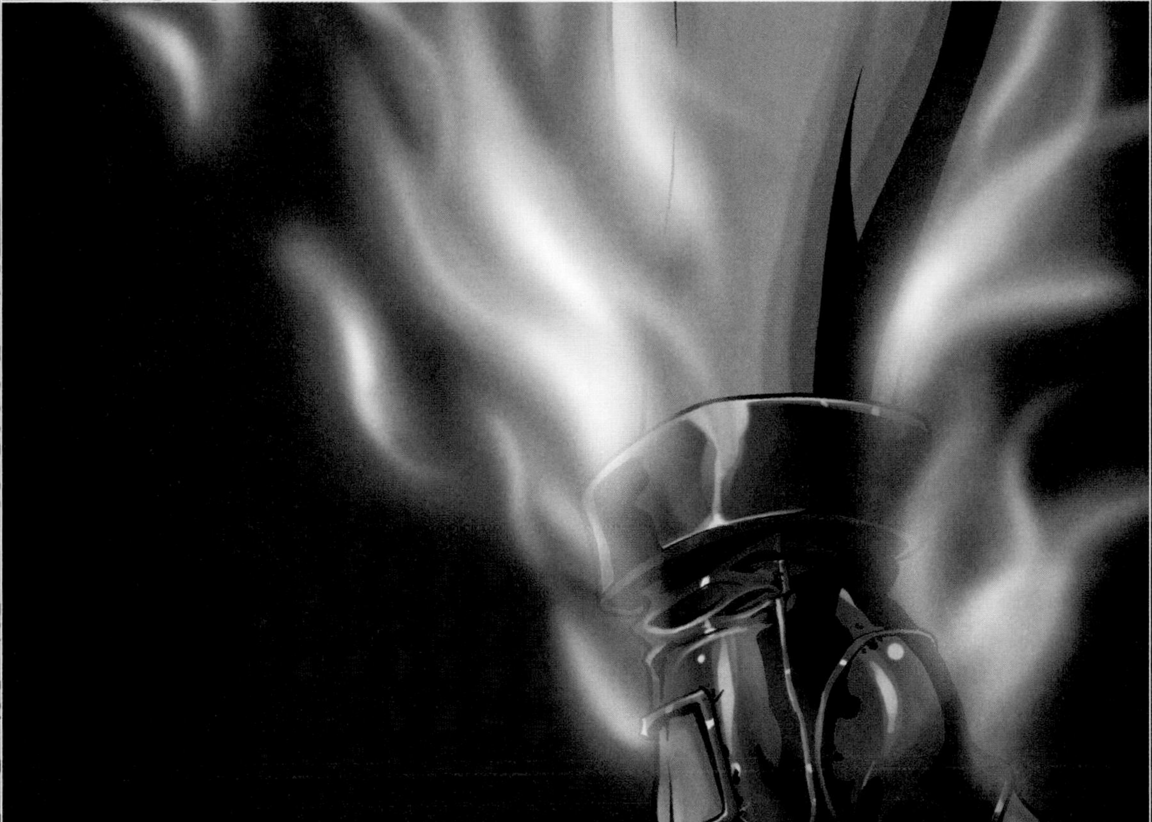

CREATOR COMMENTARY

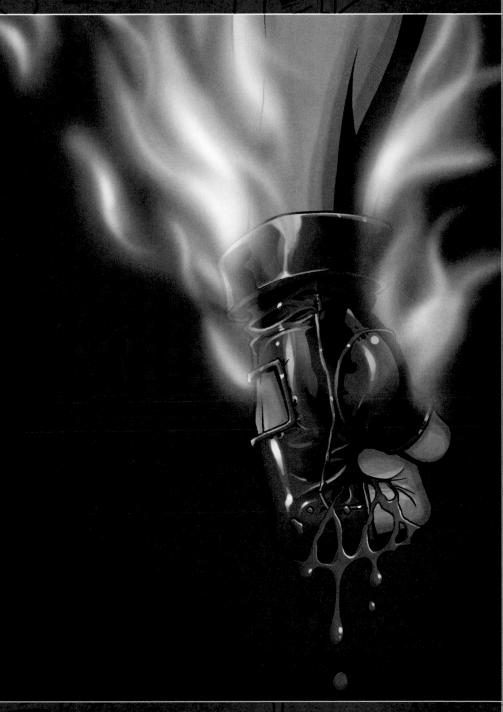

DBS: Hi, all. David Schwartz here, joined by my multi-talented collaborator Sean Wang. Sean and I are both big fans of DVD commentary tracks, and we thought it'd be both fun and illuminating, and perhaps even vaguely interesting, if we were to offer up our own creators' commentary for MELTDOWN. As we go through, we'll be giving you some never-before-seen materials to check out: unused script pages, original artwork that ended up on the cutting room floor, and more. So, without further ado, here's what comes to mind as Sean and I read back through the mini-series together...

ISSUE ONE: PAGE ONE

DBS: This was originally a full-page shot of Cal's head. Sean did a great job with it but I wanted a darker, more mysterious, more atmospheric opening, and a slower reveal of our hero, in order to slowly drag the reader into this world.

I really like what our colorists, Guru-eFX, did here. Despite the fact that Cal is clearly beaten and blood-ied, there's still a glint of sunlight shining on the edge of his mask, a subtle statement that perhaps there's still a bit of hope glowing within.

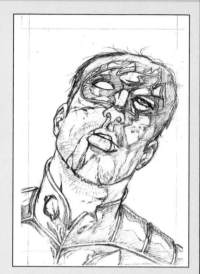

SW: Speaking of the original full head shot (shown here), I was going for some-thing reminiscent of the classic cover from the "Batman: A Death in the Family" story that showed a battered and bloody Robin.

ISSUE ONE: PAGE TWO

DBS: Our story begins with Cal bursting into Maelstrom's office, but it didn't always start that way. In fact, I had three different potential framing sequences I played with at different points in the story's gestation. One iteration had Cal seeking the counsel of a psychologist, to help him reconcile his fractured life in its final moments. Another had him seeking absolution from a priest before he passed away. Ultimately, though, the Maelstrom battle is the one that won out, and I'm glad it did. Sean was convinced that this was the way to go from the start, I vacillated a bit before agreeing.

In retrospect, it's a great choice. It gave us a chance to mix in some serious fisticuffs and dramatic action throughout the entire issue, instead of localizing it to a single battle sequence or two. I did really like the other two openings as well, but they were much quieter, more introspective, and might have been a bit too off-putting for many readers.

Here's your chance to come to your own conclusions, as we present one of those other potential openings. But, first, here are the original pencils from this page, which changed a bit in the final version:

SW: I ended up redrawing page 2 entirely since the first version just wasn't working. In panel 1, David thought it would be more dramatic for Cal to be flying towards the city instead of across it, and I agreed. I also originally wanted the last panel to be a long shot and not the typical dynamic front-on shot of a hero crashing through a window. But the side-view long shot just didn't pack much of a punch so I opted for the other.

PAGE 2 - PANEL 1

Pages two and three are pages of many small, closely-packed panels with black between them. Dark, silent, somewhat creepy. Shots that are close-ups, tight-in, very claustrophobic.

In panel one, we open in a close-up on the sleeping face of a DOCTOR. A psychologist, to be more exact.

The only light in the room is the dim glow of the city outside his bedroom window. In his late 40's, he wears a short, neatly-trimmed beard. Slightly longish hair - not so long as to be unprofessional, but not so short as to be completely unhip. Of course, now it's completely tousled from sleep - and his face is completely drenched in sweat.

PAGE 2 - PANEL 2

Is exactly the same as panel 1.

PAGE 2 - PANEL 3

Same shot - but now his eyes have popped wide open, as though something's startled him out of his sleep.

PAGE 2 - PANEL 4

He props himself up on his elbow - the sheets are wet with sweat.

PAGE 2 - PANEL 5

A close up on his beside clock as his hand reaches out to it. It's a pretty high-end piece - a Bose wave radio or something similar. It reads 1:27 A.M.

PAGE 2 - PANEL 6

He's sitting up on the edge of the bed now, a confused look on his face, as he wipes the sweat from his brow. His fine, combed cotton pajamas, wet with perspiration, stick to his chest.

PAGE 2 - PANEL 7

CU of his feet sliding into a pair of plush, cushy slippers.

PAGE 2 - PANEL 8

In the foreground is the Doctor's bed. It's large - a king-size - but one side of it looks as though it hasn't been slept in for quite some time. An empty frame sits on the nightstand, but nothing else with it - no books, or glasses, or flowers; no evidence that anyone else has shared this bed for quite some time. Clearly no wife or girlfriend (or boyfriend) shares his home with him.

In the background, we see the Doctor taking down a robe from a hook on the back of his bedroom door.

PAGE 2 - PANEL 9

A medium shot of the Doctor as he trudges down a darkened hallway, wrapping the robe around himself. No matter how hot it may be, this is a guy who would never leave the bedroom without the comfort of his robe.

PAGE 2 - PANEL 10

MCU on the Doctor's face as he stands before his thermostat.

PAGE 2 - PANEL 11

CU on the thermostat - whose digital display reads "Current Temperature: 117".

PAGE 2 - PANEL 12

Back to our CU on the Doctor's face - he's clearly confused. There's a bright, red glow coming from down the hall to his left, lighting the side of his face - but he hasn't noticed it - yet.

PAGE 3 - PANEL 1

Same shot, but now the Doctor's now turned towards the light, squinting.

PAGE 3 - PANEL 2

A shot from the Doctor's point-of-view, looking down the hallway. It's clearly an expensive home - wood-paneled walls, artwork hanging from the walls, elegant foyer tables, plants, the whole works.

A door at the end of the hall is slightly ajar, light streaming through it - blindingly bright.

PAGE 3 - PANEL 3

Same shot, but now we see that the doctor is cautiously making his way down the hall, towards the open door.

PAGE 3 - PANEL 4

Close up on his right hand, as he reaches out towards the door.

PAGE 3 - PANEL 5

Another close up, as he grasps the doorknob.

SOUND-EFFECT

Tsssss

PAGE 3 - PANEL 6

Medium shot of the Doctor, as he pulls his hand back, recoiling in pain - the knob is burning hot.

PAGE 3 - PANEL 7

Close on his hands as he wraps his right hand into the folds of his robe.

PAGE 3 - PANEL 8

CU of his right hand as he reaches for the knob again, this time keeping his hand wrapped in the robe.

PAGE 3 - PANEL 9

A close-up of the back of the doctor's head - his left hand up in front of him to block the light - tremendously bright light that's streaming over him as the door opens in front of him.

PAGE 4 - PANEL 1

A splash page.

An imposing, intimidating shot of THE FLARE, floating in the air before the Doctor, a warm, amber glow surrounding him, small flames licking his body. This is our first sight of The Flare, so it should be a really kick-ass shot. The Doctor is completely taken aback; The Flare is trying to maintain an air of superiority, while trying desperately to hold himself together at the same time.

In the Flare's glow, we can see that this room is an extremely well-appointed home office - all mahogany wood and red leather furniture; fine art and numerous certificates hanging on the wood-paneled walls.

PAGE 5 - PANEL 1

The Doctor turns to run back out the door.

PAGE 5 - PANEL 2

The Flare's hand in the foreground, shooting out a pulse of superheated air. Behind it, we see the Flare's face, one eye squinting, aiming.

PAGE 5 - PANEL 3

The pulse hits the door, slamming it shut in the Doctor's face.

PAGE 5 - PANEL 4

The Doctor takes a deep breath, pulls himself together, and...

PAGE 5 - PANEL 5

...turns back towards the Flare.

DOCTOR

The only valuables in the house are the works of art. You can take them, if you like. Then please leave.

PAGE 5 - PANEL 7

Flames dance across the face of the Flare, who smiles, easing tensions a bit as he looks down at the Doctor.

FLARE
You don't recognize me, Doctor? Not surprising.

FLARE
I understand that you've counseled a number of heroes.

DOCTOR
In my office. During the day. Generally with an appointment.

PAGE 5 - PANEL 8

Medium close-up on the Flare, his mood darkening.

FLARE
I'm sorry. I don't think I can wait that long.

ISSUE ONE: PAGE THREE

DBS: I really enjoy writing Maelstrom, because he allows me to play with some major shades of grey. Yes, he's breaking the law by peddling drugs, prostitution and the like, but is he really "evil" if he's simply giving people what they want? And, even if he is truly evil, does the fact that he funnels most of the money back to the starving, impoverished people of his homeland absolve him of his sins? I find that a really interesting dichotomy to explore. In fact, I'd love to explore Maelstrom further in a subsequent series. (Anyone interested in seeing that?) In any case, here, for your reading pleasure, is the original description I wrote about Mael, back when I sat down to write the script:

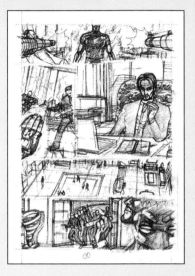

MAELSTROM:

The Flare's arch-enemy. Think a Latino Al Capone - a gangster who has his hands in everything illicit you can imagine. A smarter, hipper Scarface. And he's superpowered - able to control winds. He can be bombastic with his powers or so precise that he can create a mini-tornado an inch wide and use it to bore through a man's skull. He's spectacularly slick, and virtually oozes cool, usually in dark suits smoking Cuban cigars. Confident, relaxed, self-assured - the exact opposite of the rapidly deteriorating Flare. He came to Miami as an orphan from a small South American village, where he watched his parents brutally tortured by a corrupt, military-led administration. You almost have to feel bad for the guy. Almost. And he's smart.

He reads everything in print, but he became obsessed with legendary crime figures - Gotti, Capone, Scarface, The Godfather. When he was still young he worked his way into Miami's largest crime syndicates, then took 'em over and combined them into a massive criminal enterprise. He justifies it all by funneling the money back towards poor, oppressed nations like the one where he was born. He steals from the supposedly rich - America - and uses our money to help the people and nations that desperately need it - like a twisted, modern-day Robin Hood. Those in the struggling nations love him and come to America to join his army of felons. Those in America hate him for the pain and corruption he brings to our shores.

SW: This page also went through some changes when David asked for a tighter intro shot of Maelstrom instead of the medium shot I originally drew. He also wanted a companion shot of Cal, to give the scene that Old West face-off feel. It meant some juggling of panels, but I think the end result works much better.

Since Maelstrom would be showing up in flashback scenes as a costumed supervillain, I wanted to establish some visual cues. In addition to the purple of his shirt being repeated as the predominant color of his supervillain costume, he also sports cufflinks with a tornado-shaped whirlwind, an insignia that will also appear on his chest in the flashback scenes. And just to beat a dead horse, the tornado imagery is repeated with the sculpture in his office.

ISSUE ONE: PAGE FOUR

DBS: Here's where we introduce what's really the primary theme of our series: a rumination on the nature of heroism. Cal starts off convinced that he's no hero, but comes full circle on that about 90 pages later. It took me a while to hit on that. There were so many potential themes here, things like letting go of regret, overcoming fear, and more, that I initially wasn't sure which I wanted to primarily focus on. Then I hit on the text you see on this page, and it all just clicked into place for me. Those other themes are still prominent in the story, but they don't frame it the way that this exploration of heroism does.Sean did some great work on this page. Of course, Sean, you did great work on EVERY page, but I wanted to note this one in particular. It gives us several dynamic shots of The Flare in action, and it's really the first time we get a good look at him. Your great work here is really complemented by the amazing job that Guru did. Man, is that fire effect in panel one AMAZING or what? I can't tell you how blown away I was by this page when I first saw it colored.

ISSUE ONE: PAGES FIVE & SIX

DBS: This page features our first transition back to the past. I think it was Sean's idea to have the last panel of each present day sequence match up visually to the first panel of each flashback sequence (and vice-versa). It's a great device, as it makes the transition less jarring and eases the reader into the new time-frame. And it was a fun challenge for us to come up with the matching images and shoehorn them into the script.

SW: Of all the Present-to-Past transitions, this one was the toughest. Normally, I would have gone with an establishing shot of Cal's home, but I couldn't think of a last panel for the previous page that would have transitioned with that shot. Ultimately, I went with Cal, very tiny and curled up, being pushed out of an office window, which transitions to Cal, very tiny (as a fetus) in roughly the same position in the panel. I'll admit it's a bit forced, but the embryo shot does fit with the text being about his creation. The super-observant may have also noticed that the womb outline is very similar in shape to the Flare insignia.

ISSUE ONE: PAGES SEVEN & EIGHT

DBS: Here's our first shot of Miami in the past. Sean and I both grew up in Miami, and, clearly, I still have a really soft spot in my heart for the place. There's no other city in the world like it.

SW: In panel 1, I threw in a little visual gag just to entertain myself. Cal and his dad are in front of a hotel, but the only letters you see are H-O-T. Of course you can't really tell that it's an H since I didn't want to be TOO obvious about it.

In the original script, Cal was going to be reading a book that bursts into flames. But given that his baseball career factors in as a source of disillusionment later, I thought it would help emphasize that loss by establishing his deep love for the sport here. So we changed the book to a baseball card.

ISSUE ONE: PAGE NINE

DBS: I really love the sequence at the bottom of this page. Although this is a dark and dramatic tale, I wanted to make sure and include at least a little bit of comic relief, a few moments that'd lighten the mood slightly. This is one instance of it that I'm particularly happy with, and I think that Sean pulled it off perfectly from a visual sense. I also think it's a sequence that most guys can probably identify with - I'm sure that something like this has happened to each of us at some point.

This is also where we meet Amara. When I was a kid, I was a big fan of "The New Mutants", which is where Amara's name comes from. Character-wise, though, she's not based on anyone in particular, more an amalgam of what I thought were some pretty cool traits.

Here's a quick peek at my original character description for Amara:

Also, in panel 2, we've got a dude wearing a "CHOOSE LIFE" t-shirt. One reviewer thought this was evidence of a subtle right-wing political agenda in the book. No, it's actually just a goofy, "Wham!"-inspired shirt we remember folks wearing back in the early 80's. No political message intended, I assure you.

AMARA:

The love of his life. In fact, the ONLY girl he's had any interest in since the very first day he met her in junior high. When we first see her she's 12 - not dressed like the rest of the girls her age - she's her own individual. A 50's sock-hop dress, paired with keds and bobby socks, and whacked-out jewelry. Sort of a post-modern melange of styles. She stands out like a sore thumb, but somehow carries it off and makes it all look cool. She's insightful and thoughtful, anti-establishment, bohemian from a young age, but with a slightly rock-n-roll edge. We also see her as an adult, a woman who's suffered through a disappointing marriage, a devastating heartbreak, but who hasn't let it change who she is and what she cares about. She's still passionate, unique and excited, but more refined. She's come to terms with the fact that she needs to wear a power suit and stockings, but has learned to still make a statement with one will placed item of jewelry, or a brightly colored streak through her hair. Now a creative advertising exec, she takes her singular sensibilities and uses them to devise campaigns no other person would have dreamt up.

ISSUE ONE: PAGES TEN & ELEVEN

DBS: (Pg 10) Regarding Amara's explosion in panel 2, I still challenge any junior high science teachers out there to offer up a convincing response!

SW: I modeled the person posing for the art class on one of my art teachers from junior high. As I recall, those teachers always frowned upon us doodling comic characters in art class since they didn't view comic books as "real art." Oh, how they would be disappointed with me now.

DBS: (Pg 11) Here's where we first touch on another big theme in the book: fear. Cal allows fear to hold him back throughout his life, and it ends up being a big driving factor in his demise. His fear causes him to avoid revealing his love to Amara in his youth, from staying with her when they're unable to conceive, from stepping up as a super-hero, even from initially trying to save Sandra at the end. All that fear led to all of his pain, anguish and self-loathing, fueling those metaphorical fires within.

I originally had a really cheesy line here, one that we cut from the final version. After Amara goes on and on about the stupidity of having to memorize the periodic table, Cal responds:

> "CAL
> (sheepishly:)
> Um, you know, there's something to be said for chemistry."

ISSUE ONE: PAGE TWELVE

SW: Since the specifics of most of the Present-to-Past matching visual transitions weren't originally scripted, I tried to find ways to do them visually with similar blocking and composition. I think they tended to work best when the contexts were completely different. In this case, the previous panel has Amara and her boyfriend in the foreground, walking away from a sitting Cal. That transitions to Cal in the foreground, falling vertically from a pursuing Maelstrom.

ISSUE ONE: PAGES THIRTEEN & FOURTEEN

SW: As I recall, the Maelstrom-fight-to-baseball-game was the only visual transition specified in the original script, but I thought it worked really well, which is why I wanted to make all the other time shifts into visual transitions as well. That and I loved the use of the device in Highlander. Another gag thrown in for my entertainment: Cal's baseball number is 06 since the sixth letter of the alphabet is "F," the first letter of his future superhero moniker.

DBS: I really like the way Sean laid out panel 3 of page 14, with Cal clearly seeing Amara make out with her "skanky boyfriend o' the week". Cal's just gotten a huge hit, he's running the bases, but, even then, he's never truly got his head in the game. It's something we'll see happening throughout his life; the guy can never just focus on the here and now...until the very end.

ISSUE ONE: PAGE FIFTEEN & SIXTEEN

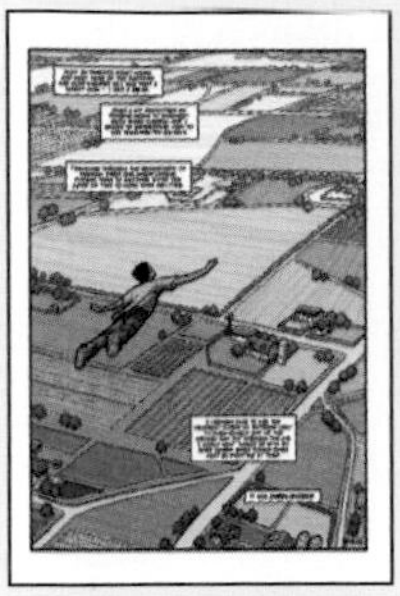

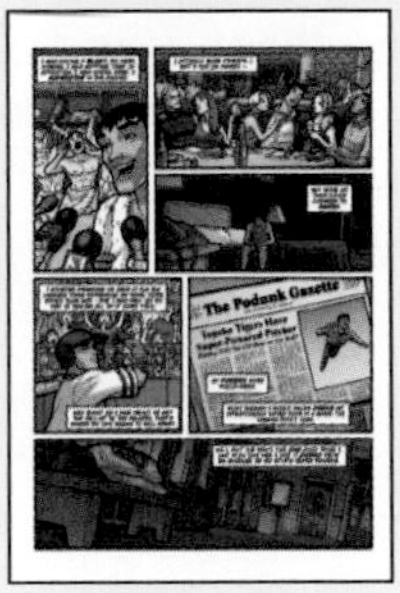
The Podunk Gazette

DBS: (Pg 15) One of my absolute favorite pages. There's a true sense of wonder here, a dream-like quality that I'm really impressed by. But, still, Cal's slightly off-center, giving the very subtle undertone that there's something slightly disquieting here, some catastrophe to come.

SW: (Pg 16) I forget what the newspaper was originally supposed to be called, but I thought "The Podunk Gazette" would be a funnier name for a small town paper. It was either that or "The Backwater Bugle."

ISSUE ONE: PAGES SEVENTEEN & EIGHTEEN

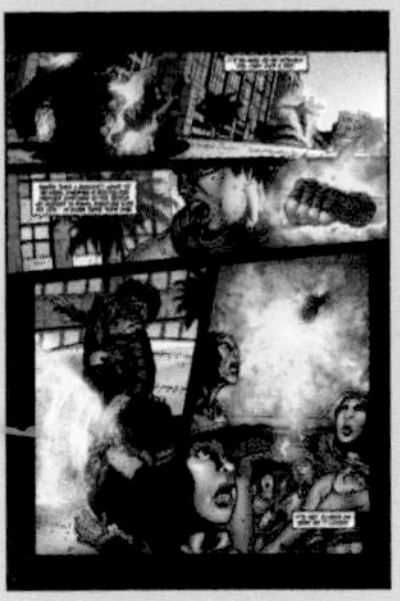

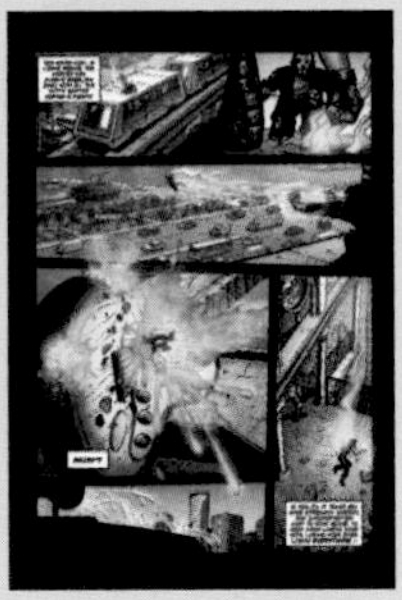

DBS: I love that we were able to get so many iconic Miami items in the series, like the MetroMover car here, Bayside on the next page, the Port of Miami later on, and so many others. I can't remember Miami ever having had a super-hero of its own, but it certainly deserves one. And, considering all of the strange crimes and tales of corruption down there over the years, it probably really needs one, don'tcha think?

SW: This was one of my favorite Past-to-Present transitions in that I think it's fairly subtle. The last panel of page 16 has Cal in the background, walking out of the locker room with his uniform left on a bench in the foreground. Cutting to the Present, Cal's again in the background, but this time he's charging forward towards Maelstrom, who occupies the foreground in the same spot as the locker room bench in the previous panel.

ISSUE ONE: PAGE NINETEEN

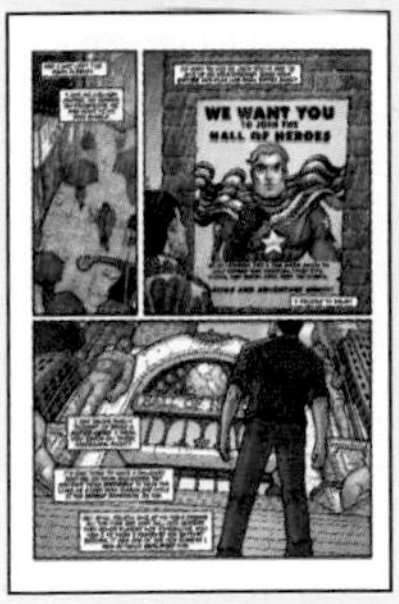
WE WANT YOU

SW: This page is the first of the Intermediate art style, starting the bridge the gap between the cartoonier Past and grittier Present.

With this birds-eye transition, Cal goes from a physical injury in the Present to an emotional injury in the Past, which I thought was nice juxtaposition. He's also the only one without an umbrella, to add to his pathetic-ness, and to draw your eye immediately to him.

The poster hero is a combination of the two most iconic "leader" characters in comics: Superman and Captain America. It's also a nod to the classic Uncle Sam recruitment poster. The Hall of Heroes is a fairly obvious homage to the Hall of Justice, although I think the statues, globe, and stars add that extra bit of grandeur. Guru-eFX originally colored it in tans and grays, but I thought it was important to give it that white marble look, like a shining beacon in the heart of the city.

DBS: I saw a poll yesterday that said that 4 out of 5 American workers don't consider their current job to be their dream job. That's a full 80% of the people out there who aren't doing what they really wanna do with their lives. Kinda sad, and Cal definitely falls into that group, as made very clear here. But, while most people are able to reconcile their lost dreams and make the best of their jobs and lives, Cal was never able to do so. He just got more and more angry and frustrated, when he should've, instead, been taking risks and finding ways to change for the better.

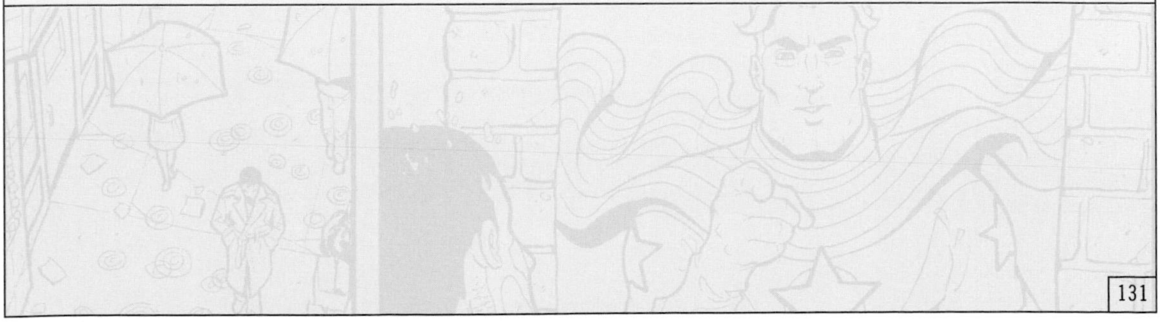

ISSUE ONE: PAGES TWENTY & TWENTY-ONE

SW: The original script had Cal getting hero experience by catching some petty criminals first before auditioning for the superteam. I thought it would be funnier if his "experience" just consisted of him practicing heroic poses in front of a mirror. Plus it seemed to fit his character more since altruism wasn't really his primary goal.

Cal's first costume was supposed to look as cheesy as possible since it's homemade, and, for me, cheesiness is exemplified by a low collar, like the uniforms in the first couple seasons of "Star Trek: The Next Generation".

I had fun getting back to my "TICK" roots here, designing some really stupid characters like the hero wannabe with the tentacle arms and the one with the light bulb head and lasso of Christmas lights. The glowing brain insignia on Neuron is also meant to be silly. And the "B" on the big guy stands for…wait for it…"Big Guy."

There was originally going to be a flashback scene around this time in which Cal completely burns off his homemade costume during his first fight with Maelstrom, leaving him completely naked and humiliated. I thought it'd be fun to have a scene with a naked Cal blocked with black censor bars on the page. While a funny visual scene, dramatically it still could have established Cal and Maelstrom's bitter relationship with their initial confrontation resulting in a very public humiliation for Cal. It would've been at this point that he sought Neuron's help in designing the more flame-resistant (and less amateur-looking) classic costume that he wears through much of his early hero years. We eventually agreed that it didn't quite fit, but it definitely would've been fun.

ISSUE ONE: PAGE TWENTY-TWO

DBS: Panels 3 and 4 were actually inspired by Beavis & Butthead. Or, rather, by that kid who set himself aflame several years back when he was trying to play with fire like Beavis & Butthead did on their show, and by the media's reaction to that event. We've also got a bit of commentary here on the media's propensity to focus on the negative and morbid, rather than on positive stories; the old "if it bleeds, it leads" mentality. I actually can't bear to watch local news telecasts anymore, for just that reason.

In the final panel, the Flare logo on Cal's shirt was a late addition to the page. We were worried that, since you don't see his face, readers might not know that this was Cal without that logo peeking out.

SW: This one tiny panel is all you see of Maelstrom from his costumed supervillain days (in Book 1 anyway). Initially I thought there might be more of him, like the previously mentioned flashback scene of his first fight with Cal, but perhaps we'll save that for the sequel…

The magazines were fun to come up with, especially some of the more ridiculous ones. I mean, "Superfast"? Just how many running heroes are there in this universe?

ISSUE ONE: PAGE TWENTY-THREE

DBS: It still pains me a bit to have our protagonist, and his lady love, smoking in our book. It was a useful device here, and Cal's comments do make clear that he takes it up out of frustration and boredom, but I really do hate the possible perception of glorifying the use of cigarettes.

Panel 4 here actually changed pretty significantly from Sean's first pass at it. It originally focused much more on Cal lighting up his cigarette, but we re-tooled it to make it more about his reaction to the sight of Amara. It served the dual purpose of heightening the drama and minimizing the cancer-stick. Here's a look at that original panel 4:

And then the replacement panel actually had Cal with his goatee - which he shouldn't have had yet at that point. I guess that's the danger of jumping around different time periods in storytelling, trying to keep all the looks straight!

Sean caught that at the very last possible second. The book was already at the printer, but there was just enough time left to make the correction. Phew!

This page actually changed a bit in other ways as well as Sean and I worked through it. I originally had Amara enter the monitor room where Cal was sitting in panel 2, and surprise him there. But, as Sean pointed out, that didn't quite make sense. They probably wouldn't just let random civilians walk into the HOH headquarters. So, we re-jiggered it and had the scene take place on the front steps. Yes, clearly, we both take this stuff WAAYY too seriously.

SW: I first drew the reptilian villain in beachwear (shorts, sandals, sun hat, etc) since I thought he could be the Cayman Caiman, a tropical island themed crocodile. But the outfit didn't register as a costumed supervillain, so I changed it to tights. He still has sandals though. With Amara, it was important for her to be immediately recognizable upon her reappearance, which was difficult since she was last seen as a teenager. I tried to use some visual cues, like the choker on her neck, which she also had as a youngster, and the star-shaped earrings, to tie back to the stars on her sleeves and circling around her when she was first introduced.

ISSUE ONE: PAGES TWENTY-FOUR & TWENTY-FIVE

DBS: We had a lot of story to fit into a mere 48 pages. So, as I was scripting the book, I was forced to have many pages with a lot of small panels and a lot of text. This is one of the spots where we were able to change that and really open things up with a big double-page spread.

SW: This double-page spread was a nightmare as the New York background took forever to draw. On the plus side, I think I have an okay eye for perspective, so I didn't have to actually draw out grid lines or perspective guides. If you look closely, you'll see the inevitable snafu here or there, but all in all, I think it came out well.

ISSUE ONE: PAGE TWENTY-SIX

DBS: Ah, our one, big sex scene in the series! Actually, panel 1 here was originally much more graphic, but we pulled it back to a silhouette in order to make the book a bit more all-ages appropriate. Here's that original version of panel 1:

ISSUE ONE: PAGES TWENTY-EIGHT & TWENTY-NINE

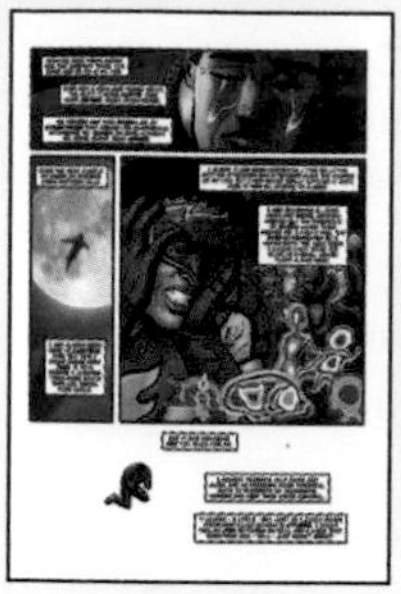

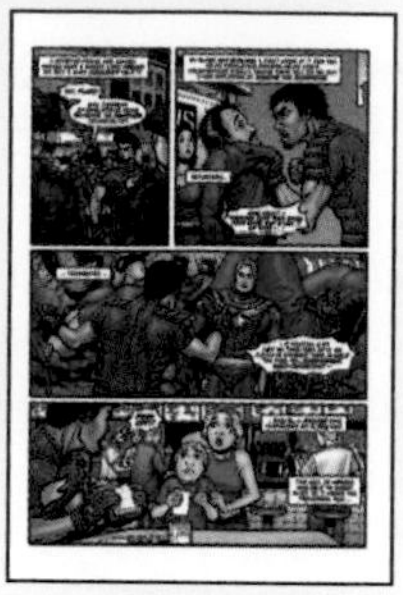

DBS: We tried to put a lot of subtle detail work into the series to make it authentic. Or, at least, as authentic as a super-hero comic book could be. The first panel here is an example of that, with Cal's tears evaporating away before they can even finish rolling down his cheek. It's a small thing, but those little touches do, I think, make a big difference in the overall feel of the series.

DBS: We debated whether to use full expletives, or to censor them by inserting symbols. At one point, I think we inadvertently had some of each. In the end, we went with the symbols, as in the final panel of t his page, in order to make the book more appropriate for the young'uns.

SW: In the original script, the last panel had Cal slapping some woman while in bed, but that seemed a bit too harsh, making him cross that fine line from unstable to unlikable. I suggested the scene of him cursing out the kid since it's still an extremely rude action, but at the same time, kinda funny. Dave loved it, so that's what we went with.

ISSUE ONE: PAGES THIRTY THROUGH THIRTY-FIVE

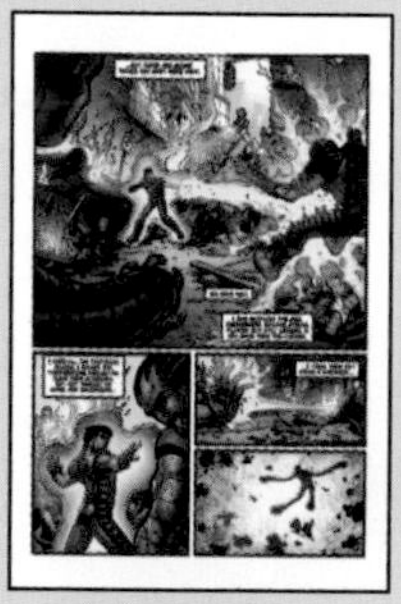

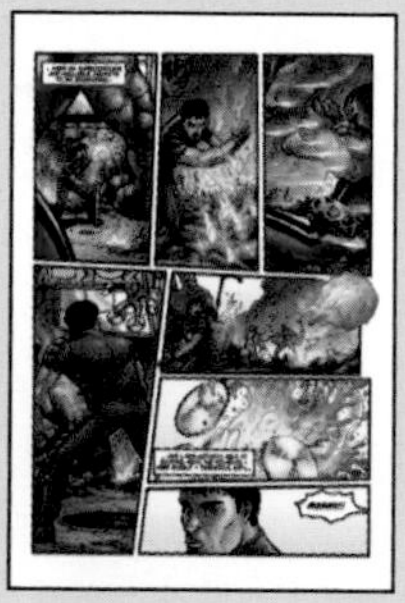

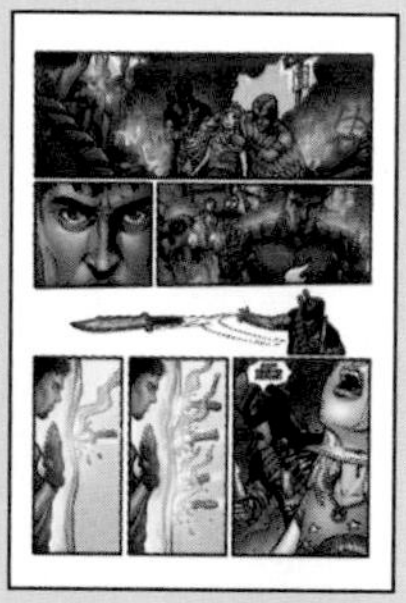

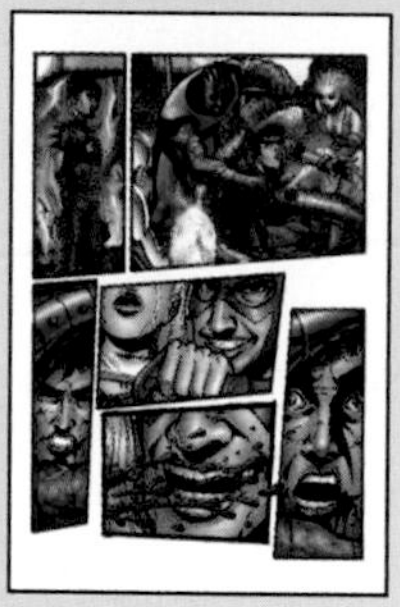

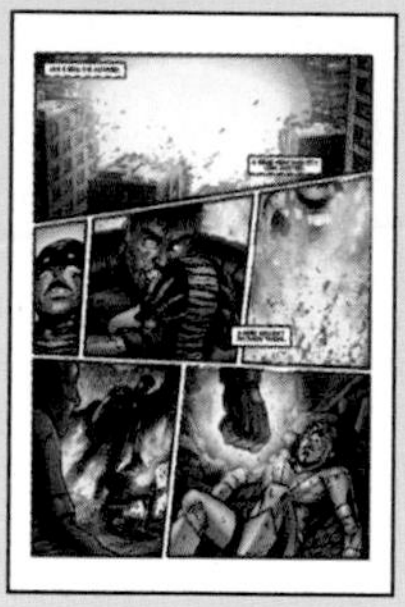

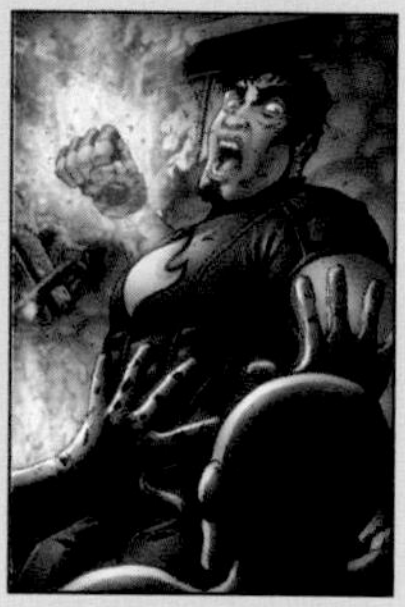

DBS: Pages thirty through thirty-six are my favorite sequence from the series, bar none. We used portions of this sequence in virtually all of our promos, because I think it really encapsulates everything the series is about: the protagonist who desperately wants to be good, but whose powers are forcing him over the edge; the transition from light and happy to dark and despairing (both visually and textually); and the pure unadulterated emotion that we put into the book; it can all be seen in these seven pages. Plus, it's got some great action, which never hurts.At one point, I think I actually toyed with having this sequence open the book, starting it off with a real bang and jumping into the action immediately. From there, we jumped back to the past, and told the past storyline linearly, without jumping back and forth, until we arrived back at this point again in the story. From here, we moved forward in the present.

SW; This sequence was the trickiest for me in that it had to transition from one art style to another over the course of 7 pages. A lot was dependent upon Guru capturing the shift in the coloring as well, which they did perfectly.

David gave me free reign with the creation of the Evil Incarnate villains, so, as a big fan of Spider-Man's rogues gallery, I went mostly with an homage to the Sinister Six. There's a Doc Ock type with mechanical arms and legs, who I imagined to be a quadriplegic. There's also a Vulture type character and a Kraven-like hunter. The silver buzzsaw guy was my Green Goblin homage in his use of personal flying gadgetry.

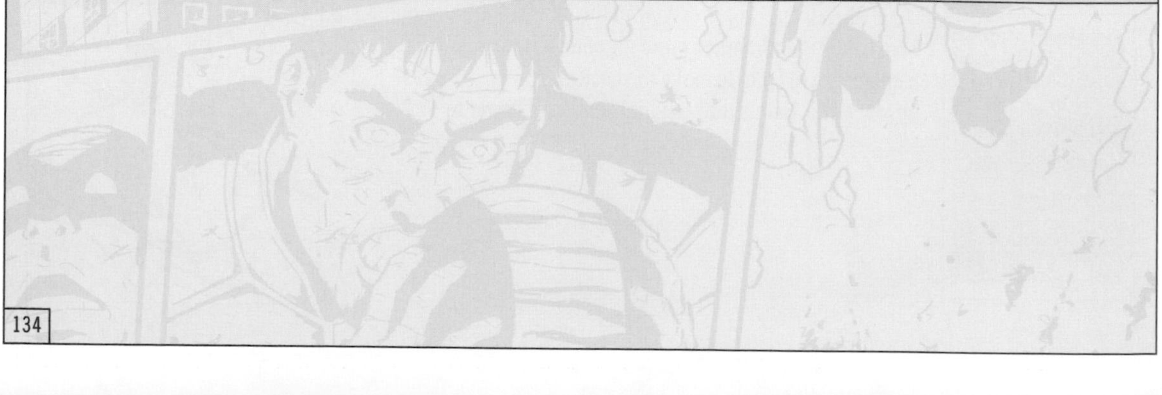

ISSUE ONE: PAGE THIRTY-SIX

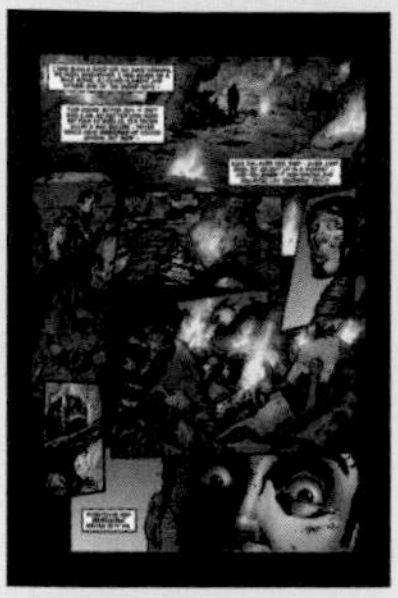

SW: This page in some ways epitomizes what I was trying to do artistically to differentiate the various styles in Book 1. In addition to getting looser with the inking and laying down more areas of black in the grittier style, I also relied on the page layout and panel composition to enhance the different looks. While the Past style has white gutters to emphasize a lighter, more optimistic feel, the Present has black backgrounds to make those pages feel darker overall. And while the Past panel layout conforms to a more static grid layout, giving it a structured look, the Present has more overlapping panels, breaking of panel borders, and other elements to give the pages a more chaotic look to match the increasingly chaotic emotions Cal is experiencing in his later days.

ISSUE ONE: PAGE THIRTY-SEVEN

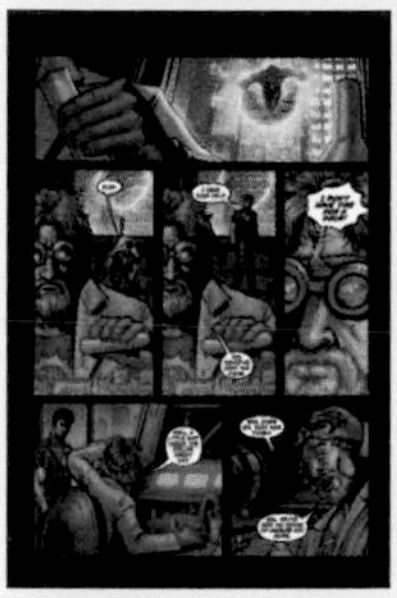

DBS: I had originally written Neuron as even more sarcastic and snarky, but thought it made him just too unlikable, so I scaled that back a bit in the final analysis. Plus, I think that Sean gave him such a kind and gentle look that it served to make him inherently more likable, helping to undercut how potentially off-putting his sense of humor might otherwise be.

SW: David and I worked a lot on this scene to make Neuron less aloof, jokey, and dismissive, since that made him seem too cold and callous. It took a number of passes to hit that fine line of having him show concern for Cal, but with that concern slightly outweighed by his fascination with the science behind it.

ISSUE ONE: PAGE THIRTY-EIGHT

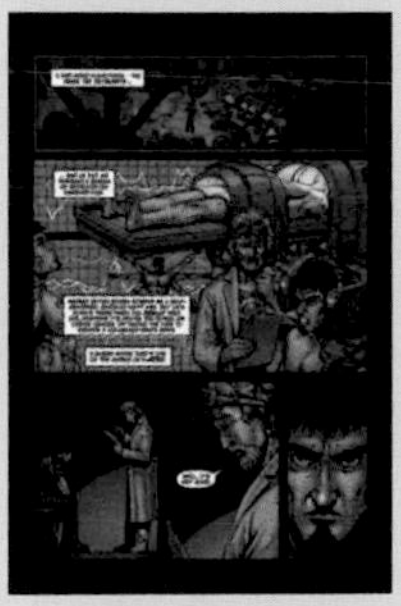

DBS: In an early draft of this scene, we flashed back and forth between Neuron giving Cal the bad news, and Cal getting physically brutalized in his battle with Maelstrom. Most of the flashbacks in the issue are at least a full page, these would have each been a single panel. The idea was to have Cal take a hit physically to match each emotional hit he was taking, to get some more action into a fairly static scene, and to really build up intensity. The problem was that it also made the scene really choppy, so we abandoned that idea pretty early on.

ISSUE ONE: PAGE THIRTY-NINE

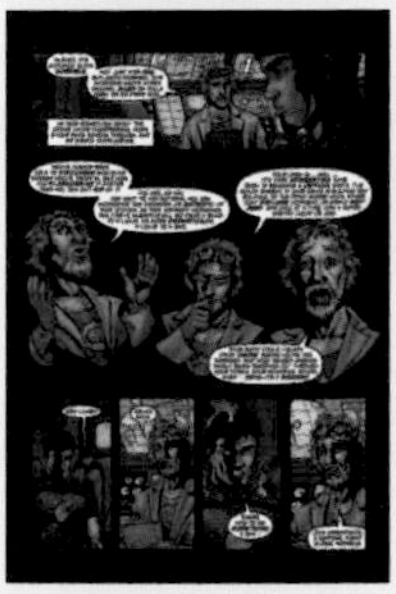

DBS: I was always a bit worried about Neuron's dialogue in the first panel. He claims that Cal's ultimate demise could result in a huge explosion, potentially leveling a city (and then mentions it again on page 41). As we see in issue 2, Cal's explosion doesn't quite hit that level. The idea is that it's because he spent so much of his pent-up energy in his final, superheroic hours, and let go of so much of his rage and anger, the explosion is reduced a bit. Plus the fact the explosion actually takes place underground, muffled by layers of rock and debris, also tones it down. But was that too subtle of a distinction? Would it be clear enough, or would it appear like a mistake on our part? I don't know the answer to that, but hopefully it didn't distract folks from being wrapped up in the ending of issue 2.

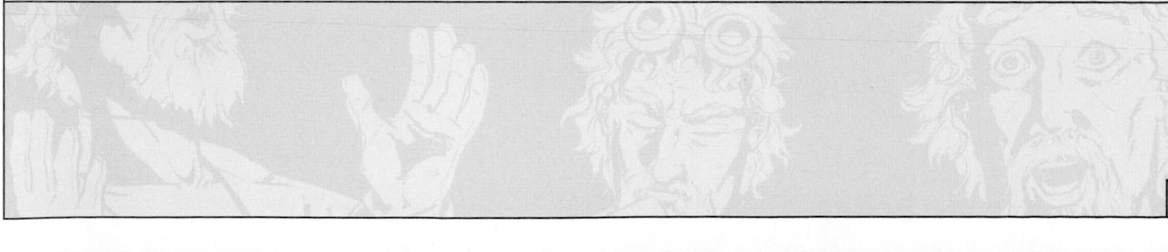

ISSUE ONE: PAGES FORTY-ONE, FORTY-THREE, FORTY-EIGHT

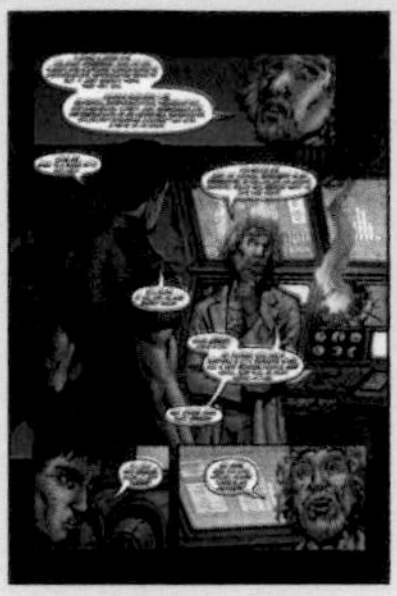

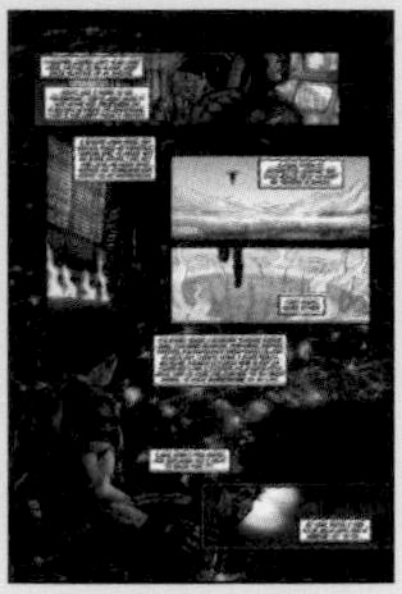

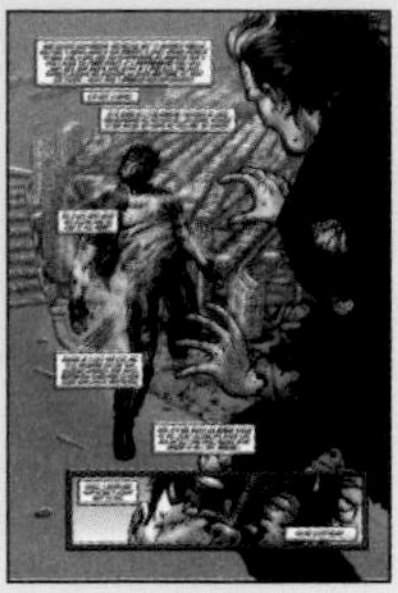

DBS: The dialogue on page 41 is actually the first dialogue I ever wrote for the series. It's intact, almost word-for-word, from the original series pitch.

On page 43 is another theme that's in a lot of my writing. The idea of procrastinating - whether due to fear or otherwise - and finding excuses to put off until tomorrow what you could do today, until you've woken up decades later and realized the most of your tomorrows are now behind you.

Originally, I had written a bit more text for page 48, trying to foreshadow the events of issue 2. But, it was way over-written, so we trimmed it down a bit. Here's a peek at that original text:

PAGE FORTY-EIGHT

A splash page that bleeds out of the panel borders. Maelstrom has lifted the Flare back into the sky, and holds him aloft with one hand. Maelstrom's other arm is cocked backwards, ready to send another mini-cyclone straight through The Flare's heart. The Flare is holding his shoulder, still in immense pain. Otherwise, he's somewhat limp in Maelstrom's grasp.

FLARE (CAPTION)
The wound cauterized instantly, but it doesn't really matter. I mean, what's the point? I can't bring myself to kill him. I set out to compromise my morals and I can't even do that right. If I apprehend him, he'll just get off again.

FLARE (CAPTION)
I'm not a hero. I've made all the wrong choices in life, betrayed and squandered my potential. I wanted to be a big star, an inspiration. Instead, I've allowed myself to be ruled by fear, to repress myself, to hurt the people I've loved.

FLARE (CAPTION)
What do I do. Do I let go? Give in? Allow him to end it all now?

FLARE (CAPTION)
Or do I fight back, make one, final push? Stay alive to see Amara again? Do I have the guts to actually face her, to apologize, to try and make amends?

FLARE (CAPTION)
Maybe if I let him kill me, it'll release all of the excess energy, and we'll both die together.

FLARE (CAPTION)
Yeah, I suppose that'd be a good way to die, but ...

FLARE (CAPTION)
What do I do?

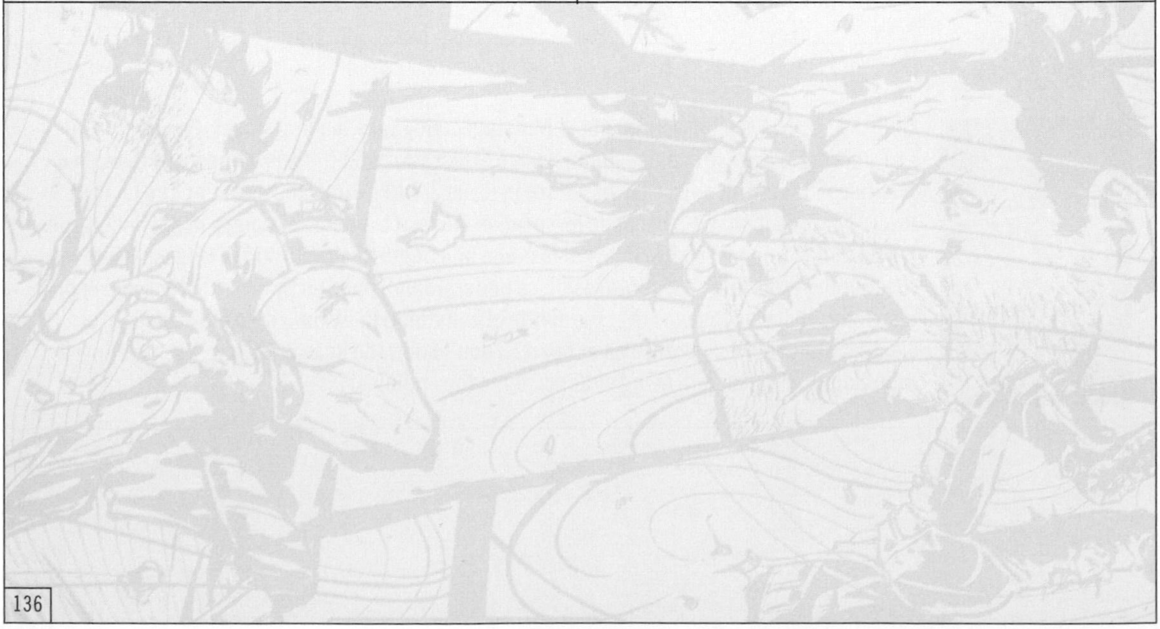

ISSUE 2

DBS: Thematically, this issue is very different from issue 1. Where issue 1 was all about RAGE and REGRET, this issue's more about RESOLUTION and REDEMPTION. So, there's a point where the anger disappears, and we see more of who Cal was really meant to be. He's a guy who's got a great heart, it's just been buried away for too many years, scarred by all of the disappointments in his life.

Structurally, this issue is also very different from issue 1. Where issue 1 was about reflecting on Cal's past, issue 2 is more about dealing with his tortured present. By dwelling so much on his past, he's really prevented himself from living and enjoying his life in the present. Over the course of this issue, he learns to leave the past behind, and, from a storytelling perspective, we also leave the flashbacks behind.

It's actually pretty scary to change things up so radically from one issue to the next, particularly given the great reaction we got to issue 1, but I'm tremendously proud of this ending, and I think it all serves Cal, and the story, incredibly well.

SW: I initially felt that Book 2 was lacking in flashbacks, given how prominent they were to the story structure in Book 1. I was afraid people would be upset by the radical change in storytelling, and for selfish artistic reasons, I also wanted to do more pages in the fun cartoony style! Gladly, the lack of flashbacks didn't seem to be an issue for most readers, although that didn't stop me from trying to get more in where I could!

DBS: But, enough of our yappin'. On to the actual pages…

ISSUE TWO: PAGES ONE & TWO

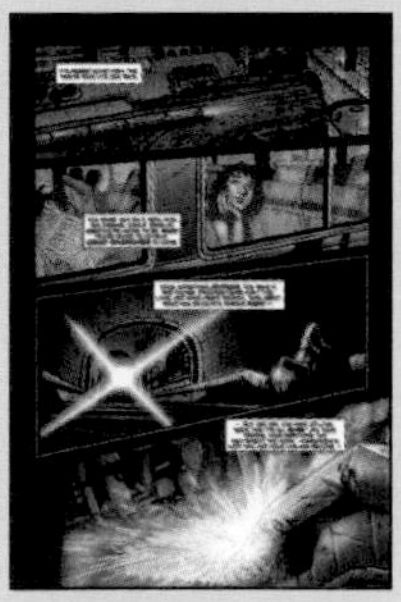

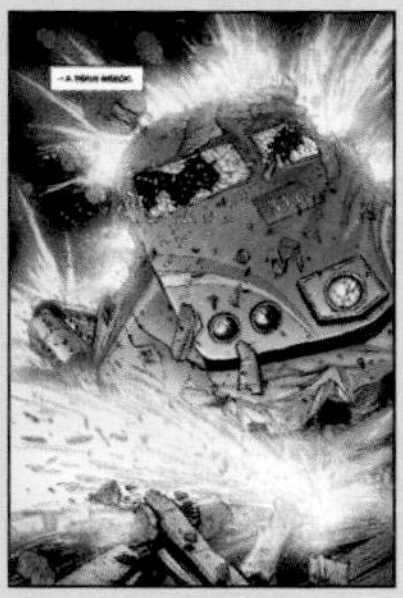

DBS: Originally, I had this text as Cal voice-over layered over a different scene. But, in splitting the story into two issues, I thought it played nicely as a prologue to the issue, a way to ease readers back into the story, and a nice precursor of things to come. I really like the dreamy quality Sean put into Sandra's face here. It sets up her character perfectly, and lends credence to the choices she makes on the final two pages.

SW: Another example of using numbers for personal entertainment while doing the art: the 3-1-12 on the train correlate to the letters C-A-L in the alphabet.

ISSUE TWO: PAGE FOUR

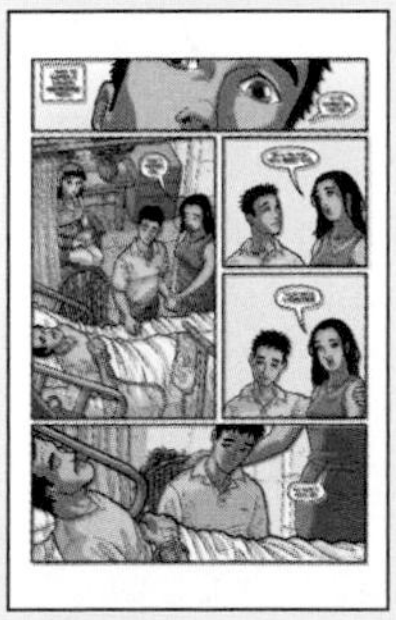

DBS: Sean and I went back and forth a bit on this page and page 6, our two lone flashback pages in issue 2. We both agreed that issue two really lent itself to a more linear style of storytelling. Plus, we had really caught up chronologically in the Flare's life-story, and didn't want to insert flashbacks that didn't serve a legitimate purpose for the story. But, we also didn't want to completely divorce ourselves from the flashbacks that readers grew so accustomed to, and that worked so well, in issue 1. Sean suggested some great flashback ideas (as you'll see throughout the remainder of this commentary), and we had fun kicking 'em around and negotiating over which ones we'd end up including. Ultimately, we didn't have room for all of his great ideas, but these two did make the cut. And, by front-loading them in the issue they provide a nice, smooth transition from the non-linear issue 1 to the more linear issue 2.

SW: I thought that it was important to show a bit more of Cal's parents in Book 2, since he leaves them in Book 1 and never mentions them again. In my attempt to squeeze more flashbacks into book 2, I tried to suggest ones that would lend themselves to the theme of death, to balance the flashbacks in Book 1 that dealt with Cal's "life." This one was meant to explain the death of one parent, introduce Cal to the concept of mortality, and also given him the will to continue the fight against Maelstrom.

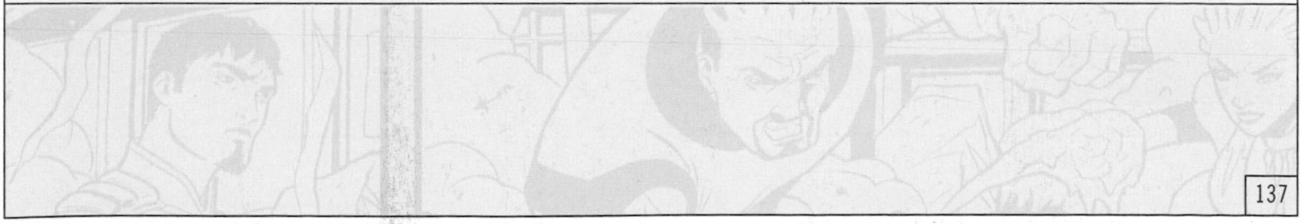

ISSUE TWO: PAGE SIX

DBS: You know, ya gotta love Maelstrom's old costume. You just don't see enough super-villains in lavender spandex nowadays.

SW: The ice villainess from the Evil Incarnate scene wasn't originally scripted to be in this scene, but she seemed like a good recurring foil for Cal's heat-based powers.

ISSUE TWO: PAGE SEVEN

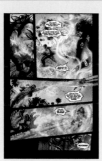

SW: David and I had a lot of fun debate about this scene. He felt the dialogue might be overkill, but for me, it was important for Cal to make the conscious decision to take out Maelstrom as a dramatic turning point as opposed to just blasting away in the heat of battle. I thought it would be interesting to attribute Cal's earlier inability to apprehend Maelstrom to a psychological block, where he subconsciously needed a scapegoat out there to blame for his failures in life. I do still feel like Cal needed some dialogue himself before unleashing on Maelstrom though, and I had suggested some lines where he says "You're wrong about everything. Our people don't need you. And I don't need you." The Robin Hood idea David came up with was a great take on Maelstrom, and I thought Cal could address or debunk that misguided notion, shortly before making his choice to end Maelstrom (and his reliance on excuses).

DBS: Yes, there was a long period of time where I was considering cutting the dialogue here, making this a silent battle page. I felt it was one of those situations where less can be more, and there are certain things that can be left unsaid between Cal and Maelstrom. But that's what was so great about our collaboration on the book; Sean and I were able to really bat things around, without any ego entering into the picture, and the book really benefited because of our back and forth.

ISSUE TWO: PAGE EIGHT

DBS: And here's where we really leave the structure of issue 1 behind. The Maelstrom battle had been our framing sequence for issue 1, but, with Maelstrom out of the way, it freed Cal up to move forward, ditch the flashbacks, and wrap up the other loose ends of his life.

Originally, when we were considering using a psychiatrist or a priest as our framing sequence, we kept the non-linear storytelling going until much further along. In those versions, the doctor/priest was the last person Cal spoke with prior to rocketing off to trainwreck, and everything else, including the Amara conversation, took place in flashback.

ISSUE TWO: PAGE NINE

DBS: We really tried to toy with the reader expectations a bit here. After book one, readers probably expected that defeating Maelstrom would be the big climax of the book. Clearly, we chose not to go that way. The climax, the big epiphany, doesn't come about as the result of a battle against an outside force like Maelstrom, it's more about the battle Cal has with himself, and that epiphany doesn't come for another thirty pages (give or take). So, we actually had Cal comment on how anti-climactic this battle ended up being.

ISSUE TWO: PAGES TEN & ELEVEN

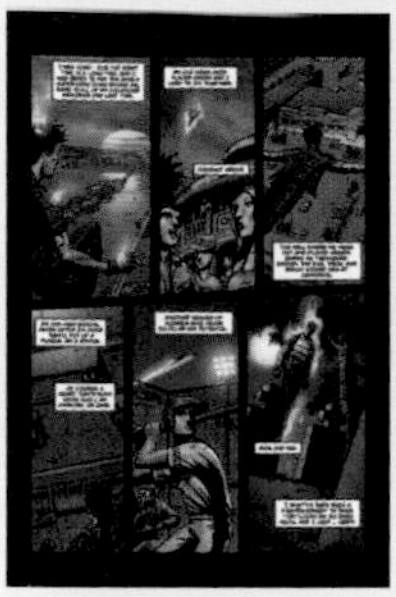

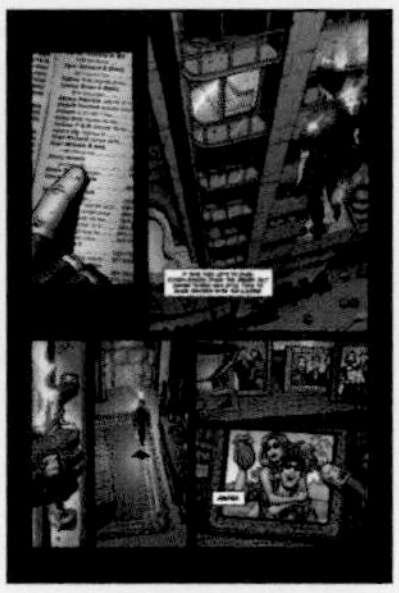

SW: Another flashback I had proposed was about the death of Cal's mother to go along with the death of his father. I suggested that Cal visit the grave in the Present, which would flash back to a funeral scene of one of the other HOH members. It would have been a nod to the fairly cliched death-of-a-superhero scenes in most comics. A continuation of that flashback would have shown the HOH hero returning to life, in even more cliched comic form. But it would have been a great way to juxtapose Cal's very real mortality with the concept of cheating death. Ultimately, the grave visitation stayed in to resolve the status of Cal's parents, but the dead superhero flashback was cut for length.

SW: The specific photo Cal looks at was originally scripted, as "a shot of Cal and Amara in happier times". I thought it would be nice to go back to one of the photos shown in the big NY aerial double-spread from Book 1.

ISSUE TWO: PAGE TWELVE

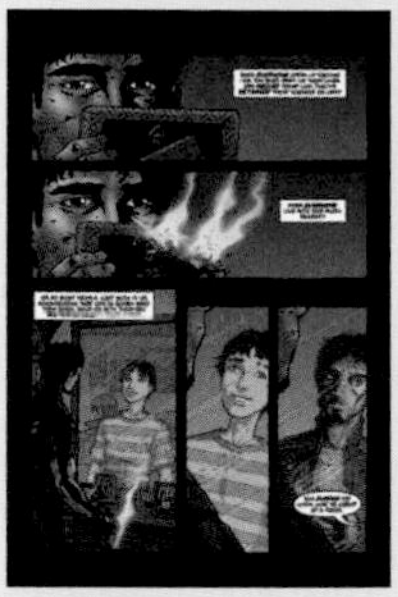

DBS: I really love this page. I feel like this one page sums up so much of the series, both textually and visually. It's all about broken dreams, burnt out memories, haunting reflections. Man, that sounds so ridiculously melodramatic, doesn't it?

SW: And this was the place for ... drum roll, please ... another suggested flashback, the most important one to me. I thought when Cal looks in the mirror, it could have segued into a flashback of him looking at himself in the mirror when first trying on his new costume. It would have been the moment of upgrading from the classic tights costume to the more contemporary leather one. Neuron would have been with him, having designed the suit for him, and would have pointed out the increased number of the boxy pad shapes. It would have explained for the first time that Neuron had been building those pads into Cal's costumes to help him control and moderate his increasingly erratic powers, hinting at the breakdown to come. I also thought there could be a good character-building moment of Cal deciding to ditch the mask with his new costume, mentioning that with his parents now dead and his relationship with Amara over, he had nothing left to protect with a secret identity. Basically, the ditching of the mask would've symbolized the desolation and emptiness he felt in life. Ultimately, again, due to a lack of space, the flashback was cut and we stuck with the original scene of him looking at his younger self in the mirror.

ISSUE TWO: PAGE FIFTEEN & SEVENTEEN

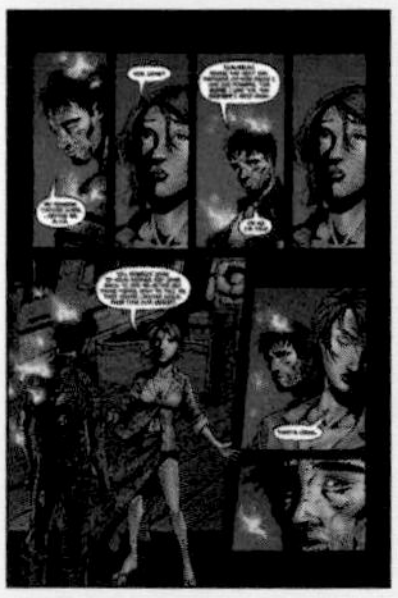

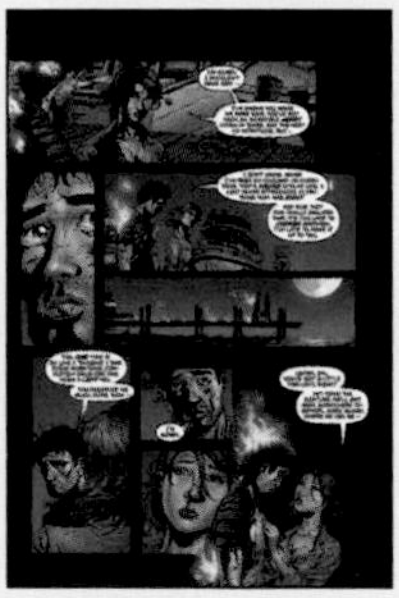

DBS: This whole conversation was pretty tough to write. When I first sat down at the keyboard, it really flowed out onto the page quickly and easily. But, then I read it back and realized that Amara had come across as really cold-hearted, especially considering that she's talking to a guy that's effectively a terminal cancer patient. So, I went back and toned it down, making her harsh reaction much more temporary, and turning her back towards the empathetic, caring person she was supposed to be.

With Sean's art, I'm always amazed by how expressive the characters' eyes are, and page 17 is a perfect example of that. Every panel here is really brought to life by the expressions in Cal and Amara's eyes.

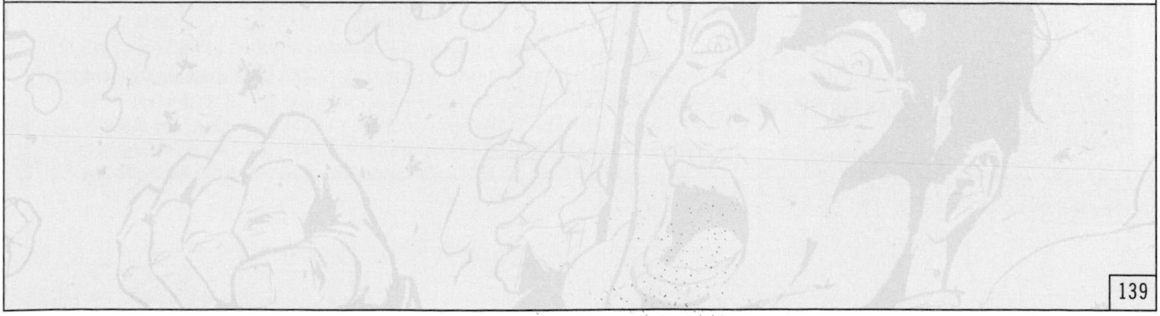

ISSUE TWO: PAGE EIGHTEEN

DBS: In order for Cal to truly be redeemed, he couldn't be forced into a final heroic act; he had to actively choose it. And it had to be an incredibly difficult choice to make. So, here we have Cal faced with the ultimate temptation: on the one hand, the love of his life, the one person who ever made him feel truly wonderful, is standing there before him and offering to make his final days as happy as they could possibly be. Or, on the other hand, he can rocket off to save some strangers in trouble. The ultimate selfish choice, or the ultimate selfless choice. He's gotta pick one or the other, and that choice is what ends up ultimately defining him as a hero. So, these next few pages are really the most pivotal points in the story.

SW: I decided to have Cal zipping up his jacket top in the last panel. I felt that after the Maelstrom fight, he'd have his jacket open in a more casual way to show that he's left the superhero thing behind him (which is also the reason he left his mask behind with Maelstrom). But with the train wreck, Cal's once again called upon to be a hero, so I wanted him to "suit up" visually for the task.

ISSUE TWO: PAGE TWENTY

SW: It's funny the amount of debate (albeit, again, in the most positive sense) you can have over the smallest things. David and I actually went back and forth many times over what Amara's last words to Cal should be on this page. I was a strong advocate for "Godspeed, Cal" as I loved the dual meaning of wishing him luck on his task while also being something you say during a eulogy. I think David wanted to avoid any religious overtones, so the line eventually became "Goodbye, Cal."

DBS: Yeah, we were really tempted to go with "Rock on, dying fire-dude", but, for some reason, that just didn't feel quite right.

ISSUE TWO: PAGES TWENTY-TWO & TWENTY-THREE

DBS: What I love about this page is that it's a great juxtaposition with page 15 of issue 1. They're both very similar in terms of Cal's pose, but the issue 1 image is light-hearted, innocent and charming, while this one is more a vision of the hell that Cal's life has become.

ISSUE TWO: PAGE TWENTY-SEVEN

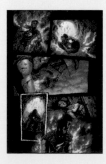

DBS: And now, the cavern scene. Tons of subtextual imagery here. First, the deep reds of the self-imposed hell that Call has forced himself into. Then, the bright light at the end of the tunnel as his life draws to an end and he shuffles off this mortal coil. I don't know that we ever intended for that level of visual symbolism, but it's there nonetheless.

SW: As far as unintended symbolism, I find it interesting that Cal has fire-based powers and Maelstrom has wind-based powers. A large turning point in Book 1 happens underwater (when he decides to save Maelstrom), while the turning point of Book 2 happens underground. So all four elements (Fire, Water, Earth, and Air) are represented. Coincidence? Yeah, probably.

ISSUE TWO: PAGE TWENTY-EIGHT

SW: For the cave-in pages I originally drew a different heap of
debris on Sandra's legs, but David
pointed out that the debris had to
look much more massive, something Cal could not easily move on
his own. It was definitely a good
call as the original pile does look
pretty tiny in comparison.

ISSUE TWO: PAGE THIRTY-TWO

DBS: Perhaps it's somewhat of a coincidence that Cal ended up here, with a big fan, in his final
moments. But, I strongly believe that it's a coincidence that's not especially far-fetched. In a
world with super-heroes, they'd be like the movie stars of our world - everyone would know them,
and lots of teenagers would be rabidly devoted fans.

SW: Over the course of this sequence (and Book 2 in general), I tried to make the art even darker
and grittier than it was in the Present day scenes in Book 1. It makes sense since the present in
Book 1 was really the midpoint of the story, so as Cal gets worse physically and mentally, the artwork should get looser and darker. I tried to reflect this also in the panel borders themselves,
which get increasingly jaggy and less gridlike in layout.

While I think Guru did an amazing job with the coloring for the entire series in general, the coloring for the last half
of Book 2 never really went quite to the extreme I was looking for. I was hoping for that coloring to get increasingly
desaturated and loose, with the colors being done in broad, simple strokes that would've even gone outside the lines
to accentuate the chaotic feel. As it is, it's very well colored, but almost TOO well-colored! I was hoping for it to
"deteriorate" much more in style over the course of the story.

ISSUE TWO: PAGE THIRTY-SIX & THIRTY-NINE

DBS: In the penultimate panel here we actually have a little joke from
Cal. He's put all of his pain behind him, and he's actually crackin' a
smile at long last...

And so, at this point, Cal's redemption is pretty much complete. You
know, 99% of the reviews MELTDOWN got were positive, but the one real
negative review we received was mainly upset about this one, lone
scene. Their criticism was that we started out with a character who
was really "bad ass", and, with this scene, we ruined his, for want of a
better word, "bad assness". Now the thing is, I never set out to write a
book about being a badass. Being a badass was a symptom of what was wrong with Cal, not what was right.

See, if you take a look at the inside front cover of either issue 1 or 2, or this trade paperback, you'll notice that it's
dedicated to Lana Meredith. That's my daughter. She's 2 right now so, pretty soon, she's gonna be reading, and one
day she'll inevitably read MELTDOWN. And I'd be doing her a disservice if I just wrote a story about a badass who never
learned, never grew, never redeemed himself. What kind of example would that be for her? Or for any of the other readers
who might pick this book up and give it a read? And, so, the redemptive ending. And ya know what, I actually really
like it this way. I'm pretty proud of it.

SW: I, on the other had, am very upset. But with the art, not the writing, or the art in this sequence anyway, as I figured out a much
better way to do it long after the book was published. At the time, I had a hard time with the choice of angles because I needed to
draw Cal lifting the huge train chassis, but that meant that I couldn't do any shots of him from the front since his face would be
blocked by the machinery. So every angle had to be from the side or the back, with his head turned, which was a bit awkward.

I feel now that I should have at some point had him turn to rest the chassis on his shoulders and back so he was facing everyone directly. It would've made for a much nicer visual of him looking forward to address Sandra and the other heroes while having the massive chunk of machinery behind his head. And symbolically, it would have read great as his final struggle with a massive metaphorical (and now literal) weight on his shoulders. Oh well.

ISSUE TWO: PAGES FORTY-ONE & FORTY-TWO

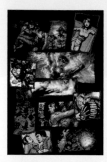

DBS: Sean had originally spotted in these flashbacks in the reverse order, starting with the oldest and heading up to the more recent. We eventually reversed it, as you can see. The idea is that, just before he goes, he slides back to a more innocent, more wide-eyed and youthful state of mind.

ISSUE TWO: PAGE FORTY-THREE

DBS: Alright folks, stick a fork in him, 'cause Cal's reached his explosive end. As you probably saw in the series pitch, he wasn't always going to die. In early drafts, Cal survived, thanks to a last minute, dues ex machina turn by Neuron. For a while, we even considered releasing two different versions of issue 2, one where Cal lived, and one where he died. Ultimately, though, we thought that Cal's death was the only ending that felt truly honest. I never wrote out the dialogue for the "alternate" ending where Cal survives, but I did outline it. We pick up in the wreckage, where Cal is sitting with Sandra...

He holds her hand. They talk. She's not afraid to die. He can feel her calm, and her bravery touches him. As a fellow Latino, she's always looked up to him as a shining example of the best the world has to offer. He finally comes to terms with himself and his life, as she helps him to understand the number of people he's touched and been an inspiration for. No matter what his motives may have been in life, the results of his actions were nothing short of miracles for the hundreds of lives he saved or inspired. As he holds her, he feels her heat slipping away, and her body turns slowly cold.

PAGES 16 THROUGH 19:

On a TV news report, we see that although several heroes came and helped, The Flare was lauded as the first to arrive, and the only one to actually bring anyone out alive. The self-obsessed heroes are lambasted, while the Flare is lionized.
Pull back from the TV to reveal The Flare exiting the wreckage with the dead girl in his arms, then collapsing to the ground beside her.

Neuron approaches and injects Cal with a serum to momentarily stabilize his system. Neuron, actually touched by The Flare's actions, had redoubled his efforts on Cal's behalf and designed a new suit for him that will both filter the light and drain the energy from his body sufficiently for him to survive.

The one hitch - he can never take it off. Not even partially, not even for a moment. If he chooses to put it on, he'll never be able to touch another person, at least not physically, but he WILL be able to help people - to continue on as a hero. He'll be able to touch people in an entirely different way for years - perhaps decades - to come. It's his choice - let go and enjoy the eternal rest he's earned, or live trapped in a suit for the rest of his days. The ultimate selfless act.

We see Cal, still weak, contemplating - his life flashing before his eyes. Finally, he puts on his new costume, then pulling it's mask over his face. It covers him completely, head-to-toe.

CUT TO:
PAGES 20 THROUGH 21:

INT - THE DOCTOR'S ACTUAL OFFICE (NOT HIS HOME STUDY) - EVENING

The doctor is closing up for the evening, saying goodbye to his assistant. He turns to close the door to his inner office and sees the new and improved Flare floating silently in his office.

During a brief epilogue, Cal thanks the Doctor. Cal explains that, for now, he's okay being trapped inside the suit - it reminds him of the import of life, of new beginnings, and of all the fences he needs to mend. Not to mention the fact that it sure beats the alternative. And, who knows; perhaps someday they'll find a way for him to live outside of the suit. In a world of fantastic powers, scientific miracles, love and compassion, anything can happen.

The Flare bids the Doctor farewell - he has a lot of time to make up for. The Doctor tells Cal that he's welcome to return anytime - no charge. As Cal soars away the Doctor mutters to himself, under his breath - But, next time, make an appointment.

CUT TO:
PAGE 22:

A splash of the new Flare joyously soaring above the skies of Miami, Amarain his arms.

END ISSUE TWO

SW: I agreed that the alternate ending would have ben a mistake, but if we had to do it, it should at least feel true to the tone of the rest of the series. David had suggested that Neuron arrive with a head-to-toe body glove suit that Cal would have to wear at all times to permanently moderate his powers. Given that, I thought it would be interesting to end with some dialogue about the concepts of being imprisoned vs being free. Basically, all his life, he's been weighed down by his negativity and self-loathing, but he finally reaches an epiphany and appreciation for life at the end. So ultimately, he's imprisoned in his new supersuit and physically more caged than he's ever been. But he's okay with that, because at least spiritually and emotionally, he's finally free of the weight he's been carrying around his whole life. And the final scene would have been him flying off in his new supersuit, but in the cartoony style, to emphasize his return to a happier outlook despite his current condition.

ISSUE TWO: PAGES FORTY-FIVE, FORTY-SEVEN & FORTY-EIGHT

SW: The group shot was a bit of a Norman Rockwell-inspired panel. It probably needed a swimming hole or old time ice cream parlor in the background though.

DBS: In the original, psychiatrist version, the basic gist of the ending was similar, with Sandra carrying on The Flare's heroic legacy, but it played out in the doctor's office. Here's a peek:

PAGE FORTY-SIX

PANEL 1

CAPTION: EPILOGUE
CAPTION: Months later.

We're in the Psychiatrist's office. Not the home office we sat in for so long with The Flare, but an actual office, in an office building. Inspired by The Flare, he's gone back into practice. Cast his demons aside and got back into the game, even though still powerless.

The Doctor's office has closed for the evening, and he sits at his computer, staring at the screen.

PANEL 2
On it, we see the end of a book he's writing:

ON-SCREEN: "Perhaps it's fitting that, in the end, The Flare turned out to be exactly what his name implied: a beacon of hope that burned far too brightly, and for far too short a time. The only question left, I suppose, is what his legacy will be. Will his light help to serve as a guidepost, inspiring others to follow in his path, or will he simply be another forgotten footnote in a barely-read text-book."

PANEL 3
Focus on the Psychiatrist, his face lit by the glow of the computer.

PSYCHIATRIST
Enough for tonight.

PANEL 4
Focus on the screen again.

He's scrolled back up to the top of his document, which reads:

ON-SCREEN: "Last Days of the Flare", written by "Anonymous"

PANEL 5
He's interrupted by a knock at the door. A WOMAN stands in the doorway.

PAGE FORTY-SEVEN

PANEL 1
A two-shot, as the Psychiatrist looks quizzically at the woman who's barged into his office after hours.

DOCTOR
I'm sorry, I've finished seeing patients for the --

WOMAN
I'm sorry to disturb you, Doctor. I'm at the end of my rope with my daughter, and I need your help.

DOCTOR
Ma'am, I'm sure that -

PANEL 2
Angle on the woman. Mid-forties. Not beautiful, but not homely, either. She has a look of great desperation on her face, as though she absolutely cannot take "no" for an answer.

WOMAN
No, it can't wait. What she wants to do - it's incredibly dangerous. She needs someone to talk to her, to talk her out of it. I hear you specialize in this sort of area and I --

PANEL 3
Her daughter steps in behind her - its Sandra - the girl we saw in the rubble - the one that Cal rescued just a few pages back.

PANEL 4
Angle on the Psychiatrist. Maybe he recognizes her from the news reports, or maybe he just recognizes the mother's desperate desire to help her child, but, either way, he gives in to the request.

PSYCHIATRIST
Ok, ma'am. Give us a few moments.

PANEL 5
Over the Psychiatrist's shoulder, we can see the daughter sit down, as the office door closes behind her, her mother having left the two of them alone.

PANEL 6
A side 2-shot, as the two stare at each other, like wary combatants, across the great divide of a large, ornate desk.

PAGE FORTY-EIGHT

PANEL 1
A 2-shot.

SANDRA
This is stupid. I don't need counseling.

PSYCHIATRIST
So, how come your mom thinks you do?

PANEL 2
Focus on Sandra.

SANDRA
Because she's scared.

PSYCHIATRIST
Of?

SANDRA
Of my getting hurt, killed.

PANEL 3
A 2-shot.

PSYCHIATRIST
And why would she -

SANDRA
See, the world needs more heroes. Not fake heroes, out for themselves, out for money, but real heroes, selfless heroes. Like back in the old days, when everything was so much simpler. We've just lost a great hero. Someone needs to take his place. Someone needs to follow his example. And, whether my mom likes it or not, I want that someone to be me.

PANEL 4
Angle on Sandra. She stares directly, and unwaveringly, into the Psychiatrist's eyes.

SANDRA
I owe him that.

PANEL 5

SANDRA
Sure, I haven't got any powers yet, but I'll find my own way. And if I die in the process, so be it. Is that so terribly crazy?

PANEL 6

Angle on the Psychiatrist, who smiles.

PANEL 7
A 2-shot.

PSYCHIATRIST
Thank you.

PANEL 8
Angle on a perplexed Sandra.

SANDRA
For...?

PANEL 9
A single shot of the Psychiatrist, clearly pleased.

PSYCHIATRIST
You just helped me find the ending for my book. Or maybe the beginnings of a sequel...

END

SW: I was a bit torn with this ending as I didn't think Sandra needed to become a costumed superhero herself for Cal to have had an impact on her. I thought she could have been shown just doing some random good deeds, as though Cal's heroism had inspired her to be a good person and help others in her own way. But revisiting the HOH auditions does make for a very fun scene, so I didn't need any convincing. And I got to draw a dog in a cape and cowl, and what more could an artist want than that!

DBS: So, there you have it. If you have any comments about the book, or questions we failed to answer here, feel free to drop us a line. We'd love to hear your thoughts. I'm at TheFlare@sbcglobal.net.

SW: And I'm at Sean@SeanWang.com

DBS: And before we go, just a few quick (but extremely important) shout-outs. First, to **RORY MYERS,** who put in a tremendous amount of time and energy not only designing the individual issues of MELTDOWN, but also designing and laying out this entire book. If you're looking for a spectacular graphic designer, he's your guy. And to **BERNARD CHANG** and **JOHN-PAUL LEON**, who, at various points in time, were set to handle the art chores on MELTDOWN, and each of whom offered up some great ideas and suggestions. And now, on to some spectacular pin-ups from some artists whose work we really admire. Enjoy!

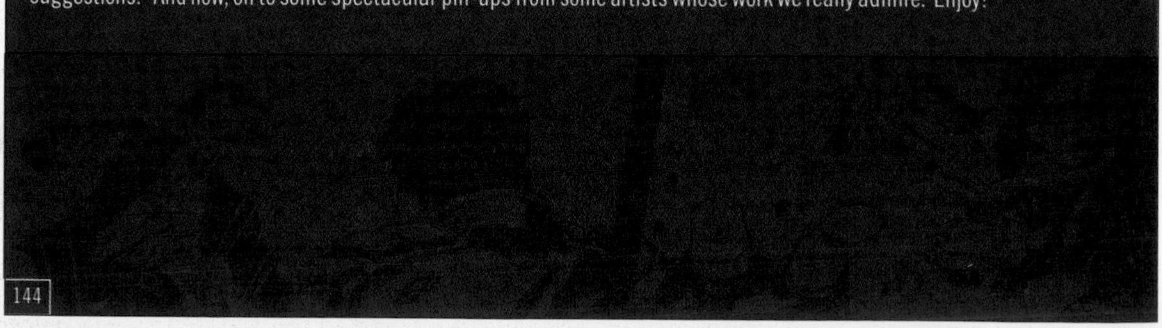

PIN-UPS

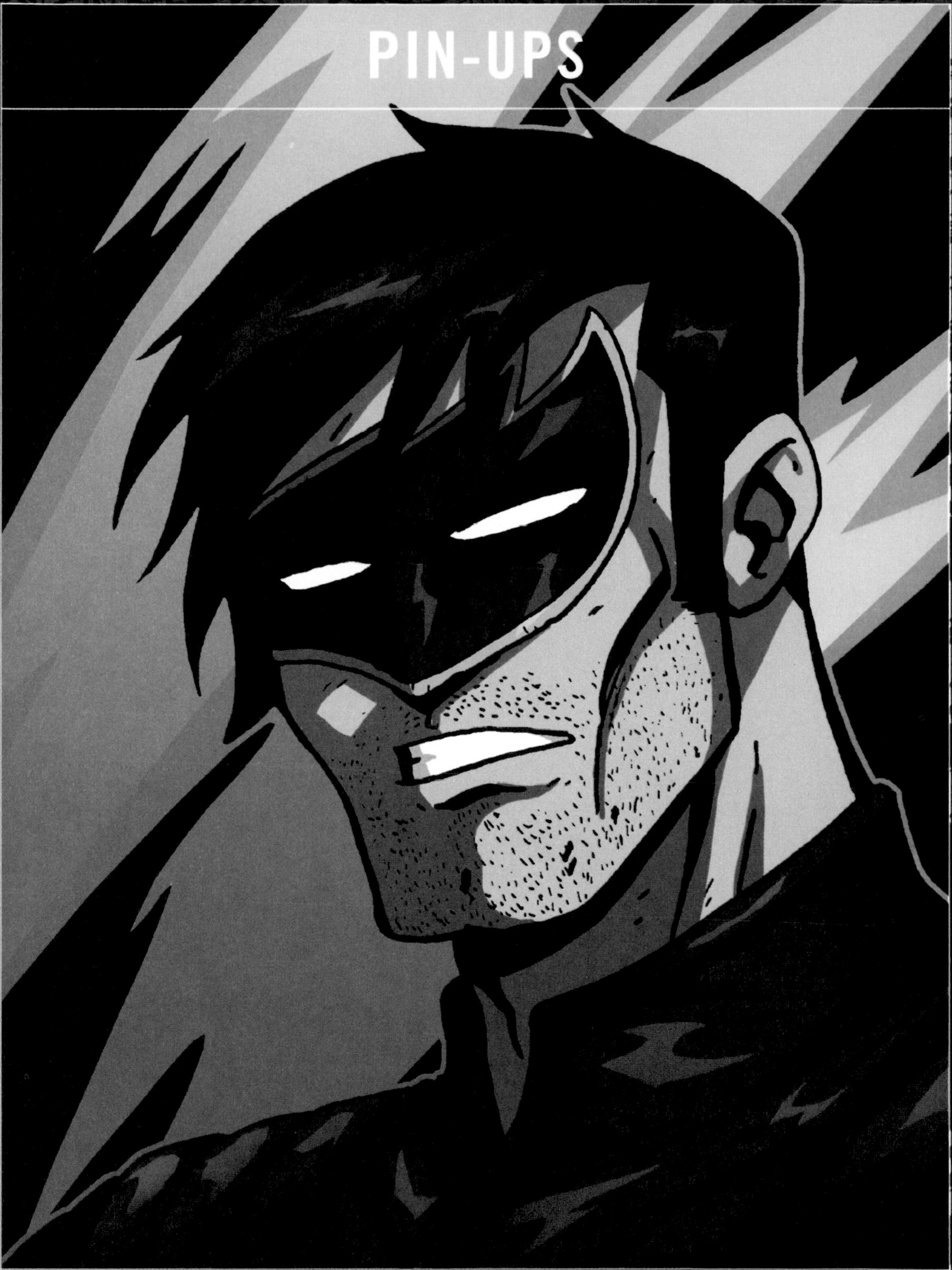

JOSH HOWARD "Dead@17", "The Lost Books of Eve" & "Sasquatch" – www.joshhoward.net

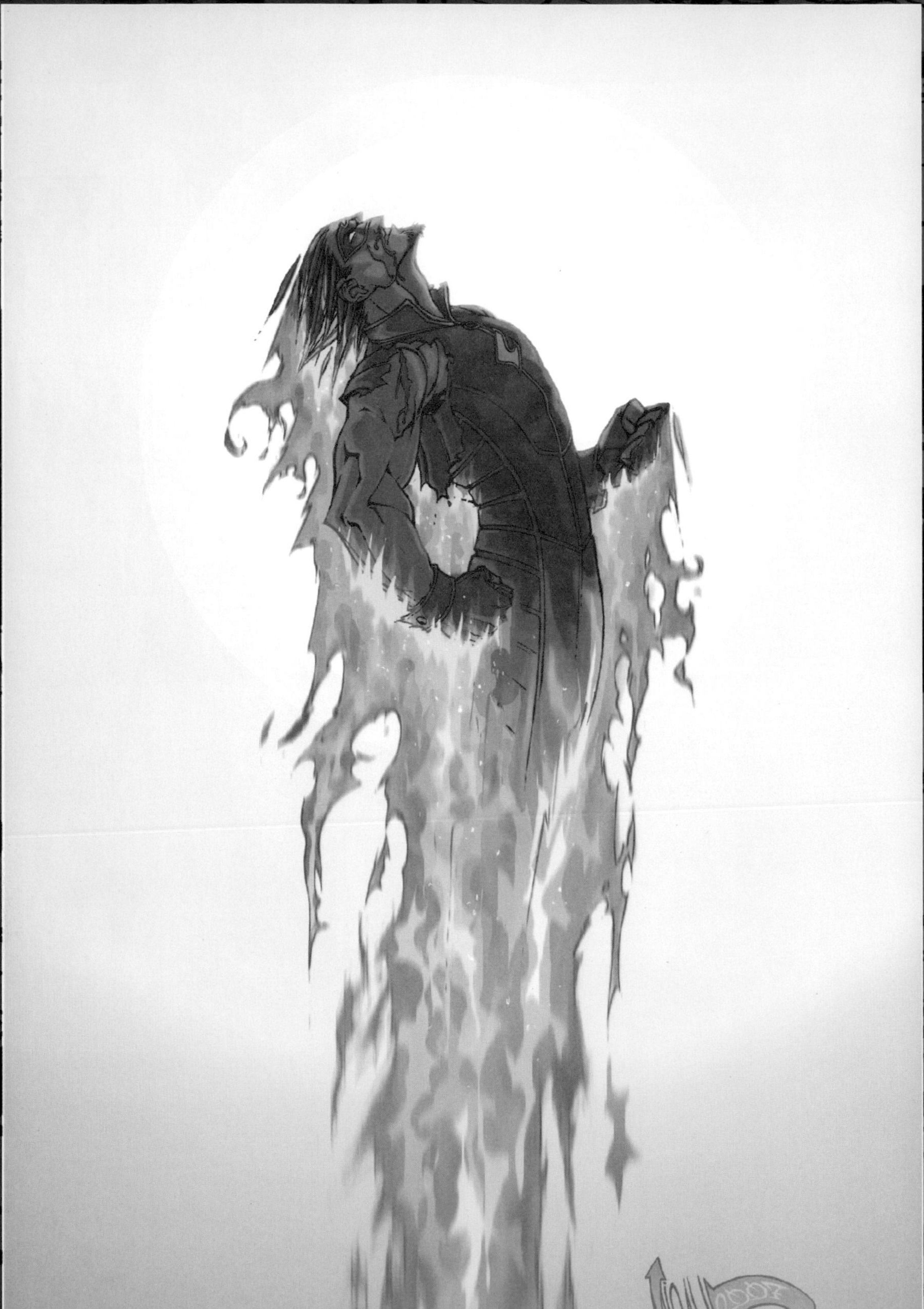

MICAH GUNNELL "Soulfire: Dying of the Light", "Shrugged" – www.sonofdavinci.com

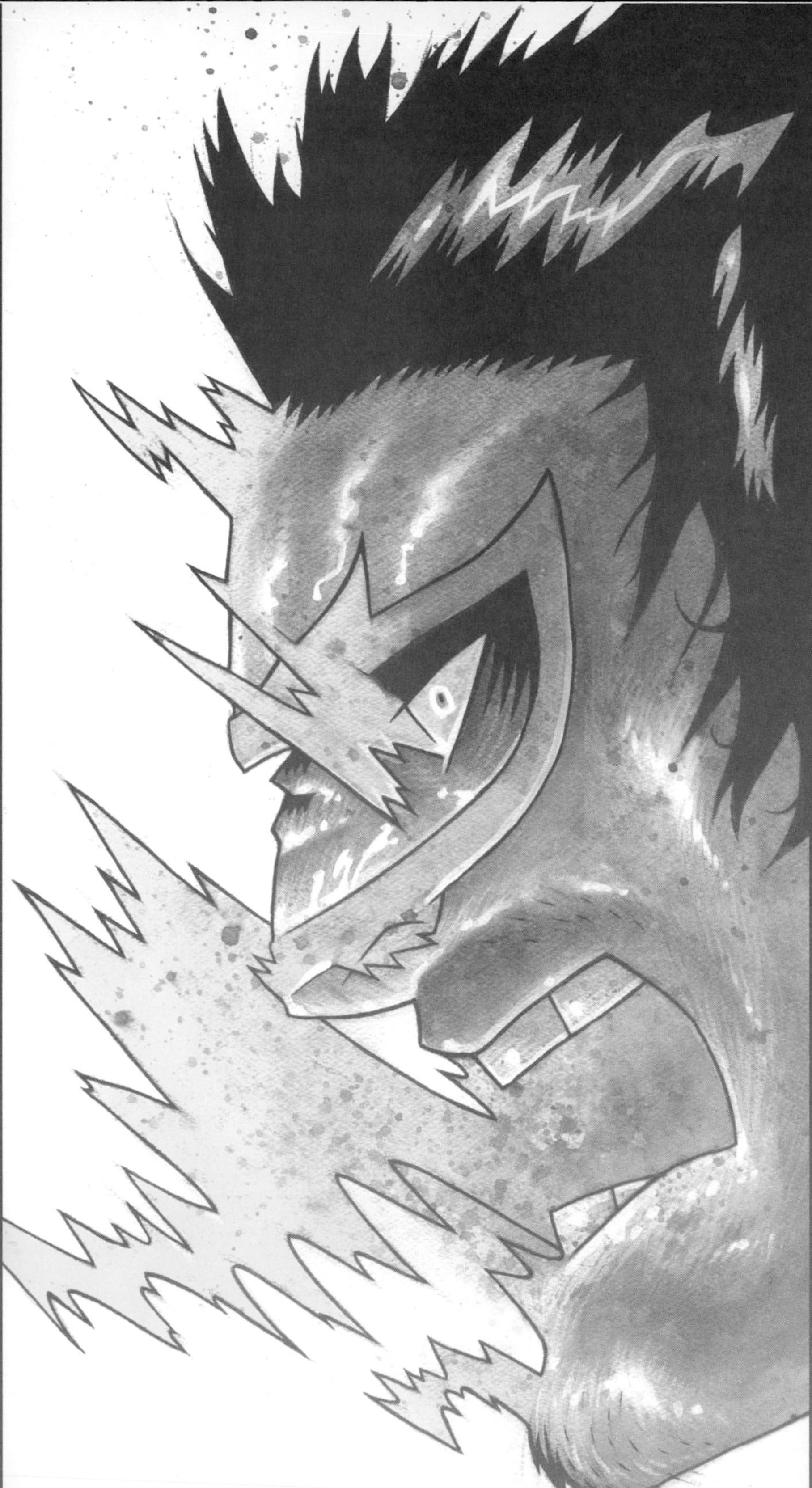

DAN HIPP "The Amazing Joy Buzzards", "GYAKUSHU!" – www.mrhipp.com

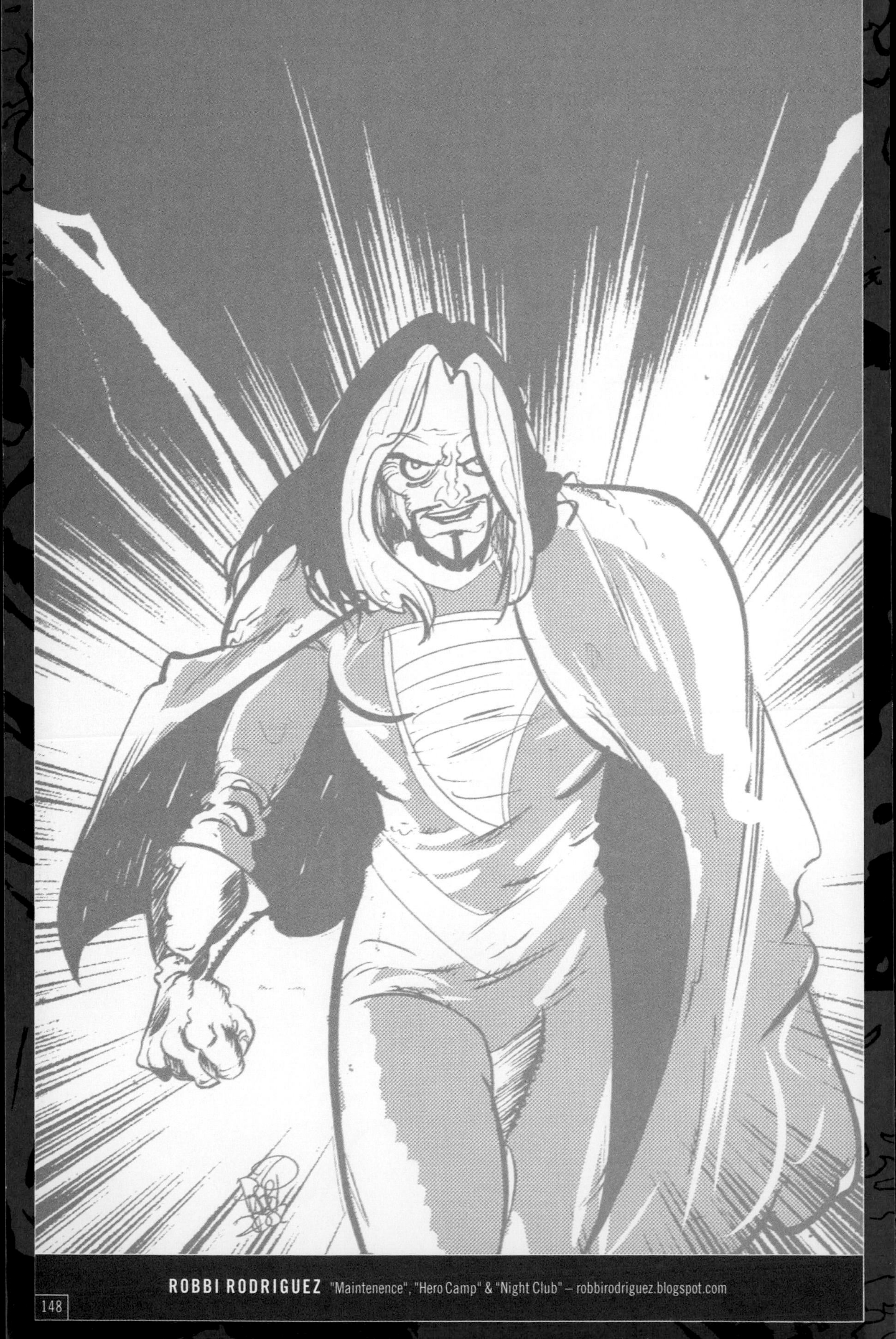

ROBBI RODRIGUEZ "Maintenence", "Hero Camp" & "Night Club" – robbirodriguez.blogspot.com

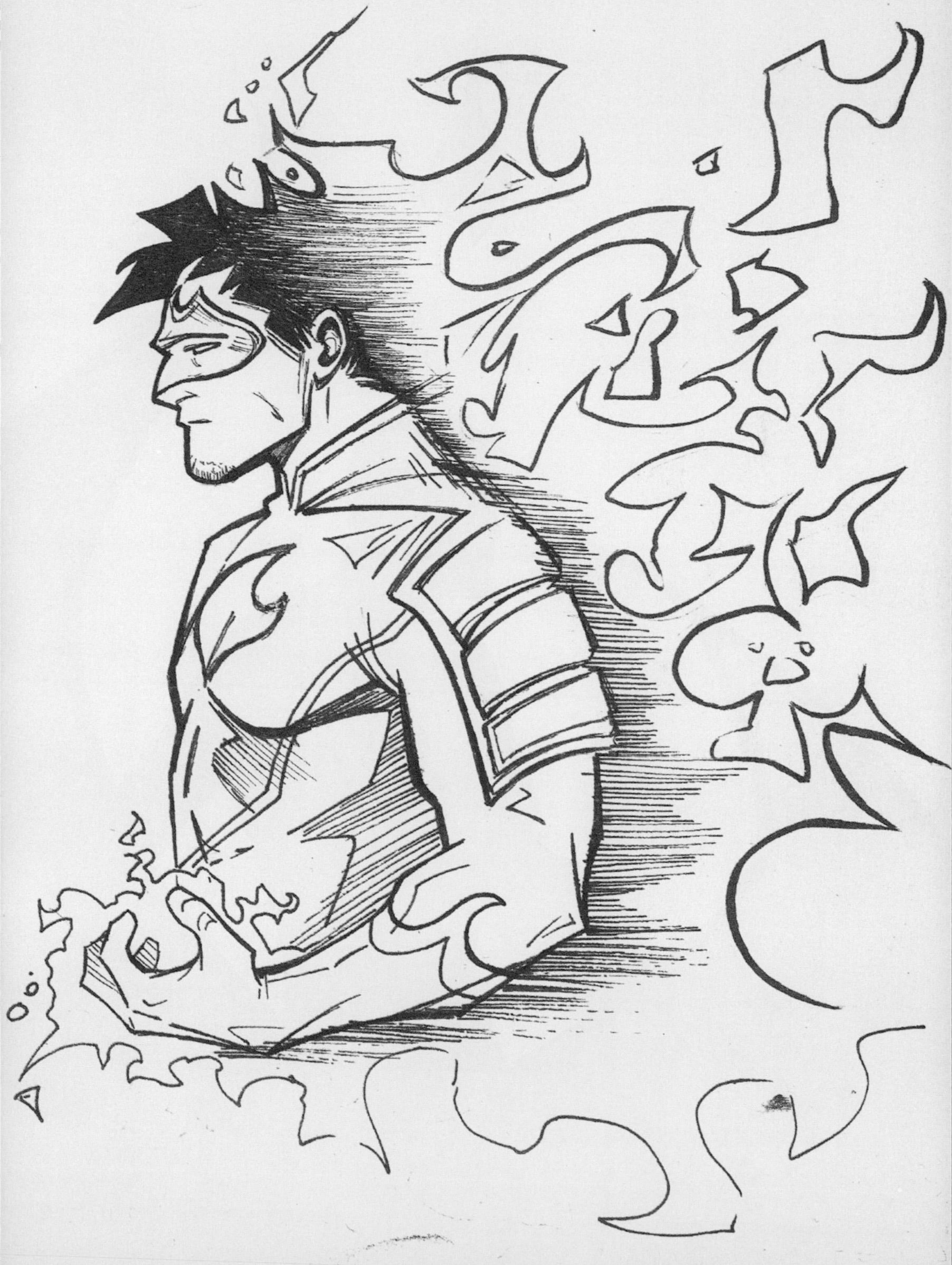

JOELLE JONES "12 Reasons Why I Love Her" – ooglygoogly.sandwich.net/joelle/home.htm

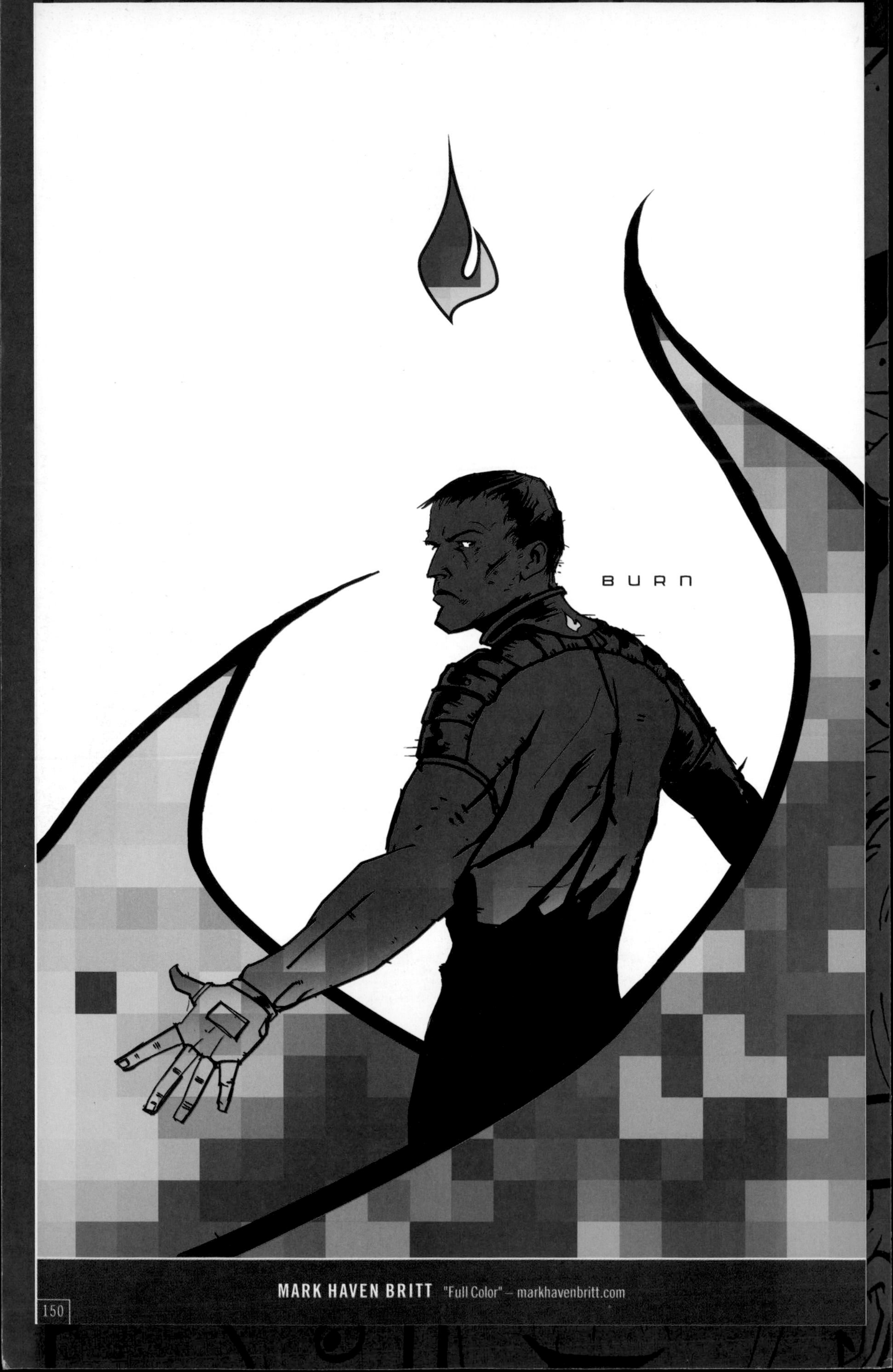
BURN

MARK HAVEN BRITT "Full Color" – markhavenbritt.com

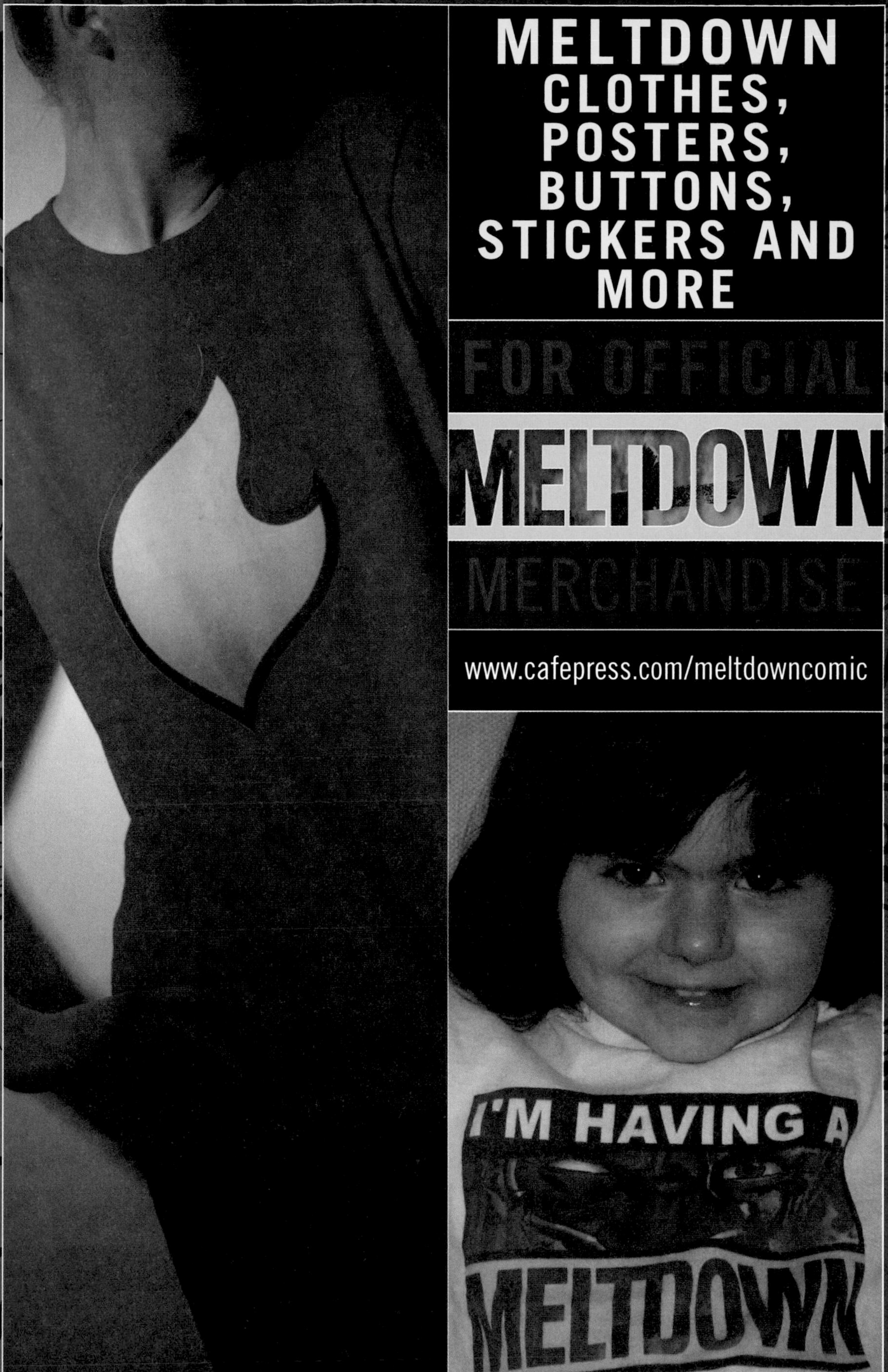
MELTDOWN
CLOTHES, POSTERS, BUTTONS, STICKERS AND MORE
FOR OFFICIAL
MELTDOWN
MERCHANDISE
www.cafepress.com/meltdowncomic
I'M HAVING A
MELTDOWN

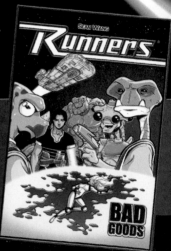